ASPECTS OF AIR LAW AND CIVIL AIR POLICY IN THE SEVENTIES

ASPECTS OF AIR LAW AND CIVIL AIR POLICY IN THE SEVENTIES

by

H. A. WASSENBERGH

MARTINUS NIJHOFF / THE HAGUE / 1970

The opinions and solutions given in this work reflect the personal views of the author.

ISBN 978-94-011-8198-3   ISBN 978-94-011-8852-4 (eBook)
DOI 10.1007/978-94-011-8852-4

For Cathérine

FOREWORD

Dr. H. A. Wassenbergh of KLM has deservedly earned, in international aviation circles, a reputation for outstanding ability akin to that enjoyed by the airline he represents. In dealing with the highly complex and difficult problems, of great significance from an airline and a government point of view, in contemporary international civil aviation law and policy Dr. Wassenbergh displays the undoubted intelligence one has come to expect from his contributions in this field.

His appreciation of the attitudes of governments, as well as of the international scheduled airlines, stems from his practical experience as a participant in the negotiation of numerous bilateral arrangements with government and airline representatives in his capacity as a responsible and dedicated KLM adviser to the Netherlands Government. Students who lack such experience may find this work requires a major effort of concentration but the reward for making the effort will be a much fuller understanding of current fundamental issues in the traffic rights field and charter flights policy as well as in the area of cooperative arrangements between airlines. The precise definition of these issues by the author reflects the considered view of the experienced practioner who has been dealing with them over a period of many years.

In the very numerous discussions one has enjoyed with Dr. Wassenbergh, very often across the negotiating table, his skill in argument and his command of his subject have been quite patent. Naturally his views reflect the outlook of the airline with which he has been so closely and constructively associated for many years but this in no way diminishes the value of the analysis he has presented of fundamental issues in international civil aviation. Dr. Wassenbergh would be the first to concede that his views are not necessarily accepted by those who have shared his experience and commitment in the international aviation field. The responses and reactions of representatives of governments to his analysis, and to his suggestions for corrective action at government level, will naturally vary according to the interests of each government in upholding the approach it regards as consistent with its own basic interests and those of its international airline.

I commend this book as a most valuable treatment of the subjects which are of concern not only to the academic student but also to those engaged in the study and application of international civil aviation agreements in governments and airlines. It would be fitting if it enjoys, as it should, wide circulation amongst such students and practicioners.

Sir Donald Anderson
Director-General of Civil Aviation
Melbourne, Australia.
April, 1970.

TABLE OF CONTENTS

List of Abbreviations XI

Chapter One

I. The Technique of government 1
II. International civil aviation regulation 4
III. National vs international approach 9

Chapter Two

I. International control of the air traffic market 17
II. Freedom classification and traffic data 22
III. The air traffic market and the exchange of routes and traffic rights 28
IV. The sixth freedom issue 32
V. Route specification 40
VI. Equal opportunity 46

Chapter Three

I. Non-scheduled and scheduled air carriers 51
II. All-cargo services 59
III. Inclusive tour traffic 63
IV. Non-inclusive tour (affinity) charter traffic 72
V. Traffic rights for charter carriers 79

Chapter Four

I. Cooperative arrangements 104
II. Aircraft lease agreements in international air transportation 114
III. Affiliation between air carriers 120
IV. Special wet lease operating authority 123

V. Wet lease agreements with charter carriers 137
VI. Blocked-space arrangements 142
VII. Summary 147

CHAPTER FIVE
Conclusion 153

APPENDIX I. Statement on US international aviation policy 156
APPENDIX II. Definitions 159

INDEX 162

ABBREVIATIONS

AAFRA	Association of African Airlines, Addis Ababa.
AF	Air France.
AGM	Annual General Meeting.
ALITALIA	Italian Airlines.
ALM	Dutch Antillean Airlines, Willemstad, Curaçao.
ATA	American Transport Association.
ATC	Air Transport Committee, Canada.
AVENSA	Aerovias Venezolanas S.A.
AUA	Austrian Airlines.
BEA	British European Airways Corporation.
BIT	Bulk Inclusive Tour.
BOAC	British Overseas Airways Corporation.
BUA	British United Airways.
BWIA	British West Indian Airways, Trinidad.
CAB	Civil Aeronautics Board, USA.
CAL	China Airlines, Taiwan.
CBIT	Contract Bulk Inclusive Tour.
CDA	Companía Dominicana de Aviación.
CMA	Companía Mexicana de Aviación.
CPAIR	Canadian Pacific Airlines.
DGCA	Director General of Civil Aviation.
DLH	Deutsche Lufthansa A.G.
EARB	European Air Research Bureau, Brussels.
ECAC	European Civil Aviation Conference, Paris.
EL AL	Israeli Airlines.
GIT	Group Inclusive Tour.
GTD	Group Travel Discount.
IATA	International Air Transport Association.
IBERIA	Spanish Airlines.
ICAO	International Civil Aviation Organization.
ICC	International Chamber of Commerce, Paris.

INS	Immigration and Naturalization Service, US Department of Justice.
IT	Inclusive Tour.
ITA	Air Transport Institute, Paris.
ITC	Inclusive Tour Charter.
ITX	Inclusive Tour Excursion Fare (on scheduled services), available only to tour operators.
JAL	Japan Airlines.
JALC	Journal of Air Law and Commerce, Methodist University, Dallas, Texas.
KAL	Korean Airlines, Seoul.
KLM	Royal Dutch Airlines.
LANICA	Lineas Aereas de Nicaragua S.A.
LIAT	Leeward Islands Air Transport Services Ltd., Antigua.
MSA	Malaysia/Singapore Airways.
NACA	National Air Carrier Association, USA.
OARB	Orient Air Research Bureau, Manila.
ONA	Overseas National Airways Inc.
PAL	Philippine Airlines.
PANAM	Panamerican World Airways Inc.
SABENA	Belgian Airlines.
SACAA	South American Civil Aviation Association.
SAS	Scandinavian Airlines.
SIT	See ITX.
TAN	Transportes Aéreos Nacionales S.A., Honduras.
TAP	Portuguese Airlines.
TMA	Trans Mediterranean Airlines, Lebanon.
TWA	Trans World Airlines.
UAA	United Arab Airlines, Egypt.
UTA	Union de Transports Aériens, France.
VIASA	Venezuelan International Airlines.

"Man is as equal as he makes himself.
The problem is the regulation of inequality."
(Auth.)

CHAPTER ONE

I. THE TECHNIQUE OF GOVERNMENT

"L'Essence des rapports entre consciences n'est pas le Mitsein, mais le conflit."
(Sartre, "L'Etre et le Néant" p. 502).

People as a collective whole lack reliable truths and nowadays are aware of it. Religion no longer gives infallible guidance, and knowledge based on science is still insufficient to compensate for the loss of the faiths which once constituted the truth and gave security.

With this development and a progressive depreciation of values, the concept of justice, for instance, as a pillar of the society of man and reflected in his laws, has lost its traditional content and therefore its original meaning for society. There is no fixed and accepted standard or yardstick for determining the demands of justice. The same is true for the concept of freedom.

One might say that there is no justice other than lawfulness. There is no freedom other than absence of conflict. And the law serves neither justice nor freedom but the development of society. Justice and freedom no longer are criteria for the development of a society; the law is. Good law is law that is effective in serving the development of a society. To give an example: If a law is discriminatory but effective in serving the development of a particular society, it is not unjust. Only unlawful is unjust. What, however, is the development of society and what is the task of government to serve this development? The task of government is to take effective measures to further the development of its State, the society. These measures cannot be more than means to be used by citizens to further develop their society. The goal of government is to provide such means. The means, if effective in serving the development of society, are the purpose of government activity. The development of society is a development without definable end. Every time a means is given which helps to develop society the end is reached as far as the government is concerned.

Which are these developments? Any which bring man to a higher and broader level of possibilities in every field of activity and enable him to lead a life which is as much as possible free from toil and repression. Man himself is the end and the goal of government. It is only necessary to define man.

Government cannot, religion no longer does. Man must define himself. But he must define himself in relation to society and more especially in relation to his own, national, community. And there is an obvious and automatic restriction imposed on this definition: man cannot define himself at the expense of his fellow men. If he did, he would deny himself, and deny that man is the goal of the organization of society and of government. He would expose himself to destruction. So he defines himself as a member of his community. Man and his collectivity thus become one and the same thing as far as government is concerned.

Man, in defining himself, creates his own freedom, his own justice through compromise.[1]

Government should enable him to do that, without, however, telling him beforehand what justice and freedom are. Justice and freedom are not static concepts and they are not State concepts. To return to our example:

If a law is discriminatory, it is not therefore unjust. It is, however, a means which is not effective, because it does not serve to broaden the possibilities for all concerned. Government should serve all its subjects because man cannot define himself at the expense of the other.

Government therefore, by having to provide effective means to serve all subjects to enable them to further the development of their society, has the task (must provide the means) to prevent definitions of man at the expense of others and thus to avoid consequences of such definitions. There are a variety of means which promote effectively the development of a society in certain fields.

Instead of trying to determine whether the means are just, it is preferable to conclude that a means is just if it is felt by the subjects to be adequate to enable them to promote the development of their society in the field concerned. So the concept of justice should be replaced by the criterion of adequacy. Note here that we have deliberately replaced "justice," which is significant in itself, by a term which is significant only in relation to something else and derives its meaning from a specific situation in society.

The bureaucratic, computerized, technocratically and technologically run State can give its subjects optimum prosperity, but it takes away a

[1] Cf. "True compromise lies in giving up something which you may regard as your natural right in exchange for some greater advantage, not necessarily to you, but to the community to which you belong." (Cecil Hourani, "The Moment of Truth," in *Encounter,* Nov. 1967, p. 10.)

sense of freedom, a sense of justice, and therefore an individual's sense of belonging to his society. A technocratic State is a depersonalized State.

A sense of freedom, justice and "belonging" results from the challenge offered by society to fight for the views which an individual wants the State to adopt. In the bureaucratic State such a fight is pointless.

The law of the bureaucratic State is objective and disinterested, a body of rules which treats individuals as objects with known qualities, potential and behaviour patterns.

In theory such law is bloodless. By definition it is effective and adequate.

In practice, however, such law nevertheless may become living law if it recognizes the continuous development of society and allows existing rules to be put continuously to the test. Only if the law of society is allowed to be continuously on trial, will there be a close relationship with the opinions of its subjects, and will the law become a living body of rules.

But making law which continuously adapts to developments is an intellectual activity. To know what is the right law, one must resort to a continuous ex-post-facto review of the effects of existing rules. Law sets rules for a given situation and the development of that situation shows whether the rules were right. As it is virtually impossible to know beforehand what will develop as a result of the implementation of certain rules, partly because one cannot predict the reaction of people to the rules' enforcement, one never knows what would have been the right law, nor what will be the right law. The right law only exists in theory and ex post facto. Moral judgement is involved when we evaluate how our law works out in practice; moral judgment can play no role before the law takes effect: although our morals can help us choose the society we want, they cannot help us determine how to bring it about. That is the work of experts, spe-

We may compromise with regard to the law we make (we must, as a

Since we all have our own preferences, we should try to separate mentally our moral judgements from our responsibility to make law. We should defer our moral judgement to the moment when the law we have made is put into practice. Making law is an enabling function: It enables the subjects to live in the manner they choose. Making law is giving society a structure and providing the activities of individuals with an infrastructure which gives them optimum freedom to live their lives as they choose.

We may compromise with regard to the law we make, (we must, as a matter of fact), but we should not compromise with regard to our morals or our principles by bringing them into play as we face our responsibilities in making law. Making law is thus a technique, a technique of Government based on continuous practical experience in the effect rules produce.

II. INTERNATIONAL CIVIL AVIATION REGULATION

"The right attitude toward law as instrumentality is the technical approach." (Auth.)

The opinions and practices of the great aviation nations, especially the USA, dominate the development of international air law and aviation policy. These opinions and practices are of particular interest because the US Government and the US Civil Aeronautics Board (CAB) are faced with the problem of regulating a true mass market both domestically and internationally and thereby are ahead of most other Governments in experiencing what is to become the general picture of air transportation in other parts of the world in future. Other countries having considerable experience of civil aviation are Canada, Japan, Australia and the USSR.

Some figures which illustrate the tremendous growth of international air transportation and prospects for the future and are an average of forecasts of Boeing, Douglas, Lockheed and the ICAO, computed by IATA in 1967, show annual growth:

in revenue passenger miles:

1960–65	1965–70	1970–75	1975–80
12.7%	14.5%	10.1%	8.7%

in passengers carried:

	14.8%	10.0%	6.1%

This means that in 1975 there will be 580 million airline passengers, 770 million in 1980, compared with 177 million in 1965.

in freight ton miles:

	19.8%	18.7%	15.7%

Compared with 1965 traffic, revenue freight ton miles in 1970 will be 2.5 times larger; 5.8 times in 1975; 12 times in 1980.[2]

The influence of the US upon the development of international air law and policy by the mere fact that the US is by far the biggest air traffic market of the Western world, is substantial.

This is not to say that other States should be bound in any way by US

[2] (*International Aviation* p. 52, September 25, 1967).
These estimates, in our view, are low. Our forecast would be close to 1000 million passengers in 1980 and a continued 18% growth of freight ton miles, 1975 through 1980.
In his Annual Report to the 25th Annual General Meeting of IATA, Doc. AGM 25/20 E, October 1969, the Director-General forecast that world scheduled passenger traffic should increase more than twice by 1975 and about four times by 1980 from the 1968 base of 308,000 million passenger-kilometers. The North Atlantic traffic is forecast to expand three times by 1975 and more than five times by 1980 over 1967. For world air freight a 20% increase per year is mentioned: fourfold by 1975, eightfold by 1980, over 1968.

views or US practices so long as they have not specifically agreed to them and the practices can be said to have received general acceptance.[3]

If a State, therefore, agrees to certain US views or concepts in bilateral negotiations with the US, it does not necessarily mean that these views or concepts need also apply in other bilateral situations.

Not surprisingly conflicts arise between the views and practices of a big State and those of smaller or less powerful States. In practice, however, the great powers in most cases have their own way. When this happens, one should be careful in interpreting such agreements as representative in any way of an *opinio juris generalis.* Even if such agreements cover principles of international civil aviation regulation, their validity in law cannot be construed as to surpass the limited framework of the agreement itself. Here we have a clear dividing line between policy as a source of international agreements and consensus as a source of international law.

To find a solution to conflicts between States with regard to regulation of international civil aviation and notably between a big and a small State, one should perhaps approach the problem by bearing in mind that the States are the *locum tenentes* of their nationals in the international sphere, not only representing their citizens as a national group but also, and more importantly, representing each individual as a subject of international society as well as of his State. In other words, a government must consider the interests of its citizens also as members of a society beyond that government's own bounds.

Such an approach makes it possible to bridge the gap between States with conflicting interests and obviate both the necessity for smaller States to have recourse to their sovereignty each time they think their rights are curtailed and for bigger States to ride roughshod over smaller States' interests. By emphasizing the rights and the interests of individuals as subjects of the international community, the conflict between the use of power, on the one hand, and a refusal to cooperate, on the other, could be solved and the further development of international society could be promoted at the same time.

This *extra-national* approach would mean that the international traffic market should technically be taken as a whole, as a composition of an innumerable number of bigger and smaller traffic streams, and not as a market made up of as many different independent markets as there are States. On the other hand, each airline should be considered according to its fitness, its willingness and its ability to provide services.

[3] Cf. D. Goedhuis, "Reflections on the Evolution of Space Law," p. 113, in *Netherlands International Law Review,* 1966, issue 2.

The operation of supersonic and wide-bodied jet aircraft in most cases will make it practically impossible to adapt the route structure to the pattern, inspired by the Bermuda principles, of capacities adjusted to various freedom categories.[4] The bilateral exchange of traffic rights, moreover, will no longer find a workable basis in the evaluation of the economic benefits which each carrier may derive from access to the national market of the other party, as there will then be a need to think in much bigger market, and even global, terms. National sovereignty will become a means for coming to terms on a global level. It will no longer be an end in itself, as a means to reserve national markets for national carriers whenever possible.

There is a need to redefine the concept of "freedom of the air." In Post-War International Civil Aviation Policy and the Law of the Air [5] the concept of the freedom of the air was discussed and the desirability and the legal foundation of greater freedom in the air was demonstrated by explaining the insufficient legal justification of many protectionist policies, practices and restrictive measures of States, and their adverse effects on the sound development of international civil aviation.

A more direct approach is an explanation and description of what "freedom of the air", in the modern sense means, based on present and future situations and the present and future requirements of both the airline industry and the public.

Of course freedom of the air does not infer complete freedom of action for carriers and the complete absence of regulations. Nevertheless, we must recognize the absence of protective restrictions for national carriers: If a need for an air service is established and a carrier is found fit, willing and able to operate that service successfully, if it harms no one and risks its own capital, that carrier ought to have the opportunity to operate the service.[6]

A carrier should be granted opportunities on the basis of its ability to compete, make a profit and ensure its self-perpetuation. It even might well be possible to establish the traffic rights each carrier is entitled to on that basis.

[4] Cf. the UK-US air agreement, concluded at Bermuda, February 11, 1946 and proclaimed as the standard pattern of bilateral air agreements.
See further p. 22 and ff.

[5] Cf. H. A. Wassenbergh, Post War International Civil Aviation Policy and the Law of the Air, Nijhoff, The Hague, 1962, second revised edition.

[6] Cf. Charles S. Murphy, then Chairman of the USCAB, before the International Aviation Club, Washington DC. November 16, 1967. "If some competitor or would-be competitor comes along and offers to provide a new service, or a better service, or a lower fare – I find myself asking this question – why shouldn't we let him do it – especially if he is risking his own money." Of course, the problem is more complicated than this.

In essence, therefore, freedom of the air is opportunity to compete. Competition leads to economic management and a maximum rate of economic progress and technological development.

However, freedom to compete is not the same thing as free competition. Competition should be confined between upper and lower limits if it is to acquire its most effective form and extent. In civil aviation this problem poses itself only after operating rights have been granted by the countries concerned to the airlines designated by each of them to operate international air services.

If we accept the reality of increasing nationalism, the desire of each individual State to have its own national airline operating international air routes to and from its territory, the fact that governments are prepared to subsidize and protect their national carriers all the way in order to show the flag wherever possible, and that governments, at the same time, want their carriers to operate as economically as possible, to contribute foreign currency to the national income, provide employment, make a profit, etc. – if we start from that reality then each government, in theory, would be able to reserve for its own flag carriers a share of the international traffic which would amount to 50% of total traffic to and from its territory.

This will be true in its simplest form if no traffic between third countries (fifth and sixth [7] freedom traffic) is allowed. As soon as such traffic is allowed, a part of the traffic to and from the homeland of a carrier must be shared with carriers of the third countries which have granted fifth or sixth freedom traffic rights to it.

On a strict *quid-pro-quo* basis the maximum which a carrier would be able to have its government reserve for it will therefore be 50% of the *value* of its home market.[8] Such carrier would then not necessarily carry traffic only from and to its territory (third and fourth freedom traffic) but also fifth and sixth freedom traffic. It would have given in return part of its third and fourth freedom traffic not only to carriers for which this traffic is also third and fourth freedom traffic, but also to carriers for which this traffic is fifth and sixth freedom traffic.

Then it would be fairly easy to determine the legitimate size of a national carrier. Problem might be what to do with the traffic a carrier is entitled to but which it is not able to carry. Here, an easy solution seemingly might be to have the carrier that is carrying this traffic "illegitimately" pay the

[7] Fifth freedom traffic is traffic which is carried between third countries.
Sixth freedom traffic is traffic which is carried between third countries via the homeland of the carrier.

[8] Cf. the policy of some States to reserve 50% of their foreign trade for carriage by their own ships.

legitimate carrier compensation for the right to actually carry its traffic.

Under the influence of US theories on the equal exchange of economic benefits in bilateral air relationships, modern air policy has become a system of bargaining between flag carriers who have been given the right by their governments to exploit the highways of the sky and to exact tolls from foreign carriers for the use of their international routes and the carriage of their legitimate traffic.

What is wrong here is that it is very difficult to speak of one's own or legitimate traffic if one is not able or willing to carry it oneself. One cannot sell something which one does not actually possess nor is able or willing to take possession of.

The efforts which are being made to define traffic by its origin and its destination are directed ultimately towards close determination of the traffic which rightfully belongs to each national carrier.

To each his own, and there would no longer be any point in competition: if a carrier is not able or willing to carry its own traffic, it sells that traffic to a carrier who is.

One could make a distinction here between the uplift and the disembarkation of traffic by foreign airlines. The first adversely affects the balance of payments of the country. The latter benefits the balance of payments (import of tourist services). Travel abroad adversely affects the balance of payments of a country and travel abroad on a foreign airline is even worse. On the other hand a national airline may be a substantial contributory factor to the balance of payments of its own country, if it has sufficient freedom to operate to and from other countries and is able to compete successfully. Therefore the operation of international air services, from the point of view of the balance of payments as well, is a matter of give and take.

The overall effect on the balance of payments situation of international air services by national and foreign carriers is difficult to assess, however, because there are many aspects to the problem. One aspect seems clear: that the stimulation of traffic to one's own country is an efficient way to improve the balance of payments. This calls for a liberal air policy, allowing foreign carriers to operate to one's country.

But to try and balance economic benefits in the field of civil aviation, either by limiting the exchange of traffic rights to the level of the operations of the national carrier or by trying to compensate for a possible imbalance of aviation benefits by requiring the foreign carrier to pay, may not be the most progressive and ultimately beneficial way to approach the regulation of international civil aviation.

Nevertheless in practice various ways and means are used to equalize the benefits derived from the operation of air services on a bilateral basis. The usual form of payment is the conclusion of a commercial agreement in anticipation of the more elegant form of a pool agreement once the operations of both carriers have reached a more balanced situation. A help here is a blocked space agreement in which one carrier offers capacity on its aircraft to the other carrier or leases its aircraft with crew to the other carrier for the performance of a number of frequencies on the route concerned. A joint venture can also be used. We will revert to this problem later.

Seeking a solution to the problem of international civil aviation policy and regulation, we have little other choice than to start from the reality that each nation is trying to gain a place in the air, and to practice the principle of live and let live. This does not mean that a far more economic solution, letting carriers most interested, fit and able to provide air transportation services do the job, should not continuously be considered.[9] A prerequisite of such a division-of-labor solution is a multilateral civil aviation agreement for which a large measure of political unity among the States is a *conditio sine qua non*.[10]

The present dispersion of effort, however, has its own laws.

III. NATIONAL VS INTERNATIONAL APPROACH

> "One cannot be free unless all are free." (Hegel)
> "All cannot be free unless all are restricted as a compromise. Our freedom is our fight against these restrictions, against that compromise." (Auth.)

The transportation of traffic has economic value; the carriage of air traffic represents a value which the States recognize as a potential source of revenue to the benefit of the national economy.

National sovereignty over the air space above its territory gives the State the means to trade in the right to transport traffic to, from, via, and also the traffic passing over, its territory.

Civil aviation is a business and therefore should make profits. A public utility service is a service which the public needs and which would not exist on a continuous basis without subsidy.

A national air carrier provides air services not as a public utility, be-

[9] N.B. Division of labor does not imply here that some States would not be able to mount successful airline operations.

[10] Cf. M. J. Keyzer, State Secretary for Transportation of the Netherlands, addressing the IATA AGM at Amsterdam, October 1969: "We shall welcome the day when the archaic system of bilateral bartering, if we can call it a system at all, is replaced by an international air framework, a multilateral system that will give every country a chance to develop its civil aviation."

cause the public could always travel on other carriers' services if the national air carrier, for some reason or other, would cease operations. It may happen, however, that some air connections would not be taken over by other carriers. Such connections, in the interest of the State concerned, would have to be provided by the national carrier, and could then be considered as public utility services, supported by State subsidies, if necessary.

But it is of use to a State to have a year-round service to various destinations available and to ensure such continuous services by seeing to it that they are provided by a national carrier. On the other hand, a national civil aviation apparatus is a valuable defense reserve.

Because of the aspects of civil aviation, air carriers find themselves to be, to some extent, hybrids. Governments are prepared to support and, if necessary, subsidize them. But since air carriers are not public utilities, they strive for profitable operations and independent managements. The mixed character of airlines explains, at least partly, the unique international regime governing international air services.

In this light air policy is based on the national interest in international air transportation and on the value of the national air traffic market. Thus a system has been created which regulates the admission by a State of carriers to its national market in return for admission of its own carriers to other national markets.

The fact that governments often refer to their national carriers as the national instrument, thus identifying themselves with the management of the carriers, illustrates the protectionist (or national) approach of States to international civil aviation regulation.

A completely different approach would be based on the recognition of the international community of man, the right of people to travel, the interests and needs of the traveling and shipping public, the advantages of cultural and economic international intercourse, and the contribution of international traffic to the economic development of the community of States and to peace.[11]

The promotion of international traffic by air would thus be to the advantage of each individual State, regardless of who carries the traffic,

[11] Cf. Charles Murphy before the International Aviation Club in Washington D.C. November 16, 1967: "But we should remember that a cardinal objective of our (bilateral air) agreements should be improved air services for the people of both nations, whether such services are performed by a US flag carrier or a foreign flag carrier." In other words, the national interest is not necessarily identical to the interest of the national carriers.

Cf. also the "Galbraith formula": "The measure of route desirability should be public convenience, not the benefit to the national treasuries or individual airlines."

a decision that should be given primarily to those best willing and able to engage in air transportation.

A purely international approach would lead to a division of labor. The main economic advantages derived from international air transportation lie, after all, with the promotion of travel (tourism) and trade, the money spent by the tourists and earned from the goods and services sold. An air policy based on a international approach to civil aviation would be a liberal one.

In this respect it is noteworthy that the Netherlands has traditionally followed a liberal policy with regard to both international shipping and international civil aviation. Being adverse to the use of power and defending the primacy of the international rule of law, the Netherlands gives priority to international interests as the sublimated national interests of all States (a practice which could be called enlightened protectionism).

The fact that Dutch shipping and Dutch civil aviation would profit from this liberal policy if it were also followed by other countries cannot be seen as an explanation of the Dutch liberal approach but merely as a coincidence and only partly a consequence. In general Dutch foreign policy is characterized by a legalistic approach to international problems and a preference for supra-national solutions even at the expense of short-term national interests.

Of course, present-day international civil aviation regulation is a mixture of national and international approaches, as, on the one hand, it allows more freedom to air carriers than could be explained if a purely national *quid pro quo* policy were pursued, and, on the other hand, it restricts air carriers more than would be acceptable if the promotion of international air traffic were the sole criterion.

With the further development of civil aviation, however the situation is changing and has come to require a different system of regulation. The mere fact of the advent of mass transportation by air, of the tremendous growth of the number of services, carriers, passengers and goods, the introduction of large capacity aircraft, makes the relevancy of the principles of national and international approaches questionable.

The application of these sets of principles takes on secondary importance in the face of an overriding need to develop a highly-specialized and efficient technique of regulation, in order to ensure the safest, fastest and most adequate transportation by air of the quantities of goods and masses of air travelers. The problem's quantity influences the quality of its regulation and solution.[12] But the growing complexity of the problem confuses

[12] Cf. Louis B. Sohn, September 1967, "UN and Human Rights," where he states that the difference between the man in the Stone Age who clubbed his fellow man with

States and leads to an exaggerated fear of competition, translated into ever stricter regulation.

In actual practice, international civil aviation regulation is becoming increasingly specific and detailed. A result is that so many details and aspects of airline operation are regulated that in general nothing is permitted unless it has been specifically authorized.

This system does not help promote the most flexible and economic airline operation. A less pragmatic and more idealistic policy seems indicated, giving more weight to the interests of the traveling public and those carriers fit, willing and able to transport them.

The *credo* of modern aviation policy, however, in the terms of the US Government, is the bilateral allocation of routes and traffic rights, resulting in an "equitable overall exchange of economic benefits derived from the establishment of air services between every two countries, including equitable opportunity for the airlines of the two countries to serve the needs of the traveling and shipping public." [13]

This is a primitive and anachronistic effort to solve a problem that is rapidly assuming supra-national dimensions. National and bilateral principles fall far short of coping with the situation. They stultify international air transportation and cripple international air travel and shipping.

Although the development of civil aviation is spectacular, with the introduction of jumbo or wide-bodied jets a completely new era has begun. We must start thinking in completely different terms. We must approach civil aviation, government, carrier and user aspects, from a detached, which is an extra-national, point-of-view and then determine the role of each individual State in international air transportation. This is not to say that we advocate an internationalization of airline operation (although the idea certainly should not be excluded), nor that we plead for multilateralism instead of bilateralism, in order to meet national requirements with an extra-national approach. The machinery of bilateral air agreements could very well serve the purposes which we have in mind:

An extra-national approach to international air transportation entails finding the most efficient technique of regulation. This may well be laid down in bilateral agreements geared to enable the smooth working of the international air transportation system.

The task of governments is to enable their citizens both to trade and travel internationally and to engage in the economic field of air transportation (to operate an airline). It may be necessary for the government,

a rock and the President who orders the H-bomb to be dropped on a city, is of a gradual nature. The quantitative change of the efficiency of the weapon has brought about a qualitative change in the result: to "beat to death" and to "wipe out," respectively.

[13] Cf. US-Canada air agreement of January 1966, article I (b).

however, "to restrict in order to enable" to a certain extent. The government must know what precisely it should enable.[14]

In aviation the government should, by virtue of its sovereignty, enable and ensure the safest, fastest, most efficient and most varied international air transportation possible. It should enable air carriers to carry as many passengers and goods as they can in the most economic way. It should enable the most economic operation of an airline by its own nationals.

It should not, however, protect its national carriers and support their operations by artificial means to keep them alive. The government should regulate international civil aviation, not protect its national airlines. It should protect the system as a whole. And we have tried to indicate that a system based on protection of the national airlines cannot be adequate in a mass-transportation era.

Next to the certification of their national carriers and the admission of foreign carriers, governments have three ways of regulating the operation of international air services: route grants, capacity control and tariff control.

Route grants and capacity control are both in the hands of the foreign governments of the countries to and via which a State wants its carriers to operate. But such route grants and capacity control lack clearly defined criteria for the determination of "who may carry what, how much, and where." It is customary, however, to take the carrier's home market as a basis for determining the extent of its right to international air transportation.

With regard to tariffs, governments try to prevent harmful and wasteful competition by requiring prior approval of fares. They could also claim the powers to disapprove and alter rates or practices, to suspend new rates and to prescribe lawful fares and rates. Thus governments could determine, to a great extent, the conditions under which carriers would be allowed to compete in a market. However, because of the worldwide interdependence of air fares, governments could achieve this only on a multilateral basis.

As it is, governments do indeed normally have the power to approve or disapprove fares quoted by the carriers, and as a rule governments do not allow fare competition. They normally do not have the power (nor, for that matter, the know-how) to set unilaterally, except for non-scheduled

[14] Cf. Wassenbergh, *op. cit.*, p. 155: "The criterion must, in fact, be the *purpose* for which a State, in the face of a given situation, wishes to use the sovereignty over land, sea and air."

Cf. also Professor J. G. Sauveplanne in a remarkable article entitled: "Freedom and Sovereignty in Air and Outer Space," *Netherlands International Law Review*, Year 1965, Issue 3, p. 243: "Sovereignty in the air therefore is not a territorial, but rather a functional, concept."

services, fares.[15] They may do so, however, by common agreement.

An extra-national and adequate solution to the problem of modern international mass air transportation regulation should establish a technique of regulation, that is, should avoid starting from the preset principles and rights of individual countries and carriers to traffic shares and the like.

Modern positive law, which regulates human activity in society as a technique, takes activities as they occur as a collective whole and disregards the why or other underlying motives of an individual nature.

This could be seen as a reverse approach to a legal problem; nevertheless such matters as freedom, order and justice in modern mass society can only have meaning and be attained if the rule of law, rather than individual opinions, principles or preferences, emphasizes collective involvement.

The major purpose of the rule of law should be to serve the actual unimpeded and disciplined development of society and to avoid conflicts in the widest sense. Conflicts impair the freedom of man in society and are detrimental to the development of society.

These criteria can appropriately be applied to international civil aviation where the efficiency of the collective carriers and the satisfaction of the collective users can be established to a reasonable extent for in this instance the function of the rule of law can be closely defined. The legal order which we have in mind would be neutral, since the technique of the rule of law has the neutrality of a scientific approach to the problem of man in society. For instance, as we have argued, the word "justice" should not be taken in its usual sense, but should be translated to mean "adequacy," or "adapted to the phenomena of man and State, their attributes and their activities in society".

The scientific character of the legal technique of regulation implies an important educative element, showing that in a given situation it is a framework, a prerequisite, a catalyst for the optimum development of society, since it enables optimum constructive activity and prevents or solves conflicts. To regulate the activities of man in society, prior attention should be given to regulations enabling and even stimulating the activities which contribute to the prosperity and the further development of society. Restrictions can and should be imposed to prevent or resolve conflicts and to ensure optimum development in a given situation. This means that with regard to international civil aviation regulation not the freedom of

[15] Cf. e.g. "British Air Transport in the Seventies," the Edwards Report of May 1969, H.M.S.O. p. 170: "Given the intention to regulate international tariffs we have no alternative system to suggest as a replacement for IATA." (the International Air Transport Association of the scheduled air carriers, which sets fares and rates by unanimous vote).

the carriers is at stake, nor the freedom of the traveling public, but the development of international aviation.

The technique of the regulation of international air transportation, that is, the extra-national approach, should focus on the situation of the international air relationships of States and of their nationals as a collective whole rather than on the situation of each State and its nationals, individually.

A difficulty is that in the international situation one cannot properly speak of an international society but only of a community of States. International civil aviation regulation therefore is intra-state regulation and as such has a character and structure different from national legal disciplines. States are sovereign entities of widely divergent importance, development, political structure and power. One could say that States can be compared with political parties without, however, being represented in a single congress or parliament with the power to draft worldwide legislation and enforce its observance. The UN with its specialized agency for international civil aviation (ICAO) has so far not attained this goal.

Nothwithstanding this difficulty, however, it is possible for States to act as if they and their nationals form part of an international society and consequently to approach the problem of international aviation regulation in a scientific, adequate, technical way. We do not wish to go again into the philosophical problem of good and bad law, but when we advocate a certain approach to the problem of the rule of law in society, it is with the very intention of avoiding a choice between good and bad law.

We wish to establish which rule of law is adequate and which is inadequate in a given situation, from a purely technical point of view. To give an example: we do not wish to base a system of law upon such a principle as that "all men are created equal". They are equal to the extent that they present themselves as equal in a given situation at a given time.

Similarly, when we speak about the prevention, avoidance and the solution of conflicts as the *raison d'être* and the purpose of the rule of law, we mean by conflict a situation which presents itself as such.

In such situation we should try and find an adequate solution. This may be different from what would be considered a just solution if certain principles were allowed to play a part.

Our hope for the solution of international aviation problems does not lie with our principles, nor with a purely rationalist approach, but simply with our knowledge of the mechanics of society.

There is a technical truth beyond our own personal truths and we should try to discover what that technical truth is to arrive at ideal solutions.

The national approach mentioned above is obviously the most primitive solution to the problem of international air transportation regulation.[16] This theory completely fails to recognize the existence of an international legal order, a community of States governed by a set of *sui generis* rules, governed by international law rather than by a system of intra-State law where national laws fight for priority in the international sphere.

We stress that international air traffic must be considered as a whole and that international air transport regulation must be de-nationalized in favor of extra-national regulation.

Each nation should strive both to stimulate traffic and to obtain the greatest possible share. In practice, however, the accent lies on traffic shares. Nations choose either liberal or protectionist policies, depending on their national circumstances. A protectionist policy aims at obtaining a 50% share of the traffic on the routes to and from the home country. A liberal policy allows commercial competition to determine market shares, at least to a point.[17] Today the choice is no longer between protectionism and freedom. The problem of civil aviation regulation is adequacy.

After a number of bad years in the late fifties and the early sixties international civil aviation took a turn for the better in 1963. In a period of prosperity and expansion restrictions are felt by those who take advantage of the boom to be obstacles rather than protection.[18] Opinions change with circumstances. This does not change the need for adequate regulations adapted to circumstances. Adequate is not the same as opportunistic.[19] It is a new concept of freedom.

[16] Illustrative of a national approach is a statement by the US CAB that its recommendations to the President have taken due account of any allegations that the grant of a permit will be detrimental to the interests of US carriers and thereby to the public interest.

Cf. Explanatory Statement. Notice of Proposed Rule Making P.S.D.R.-21, Docket 20029, July 10, 1968, Part 399.211.302. re Filing and Processing of Certain Applications for Foreign Permits.

Cf. also the US doctrine of "equal exchange of economic benefits".

[17] Cf. Stephen Wheatcroft, *Air Transport Policy,* 1964, p. 74, where he remarks that if a country's share falls below 40%, it would (naturally) turn towards measures for restricting foreign competitors.

[18] Cf. Mr. S. Tipton, President of the American Air Transport Association, in an address delivered in Washington D.C. on June 1966, on "The Success Story of World Civil Aviation": "I have stressed the dynamic economic growth of the industry as a reason for the growing obsolescence of restrictive practices."

[19] Cf. also the statement of Jacques Boitreaud, the Secretary General of the French Civil Aviation Department, quoted by the journalist Jean Marie Riche in *La Vie des Transports,* December 1966; "Il est vraisemblable, d'ailleurs, que pour tenir compte de la diversité de ces éléments (sociaux, politiques et économiques) dans les différents pays, comme aussi de l'inégale importance des compagnies aériennes, on sera conduit de plus en plus à délaisser une conception protectionniste et de stricte équilibre des droits de traffic, pour la recherche de formules plus souples de coopération et d'échanges, notamment et en première urgence dans le cadre européen."

CHAPTER TWO

I. NATIONAL CONTROL OF THE AIR TRAFFIC MARKET

In the face of the continued increase of the number of airlines and the expansion of their services, and the introduction of aircraft with ever bigger capacity, governments are inclined to ever further regulate airline competition, as a defensive reflex.[1]

They can do this by allowing only a limited number of foreign airlines to operate into their territory, by limiting the granting of routes to foreign carriers, limiting the number of frequencies operated by foreign carriers over existing routes, restricting the number of passengers which may be carried on routes or route segments, limiting the operation of all-cargo services or the amount of freight to be carried, limiting the days and hours foreign carriers may operate over routes also operated by nationals carriers (to avoid duplication of services), restricting the operation of charter flights by foreign carriers, etc.

On the other hand governments have a responsibility to further the development of international civil aviation and to promote international air services in the interests of the traveling and shipping public.

Moreover they cannot ignore the obvious benefits to the national economy of attracting international air services and foreign passengers to their country.

Governments thus are faced with conflicting objectives: the protection of national carriers and the promotion of international air traffic to their country.

In practice priority is given in most cases to the protection of national carriers.

When the US carriers' share of international air transportation declined the US Government was accused of following a "give-away" policy

[1] Cf. e.g. ICAO Assembly, Buenos Aires, 1968, Doc. A16-WP/33-EC/5, 8/7/68, p. 5 B: "Exchange of Commercial Rights".

and an investigation was ordered which resulted in the Smathers Report of April 1956.[2]

One of the report's conclusions was that "no foreign flag airline competitor to the US flag carriers should be allowed to prosper at the expense of the US by engaging in traffic to which it does not have a primary entitlement."

Because many foreign airlines are supported by their governments, while the international air transport system of the US is maintained by private enterprise, the US government should not bargain away too frivolously the value of its market. This simply would not make "good business sense".

The instrument for carrying out a "businesslike" policy, it was stated, could be found in the Bermuda capacity principles incorporated in most bilateral air agreements concluded by the US.

We may note here two key concepts for the granting of air routes and the determination of capacity:

- the value of the (US) market and access to it (the granting of *routes*);
- the traffic to which a carrier has a primary entitlement (Bermuda capacity principles, the granting of *traffic* rights).

Among other things, the report stressed that by granting a foreign air carrier access to the New York air traffic market alone, New York being the largest single market in world air transportation, "a traffic flow is established which is so great a value that the foreign State should offer US carriers access to a second city in its homeland to attempt even in limited measure to match the American grant."

The argument that the foreign cities are an inseparable ingredient of the value of the US market – "unless there is a place to go to there is no market to serve" – and that therefore both sides have an equal claim to the value of the US market, was countered by pointing to the possibilities offered to a foreign airline, by virtue of the "geographical location of its homeland" (sixth freedom traffic) as well. This 1956 argument is still prevalent in the US today. The value which a carrier obtains under an air agreement is dependent upon its access to the market opened to it. This access may be more favorable to the carriers of the foreign country, for reasons of geographical location, than to US carriers.[3]

[2] Cf. US Senate, S. Report No. 1875, 84th Congress, 2nd Session, Report of the Ctee on Interstate and Foreign Commerce, *passim,* Washington D.C. April 30, 1956.

[3] Cf. Frank E. Loy, "Bilateral Air Transport Agreements: Some problems of finding a fair route exchange". McGill University, Montreal November 1967: "What we are looking for is the value (in terms of access to market) which a carrier obtains from an agreement, and this value is either there or not, regardless of the freedom category of

Today the accent has shifted somewhat from the freedom classification of the traffic to the geography of the foreign country. With today's tourist traffic making round trips with a multitude of stops in various countries it is difficult to find an acceptable definition for sixth freedom traffic.

We have mentioned earlier that both sides could claim an equal right to the value of the (US) market. And indeed it seems logical to us to say that a market consists of traffic, any traffic, moving on routes between cities in the homelands of the States entering into a bilateral agreement. Both sides have one and the same bilateral market to bargain with. Another matter is whether the national carriers of both parties will have an equal opportunity (equal access?) to participate in the carriage of the traffic which moves on the routes concerned. In other words, does a foreign carrier have a better opportunity, (better access) because it can carry traffic to and from points beyond its homeland more easily than US carriers can?

While the carriers of both parties have points beyond their homelands to and from which they may carry (sixth freedom) traffic on the routes concerned, there may be differences in the geographical position of the homelands themselves. Once we consider any route as an integral part of the whole world network of international air routes, however, these differences become of secondary importance and moreover can be made to disappear for the greatest part through adequate scheduling of services and adequate sales promotion.

On the other hand, carriers carrying sixth freedom traffic will always have to make an intermediate stop in their homeland and to change the line number of their services and probably the aircraft as well, while the carriers of the other party may operate direct services to the points concerned under the terms of bilateral agreements concluded with the States where these points are situated. The value of sixth freedom traffic therefore should not be exaggerated.

No carrier, however, need have its government conclude an air agreement with any State to carry this traffic so long as the carrier makes no commercial intermediate stop in the territory of that State.

The carriage of such traffic is thus an advantage derived from the agreement by a carrier flying via its homeland, but it is not an advantage for the carrier flying direct from its homeland. For instance, a foreign carrier obtains access to third country markets via its homeland and US carriers have no need to conclude an agreement with the foreign country con-

the passenger." Loy reasons that the value of most franchises is heavily dependent on what he calls the "accident of geography". (p. 18).

cerned to obtain the same access. Here is where geographical location comes into play, at least in practice. In other words, in practice a distinction can be made between terminal markets and transit markets, depending on geographical location and of course on size. The USA is chiefly a terminal market and so are peripheral States. A country like Holland is, to a great extent, a transit market.

We have stated that each separate route constitutes a separate opportunity, and is thus a separate bilateral market and that this is so because of the technique of bilateral route exchanges. Because of that same technique we cannot consider a route to be a separate market in the sense that this market is defined by traffic which has its "true origin" and its "ultimate destination" in the terminal points (and possible intermediate points) of the route.[4]

We cannot define a market only by the traffic generated at a single point. Since traffic moving on a route may be sold, may "originate" or have its "destination" at any point in the world, each route should be considered to be an integrated part of the worldwide route pattern of all airlines' air services.

When the Smathers' report states that KLM, for instance, by carrying sixth freedom traffic, acquired in 1963 an estimated $ 9,273,000 from the US as opposed to the $ 53,000 acquired by US carriers from Holland, this statement only indicates that US carriers evidently did not make optimum use of the possibilities available under the US-Netherlands air agreement.

It is true, however, that if, for instance, a US carrier serving a point beyond Holland wants to include Holland as intermediate point, it should be prepared to accept, in return, that the Netherlands carriers obtain, together with the possibility of transporting traffic between Holland and the US, the possibility of carrying traffic via Holland between points beyond (in Europe, etc.) and the US as well (sixth freedom traffic).

The value to the US carrier of the inclusion of Amsterdam in its service would be calculated by the US carrier on the basis of the additional traffic to be gained between the US and Amsterdam and between Amsterdam and points beyond Holland.

On this US service between the US and a point beyond Amsterdam, the

[4] Cf. Stephen Wheatcroft in his excellent book on "Air Transport Policy", 1964: "... scheduled air transport is not a homogeneous commodity, but a different commodity on each route, in other words each route is a separate market." (p. 55).

Cf. also Mel Brenner (TWA) in "Discussion of Airline Load Factors and Capacity", August 1969, commented in *Aviation Daily* of September 4, 1969: "Every schedule is a separate, distinct product ... has its own specialized appeal to a portion of the market."

inclusion of Amsterdam would make the Dutch carrier a competitor in the market between that point and the US without the US carrier gaining anything in return *in that market*.

Of course the possibility of transport between the US and Holland makes it possible for the US carrier to take traffic between points beyond the US (Mexico, the Pacific and the Caribbean) and Holland, as well. Speaking geographically, this possibility is not as obvious as the one obtained by the Dutch carrier to and from points beyond Holland. Moreover, in the US the CAB awards various routes to different carriers so that routes to and from points beyond the US and connecting in the US with ex-Holland routes will not be granted to one and the same carrier, so optimum stimulation of this traffic is not guaranteed.

In the exchange of rights between governments, however, the US government does indirectly obtain the possibility of having traffic carried by US carriers to and from points beyond the USA to and from Holland. The USCAB could take steps which would turn this possibility into a valuable one in view of the great distances and the corresponding high fares involved by allocating such routes to one and the same carrier.

It is true that the US government may not be interested in doing this because US carriers would stand to lose more than they would gain: penetrating these markets would require too much effort in competition with the market's home carrier and it might be possible to carry the traffic concerned more profitably under other bilateral agreements, which would avoid additional competition by the other carrier.

Such pragmatic reasoning, however, tends to carve up the worldwide air traffic market to the detriment of both air travelers and carriers and to the detriment of the development of the markets of the smaller States.

Moreover the above argument is valid only for sixth freedom traffic which, in our example, does not propose to stop in Holland and passes through in direct transit. Traffic which makes a stop in Holland is of direct value to US carriers under the US-Netherlands bilateral air agreement.

Finally and of particular interest is the advantage derived by US carriers from a bilateral air agreement to carry traffic between any US point and the other country even if only a limited number of routes is specified in the agreement: through equipment interchange arrangements with domestic US carriers one-plane through services can be provided to any US point. Foreign carriers are not allowed to make such arrangements.

The guiding principle of US air policy is to arrive at an "equal exchange of economic benefits" under bilateral air agreements and to make capacity control possible on the basis of statistics indicating the "true" origin and "ultimate" destination of the traffic.

It might be more adequate for US carriers as well if they were to view the conclusion of an air agreement as the construction for their carriers of new highways open to the traveling public at large. Or in other words, the exchange of routes under an air agreement should not be based on the traffic-generating power of the contracting parties, which leads to withholding routes because sixth freedom traffic might be carried, or because the rights exchanged might be exploited by the designated carriers in some other way exceeding the potential of their home market.

It should be noted that US air policy at the time of the Smathers Report concentrated on finding ways and means to restrict the growth of foreign flag carriers operating to or wishing to operate to the US, using a system of regulated competition, and was not so much concerned with the *quid pro quo* for US carriers in foreign countries. Accepting the fact of restrictions placed by foreign governments on the operations of US carriers, the US hoped to be able to reserve its own traffic market for its own carriers as much as possible. The US, at the time, was on the defensive.

In practice, however, US carriers for the greater part still exercised far more route and traffic privileges in other countries than the carriers of these countries did in the US. Restrictive tendencies in the US were directed mainly against carriers in a position to carry the sixth freedom traffic between the US and points beyond their homeland.

II. FREEDOM CLASSIFICATION AND TRAFFIC DATA

In the present technique of international civil aviation regulation, traffic restrictions are based on the precedent of the Bermuda capacity clauses of bilateral air agreements.[5]

Although the language of the Bermuda capacity clauses is vague it is possible to summarize its main implications as follows:

a) the backbone, so to speak, of air carrier traffic, has to be the traffic between the country of which the carrier is a national and the countries of ultimate destination of the traffic (third and fourth freedom traffic);

b) the opportunity to carry traffic between third countries (fifth freedom traffic) is a secondary and restricted privilege;

c) capacity should be adapted to the amount of the "primary traffic"

[5] Cf. for a very clear and objective view on the problems of the Bermuda principles, Albert W. Stoffel "American Bilateral Air Transport Agreements on the Threshold of the Jet Transport Age," the *Journal of Air Law and Commerce,* Vol. 26, 1959, No. 2, North Western University.

mentioned under a), allowance being made for additional capacity for the "secondary traffic" mentioned under b);

d) control through bilateral consultations can be exercised on an *ex post facto* basis, if one party finds that its carrier(s) are being handicapped (notably in their primary traffic) by the carrier(s) of the other contracting party (the latter having only a secondary right to this traffic).

The implication of the *ex post facto* review is that the Bermuda principles presuppose a liberal route grant, in any case of terminal routes, (routes which have their terminal point in the territory of the other party), and that they do not allow for a predetermination of capacity and frequencies.

Different and more restrictive applications of the Bermuda capacity clauses may be explained by the fear that strong carriers will make use of the rights granted to them without regard to sound commercial principles and operate services without sufficient economic justification (dumping).

Another reason to adopt a restrictive attitude towards route grants and the capacity permitted on the routes granted is the fear of sixth freedom traffic.

This kind of traffic developed as national carriers built their networks around their home countries with their home bases as the hubs of their services.[6] In the home country traffic is transferred from one service of the airline to another for onward international air travel.

As regards the regulation of this traffic, Stoffel rightly states: "It has not been possible to solve this problem since it does not seem practical to specify what traffic an airline may carry from points back of its homeland. One clarifying step would be to agree on the freedom category of such traffic." [7]

Clarifying the freedom category of sixth freedom traffic, e.g. by classifying it as having the character of fifth freedom traffic, thus bringing it under the capacity principles of bilateral air agreements, would result in the application of the usual fifth freedom restrictions to the carriage of sixth freedom traffic.[8]

Moreover sixth freedom traffic would then be eliminated from the traffic on which the capacity of a service should primarily be based (the

[6] N.B. Routes granted in bilateral air agreements or otherwise always have the home country of the airline to which the routes are granted as their starting point.

[7] *Op. cit.*, p. 130.

[8] Cf. ICAO Doc. 7586 C/883 June 24, 1955, p. 65: "It should be noted that in the US view sixth freedom is merely a designation given to a specific type of fifth freedom traffic and it is subject to any provisions of bilateral agreements which relate to the fifth freedom."

third and fourth freedom traffic of the country of which the airline is a national).

There seems to be no legal basis for making sixth freedom traffic subject to the capacity provisions of bilateral air agreements. Capacity principles govern the bilateral air relationships of the States and their application cannot surpass the geographic scope of the air agreement, which is defined by the route pattern as specified between the contracting parties.

Any review of capacity in the light of the traffic carried should confine itself to the relation between the capacity offered and the traffic carried on the routes specified, between the point of origin, the point of destination and the intermediate points of these routes on the one hand, and the points in the territory of the other contracting party on the other.

Of the traffic carried from or to a point not specified in the route schedule attached to the air agreement (off-route point), via a point on the route as specified, to or from the territory of the other contracting party, only the on-route portion falls under the traffic to be considered when reviewing the capacity requirements which exist on that route.[9]

In applying the capacity principles of bilateral air agreements, sixth freedom traffic can therefore be considered only as third and fourth freedom traffic (traffic carried on the on-route portion to or from the home country of the airline concerned).

There is no clear definition of the origin and the destination of traffic. In practice the points on the routes at which traffic is embarked or disembarked were (and still normally are) considered as such. Sixth freedom traffic therefore automatically becomes part of the third and fourth freedom traffic carried on the route. In this case the traffic which an airline carries to and from points beyond its homeland is of no concern to the other contracting party under the bilateral air agreement (the carriage of traffic, embarked in the US, by a Belgian airline between Brussels and for instance Frankfort or Zürich would be of no concern to the USA under the US-Belgian air agreement).

Unless a definition is agreed upon as to what are to be considered the demands of traffic to and from a country, that is, as long as in bilateral air agreements routes are exchanged which have the home country of the carrier to which the routes are granted as their starting point without

[9] Cf. Foreign off-route charter service investigation (Docket 7173, p. 8): "The Board has always construed the foreign air carrier permits as authorizing, and the carriers have regularly scheduled flights from a US point named in the permit to a point beyond the homeland terminal, provided the flights are operated via the described homeland terminal."

specifying points beyond the homeland, there seems to be no legal basis for any other application of the capacity provisions of bilateral agreements.

The big problem with statistics is defining the origin and the destination of traffic.

Origin normally would be the first place mentioned on a traveler's ticket, the point where he embarks by aircraft. His destination would then be the last place mentioned on his ticket, the point where he disembarks for the last time. In case of a round trip journey, however, one could say that the destination is the furthest point mentioned on the ticket, to be measured in terms of direct great-circle distance, or the great-circle distances of the stages flown.[10]

The matter is important because of the implications the compiling of origin and destination statistics has in applying restrictive measures. It is probably because of this implication that agreement on a definition of traffic statistics at the multilateral level seems impossible.

In this way the already highly controversial Bermuda principles also unfortunately bar the collection of detailed international traffic statistics.

As it is, most countries and airlines agree to the collection of "on-line" statistics or even system-origin-and-destination statistics. On-line, the origin of traffic is seen as the point where the traveler embarks on a specific service, defined by line number, and the destination the point where he disembarks from that service; within one airline's system the origin is the point where he embarks on a service of a certain carrier and the destination the point where he leaves the services of that same carrier, for instance when he embarks a connecting service of another carrier.

Agreeing on an exchange of more detailed or more extensive traffic information is difficult because of the wide variety of interpretations, resulting, among other things, from different air political concepts and from the lack of agreed definitions for such terms as true origin, ultimate destination, stopover, transit.

As a matter of fact it is virtually impossible to determine the "true origin" and the "ultimate destination" of traffic as it is impossible to control how a passenger ultimately uses his ticket. If he changes to another airline, the other airline's documents are not available to the airline that issued the ticket in the first place; as the validity of a ticket extends to one

[10] N.B. Origin and destination of traffic can be defined in many ways: e.g. Directional origin and destination, ticket origin and destination, system origin and destination, coupon origin and destination, effective origin and destination, purpose destination, stopover destination, line origin and destination, route origin and destination, etc.

year, it is impossible to know the duration of an en route stopover if the passenger proceeds on a different airline afterwards.

It is not traffic which has a determinable origin and destination, but the carriage of traffic by an airline which has.

Thus the ticket should not be the criterion for determining the origin and the destination of traffic. The ticket is both a ticket and a voucher and as a voucher it makes the determination of the origin and the destination of the passenger impossible.

In January 1961, the US CAB instituted an investigation of the terms, conditions and limitations of foreign air carrier permits in order to try and impose a new condition pursuant to which foreign air carriers should be required to furnish traffic data to the Board and submit their schedules for aproval to the Board.[11]

These new conditions would have enabled the Board not only to limit grants to foreign carriers of new routes, but also to limit the carriage of secondary (third country) traffic (including sixth freedom traffic) by adapting the capacity of foreign carriers to the traffic requirements of their home markets as defined by the CAB.

Notwithstanding increased competition by existing and new carriers the US carriers' relative share of traffic rose again after 1963/64. In 1950 this share had been 59.5%, in 1962 it was only 36.6% over the North Atlantic.

It was during this period that the new US international civil air policy was drafted and, on April 23, 1963, released by President Kennedy.

Not surprisingly it maintained the relatively liberal approach of US civil air policy laid down by President Eisenhower in May 1954.[12]

The civil air policy of the US recognizes the principle of an "equitable exchange of economic benefits" under bilateral agreements. In practice this means that even if no adverse effects on the operations of US carriers are feared, no routes are granted if they could produce an "unbalanced" situation. However, the US Government departs from this principle if political, military or other non-aviation considerations are involved, such as the "give-away" route grant to West Germany in 1955, the US-Iceland air agreement, the granting of Seattle to SAS in 1968 and Houston to KLM in 1967.

Frank Loy, in the speech referred to above, disapprovingly mentions a

[11] Cf. CAB Permit Investigation, Docket 12063, Order E-16288, Jan. 18, 1961. Recommended Decision of June 21, 1962. See, however, pp. 28 and 103.

[12] N.B. "liberal" only because the US, as a rule, does not impose capacity limitations on the operation of routes once granted.

variety of trades such as a route for a technical assistance program, a route for support in ICAO, etc.[13]

The principle of an equitable exchange of economic benefits under bilateral agreements was reaffirmed in the 1963 statement. The new policy remained vague and cautious in its wording, thus leaving room for opportunist solutions in bilateral negotiations.

In the course of 1963, however, the US State Department and the CAB made abortive attempts to reach an understanding with a number of European countries especially on the sixth freedom issue.

But, as the sixth freedom problem solved itself more or less ,with the ever-growing number of direct flights and their marked competitive advantage over flights with an additional stop and usually a change of aircraft in the carrier's home country, and because it was felt that restrictions on sixth freedom traffic would scuttle the 1963 aviation policy, which opposed "arbitrary capacity restrictions", these US moves created mistrust and confusion and were not pursued.[14]

Furthermore the CAB refrained from investigating further the terms and conditions of foreign air carrier permits. Nor was a later CAB effort in 1965 to impose restrictions on the volume of off-route charter service performed by foreign air carriers pursued.

These efforts to make it possible to curtail the operations of foreign carriers were undertaken in the absence of a pressing need for protective measures and without a clear indication that US public interest would be served by them.

They may have stemmed from uneasiness and the fear that other countries could place limitations on US carrier operations without the CAB having appropriate means to retaliate.

In this light may also be seen the introduction of two bills by Senator Warren G. Magnuson in April 1966.[15]

[13] N.B. The strengthening of political relations through a fair exchange of operating rights cannot be ignored as a major factor in air policy.

[14] Cf., however, Charles Murphy, Chairman of the CAB, before the Aero Club in Washington on March 1, 1966: "Although more than 60% of all international air passenger traffic to and from the USA consists of the travel of US nationals, US flag carriers handle less than 49% of this traffic. In the important market between the US and Europe, the US citizens account for 61% of the travel, yet the US flag carriers receive only 40% of this market. It is extremely difficult to establish and maintain arrangements with other countries which give US flag carriers an equal opportunity to participate in the traffic." Cf. also ITA Study in ECAC/ECO-II/2-WP/3 of September 1969: in 1968 US citizens represented 62.4% of the total traffic between the US and Europe; US airlines performed 46.1% of the passenger traffic, against 40.4% in 1964. (p. 9)

[15] Cf. S. 3197 and S. 3198, 89th Congress, 2nd Session, April 6, 1966. Neither of the Bills was enacted.

The first intended to enable US carriers, through interim exemption, to compete with foreign flag carriers pending final CAB certification under Section 401 of the Federal Aviation Act of 1958 as amended. The second bill, which was passed by the Senate in September 1966 would have enabled the CAB to retaliate if restrictions are imposed by a foreign government on US carrier operations contrary to rights previously agreed upon, and could have ensured or, as the case may be, enforced a liberal attitude on the part of foreign Governments, at least with regard to the operations of US carriers. In 1970, such retaliation was made possible (Part 213).

The danger of regulatory measures in general is their catalytic effect, the escalation of regulations. Already international civil aviation is overregulated in many respects. The national approach to the problem of international civil aviation regulation has led to a highly complicated system of capacity regulation, in particular.

At the risk of oversimplification, one could say that in US civil aviation policy the emphasis is shifting once again from efforts to restrict foreign operators to efforts to safeguard and improve the position of US carriers in other countries.

The lesson derived from recent world history and especially from US aviation history is clear. Fear, source of all kinds of protective measures, proved unjustified and nearly led to regulatory action which in actual fact might have contributed to bringing about the very situation which these regulations intended to prevent: a further weakening of the competitive situation of US carriers in the world.

Efforts to confine each flag carrier as much as possible to its own national market, where traffic originates or terminates, set the clock back by frustrating the further development of transit markets. In the last analysis the development of these markets is the most effective means for promoting world-wide air transportation and a global rapprochement of nations.

In August 1969, President Nixon ordered a new study of US international aviation policy, noting that economic, political and technological developments since 1963 called for a fresh review of major aviation policy questions. A summary of this new policy is given in Appendix I.

III. THE AIR TRAFFIC MARKET AND THE EXCHANGE OF ROUTES AND TRAFFIC RIGHTS

The Navigation Act of 1651 stipulated that the "right to carry traffic between two countries belongs equally and exclusively to the carriers of those countries." [16]

[16] Cf. Mercantilism, a purely nationalist approach which advocates government in-

Professor Ferreira, of Argentina, claims the "right of each State to dispose of its own traffic as being in keeping with the sovereignty and equality of States."

He concludes that "*El tráfico de nación a nación es una unidad, un todo, una síntesis de su commercio mutuo.*" [17]

But modern traffic increasingly cannot be broken down into independent bilateral units. Modern traffic becomes a global unit.

The doctrine of a State's own traffic often is promoted by governments whose carriers may be less competitive and are trying to make up for their lack of commercial acumen by advancing the theory of the right to reserve to their own carriers traffic to and from their States and consequently condemning those carriers who carry other than their rightful traffic. Thus in a report published in the French Official Gazette of Dec. 1, 1967, it is stated that "Certain States with a modest national market, like Holland with KLM, have become masters in the field [of combining routes permitting the transportation of traffic that has little connection with any activity in the home country]." [18]

The report goes on to state that, "If industrialized countries are experts in the field [of negotiating traffic rights and combining the use of them], the newly independent States do not always have the necessary skill to avoid being duped . . . The role of France through the intermediary of Air France and UTA consists precisely of protecting the interests of these States, at the same time taking care that the interests of France, which in general coincide, are defended." [19]

It is doubtful whether the doctrine of a State's own traffic is in the best interests especially of the newly independent States. The contrary may be true. It may be that France wants to reserve the traffic between these States and France for French carriers and the carriers of these States, who are assisted by French carriers. The traffic between new States and other States would then be shared among the carriers of these States. Such a system results in a dispersion of effort on the single basis of the national market of the newly dependent State concerned.

The role of French carriers outside bilateral relationships with France,

tervention in and direction of economic life as necessary to promote the prosperity of the State. In the international sphere this theory is bound to lead to power politics.

[17] Cf. Javier Rubio García-Mina in "Iniciación al estudio del mercado de Transporte Aéreo," IV (E), *Ingeniería Aeronáutica,* July/August, 1965, p. 15.

[18] It may be interesting to note that the traffic carried by KLM in 1967/68 consisted for about 60% of third and fourth freedom traffic, about 19% of fifth freedom traffic and 21% sixth freedom traffic. These percentages are calculated on the basis of ticket coupon origin and destination statistics.

[19] Cf. *Journal Officiel de la République Française,* No. 20, Dec. 1, 1967, page 871.

apart from technical and operational assistance, would be obscure. Or would it be the role of French carriers to see to it that the new State's carrier obtains its "rightful" share of traffic with other States as well? The carrier of the new State might be able to obtain a much larger share of international world air traffic than its rightful share as calculated on the basis of the own-traffic doctrine. Much would depend on the national ability, the geographical situation, tourism, trade and other relations with other countries, the choice of possible partners for cooperation in the field of civil aviation, etc.

Moreover the national market of new States often is still in a state of development and therefore may offer a rather small basis for the development of a viable national flag airline.

Unfortunately, protectionism has a snowball effect. A country like Brazil for instance, restricts overflight and frequencies through its territory to prevent as much as possible adverse effects on Brazilean flag airlines and their carriage of traffic between the countries south of Brazil and the countries north of Brazil, especially Europe. As a result of protectionism of other countries, especially European countries, Brazil has concluded that it has to protect its interests by bargaining strictly on a reciprocity basis, keeping out carriers transporting third country traffic even if this is traffic between two countries neither of which is Brazil (traffic via Brazil). In other words Brazil does not want deviation to third carriers of traffic between third countries via Brazil, the markets of which are not available to Brazilean carriers without Brazil having to offer reciprocal rights to the carriers of such countries in return. To give an example: To transport traffic between Buenos Aires and Europe via Brazil, Brazil has to offer traffic rights to the Argentine carriers between Brazil and Europe in return. Therefore Brazil does not want to grant overflight rights to permit third carriers to carry traffic between Buenos Aires and Europe, as this would mean competition for the Brazilian carriers carrying this traffic via their own country in sixth freedom.

In this way, Brazil extends its "own" market in conformity with the power it can exercise over air services transiting the territory of Brazil, to improve its negotiating position. There are still other ways to make the most of its power over the national market under a system of "calculated" protectionism.

Some (airlines for instance of) developing countries not yet able to fully exploit the own national traffic potential or claim full reciprocal rights for immediate use resort to such methods of compensation as charging for the use of their air space and the carriage of traffic to, from or via their territory by foreign airlines. This "royalty" system is applied by some countries under various disguises and even in rare cases openly.[20]

Payment in various forms, like commercial or cooperative agreements by foreign airlines, to national carriers for traffic carried on certain routes or segments is likely to become more frequent to compensate for "unbalanced situations." There are many definitions for an unbalanced situation. Some may hold that a balance exists if there is a 50/50 split of the market concerned. Others, if there is "fair and equal opportunity" for the carriers of the two States. The US adheres to the principle of the "equitable exchange of economic benefits," which means, in terms of routes, an equitable exchange of "access to markets". The Netherlands Government is inclined to find a balance through mirror reciprocity in route exchanges. If we talk here about an "unbalanced situation," we refer to an imbalance of revenues derived by the respective carriers on the routes exchanged, on the one hand, and an imbalance of the rights exchanged and actually operated, on the other. Of course a system of payments can only be applied in a competitive situation. If the operations of a foreign carrier have no adverse effect on the operations of the national carrier (for instance, because the national carrier does not operate the routes in question), any payment by the foreign carrier to the national carrier would amount to a royalty, a subsidy or even a type of financial aid. It does nothing to improve the competitive strenghth of the national carrier, on the contrary.

Clearly a system of payments by foreign carriers to national carriers for traffic carried on certain routes or route segments will have further adverse effects: It will result in lower revenues for the carriage of that traffic. This, in turn, will discourage these carriers from applying for lower fares in IATA for the routes concerned. And this will be to the detriment of further development of traffic on these routes.

Moreover such payments tend to distort the competitive situation and in a way are a penalty for success.

To have to "buy", as a foreign carrier, all passengers and the cargo carried on certain routes or route segments which are in excess of the traffic the national carrier carries on routes operated to, from and via the territory of the foreign carrier, seems to be a system which lacks the "justification" of pool agreements between carriers. It means that a national carrier can peddle the traffic to and via its country to the highest bidder, that is the

[20] Cf. Zambia, which in 1967 required the payment to Zambian Airways of 15% of the net revenues derived by foreign carriers from the exercise of third and fourth and fifth freedom traffic rights in Zambia, pending the exercise of reciprocal rights by Zambian Airways.

foreign carrier interested in and able to transport for the lowest revenues, for instance because of its size or efficiency, or because of subsidies.

To place the conduct of a nation's air policy in the hands of the national carrier, even if the carrier is government-owned and government-controlled, is contrary to the national public interest. A company naturally views this interest in the light of its own balance sheet, after all.[21]

Governments should not allow their national carriers to "negotiate" payment for traffic rights unless the exercise of such rights will adversely affect the traffic of the national carrier. In such cases a solution may be found which, as an interim arrangement, also meets the requirements of the foreign carrier who otherwise would not have been able to exercise its rights.

Payment for traffic rights is different from charges imposed on the carriers for the use of airport and air navigation facilities. For these charges services are rendered. Payment for traffic rights can be merely a temporary compensation for the losses which the national carrier expects to suffer as a result of the additional competition on the route or route segment in question.

As a rule it is not easy to assess such losses, and the governments concerned should supervise such transactions.

IV. THE SIXTH FREEDOM ISSUE

The world air traffic market is far bigger than the sum of the bilateral air traffic markets. Each State forms part of this world market. The relevant "bilateral" relationship should be between each individual State and the rest of the world, which is not the same as between a State and each of the other States. A State is not only origin and destination, but also a junction, of international air services and, consequently, international traffic. As such its importance can be measured. This importance could be a basis for its share of international traffic. Other factors could be considered relevant, as well, such as the ability of a carrier to perform air transportation services.

How can the importance of a State as the origin, the destination and as a junction of international traffic be measured?

A comprehensive interpretation is given in an "understanding" reached between the US and the Scandinavian countries in June 1966.[22]

[21] Air talks on this basis, placing the emphasis on the (short-term) interests of the national carriers, may adversely affect the wider interests of the overall relationship between the countries.

[22] Cf. Agreements between the US and Sweden, Denmark and Norway, effected by

Here, as is usual in present day air policy, the problem was approached by defining the capacity which a State is "entitled" to operate on international routes. Although, as we have explained, we consider this approach, which apportions capacity instead of stimulating the traffic over the international "highways of the air", to be wrong, it does illustrate the current definition of an "air traffic market".

The air traffic market to which a designated airline is entitled consists of traffic to which the airline has a "primary entitlement" and traffic to which it has only a "secondary entitlement".

Traffic of primary entitlement is defined as "the traffic whose initial origin or ultimate destination as shown on the ticket or waybill or combination of tickets or combination of waybills, is in the country of which the transporting airline is a national, whether or not the traffic passes through, connects at, or stops over for any length of time within the period of validity of the ticket at any point or points en route," and also "the traffic stopping over for twelve hours or more at a point in the country of which the transporting airline is a national."

Traffic of secondary entitlement is defined as "the traffic having neither its origin or destination (ultimate destination), as shown by the ticket or waybill or combination of tickets or combination of waybills in the country of which the transporting airline is a national, irrespective of whether the initial origin or ultimate destination of the traffic is intermediate to (fifth freedom traffic), or beyond (sixth freedom traffic) the terminals of the route over which it is transported" and also "the traffic which passes through, connects at or stops over for less than twelve hours at a point in the country of which the transporting airline is a national."

Furthermore it is clearly stated that the rights of the one carrier to provide capacity for sixth freedom traffic shall not alter the right of the other carrier to provide capacity for *all* traffic whose initial origin or ultimate destination is in the country of which the latter airline is a national.

In other words the bargaining position of each party vis-à-vis a third country is not affected because sixth freedom traffic is regarded as traffic

Exchange of Notes signed at Washington, June 7, 1966. TIAS 6026.

The agreed definitions of origin and destination of traffic read as follows:

"(a) for a one way trip the initial origin is the first point and the ultimate destination is the last point on the ticket or waybill or combination of tickets or combination of waybills;

(b) for a circle or round trip a directional criterion will apply, i.e., the landing point farthest from the initial origin of the trip out, on the basis of the great circle distance, as shown on the ticket or combination of tickets, is the ultimate destination on the trip out and the point of initial origin on the return trip."

primarily entitled to the airline in whose country it makes a stopover of at least twelve hours.

Another example where the sixth freedom traffic received attention is the USA-USSR bilateral air agreement concluded at Washington DC on November 4, 1966, the Annex of which states (art. 3): "The designated airline of the USSR shall have in the territory of the USA at the terminal point of the agreed route the right to land for technical and commercial purposes as well as to use alternate airports and flight facilities for these purposes. Such airline shall have within the territory of the USA the right:

1) to discharge passengers, baggage, cargo and mail coming from the USSR or points beyond the USSR in third countries and destined for the USA or points beyond the USA in third countries; and

2) to pick up passengers, baggage, cargo and mail coming from the USA or points beyond the USA in third countries and destined for the USSR or points beyond the USSR in third countries." The route in question is the route Moscow-New York and return, non-stop in both directions except for agreed technical stops.

Under existing bilateral agreements, unless otherwise provided, it is taken as a matter of course that an airline of either party transports traffic to and from points beyond its homeland without specific mention being made of such right in the agreement, as long as a stop is made in the carrier's homeland, the flight number (line number) of the service is changed at that stop and, in some cases, this traffic does not constitute the primary objective of the service (which is the case in countries who make no distinction between sixth and fifth freedom traffic).[23]

In the field of charter transportation, the Caledonian Case is a good example.[24] Here again the US demonstrated its preoccupation with the sixth freedom: "The holder (of the permit) shall not engage in foreign air transportation between the US and any point or points, other than a point or points in the UK, nor shall it hold out to the public that it provides such service."

Upon the request of PANAM the CAB amended the wording of the

[23] Cf. e.g. US CAB Proposed Rulemaking July 27, 1967, Parts 216 and 375, Explanatory Statement: "A beyond-homeland point would not, however, be considered as unauthorized." In the adopted regulation ER-525, effective Jan. 15, 1968, Part 216, 1(a) (Note), however, the CAB changed this wording (as a result of an objection of PANAM that by implication foreign air carriers would be entitled to conduct through single plane flights from beyond homeland points), by speaking of "authorized beyond homeland traffic"; thus the CAB avoided the issue.

[24] Caledonian Airways (Prestwick) Ltd. Order E-19710, June 17, 1963 (temporary permit). Order E-22978, Dec. 5, 1965, adding inclusive tour authority. Order E-24413 amended permit, served Nov. 16, 1966, and Order E-25017, served April 21, 1967.

condition which was intended to preclude carriage by Caledonian between the UK and the USA of traffic to and from points beyond the US and the UK: "(1) ... the holder shall not engage in foreign air transportation between the US and any point or points, other than a point or points in the UK, or transport any person whose journey, by any means of transportation, begins or ends at a point not in the US or the UK..." [25]

The CAB interpreted the beyond-homeland restriction to include a prohibition to hold out or sell in the US charter flights originating in the US for the carriage of passengers between the US and Europe who would make a bona fide stop over in the UK. Caledonian, however, would be entitled to carry charter passengers across the Atlantic from the US to the UK and return, who, in connection with such trips, made trips by other carriers between the UK and the continent.[26]

Of course a delimitation of the traffic which may be carried is more in line with the character of charter company activities than it is with the activities of scheduled airlines who offer their services to the public at large.

A sixth freedom restriction on scheduled services leads to such incongruent clauses as the one in the Canada-US bilateral air agreement of Jan. 17, 1966, reading: (article III (d) "the routes specified in the Schedules annexed to this agreement shall be operated and promoted as routes between the US and Canada. Should a designated airline of either country provide a service to points beyond its home country in connection with such routes, public advertising or other forms of promotion by such airline in the territory of the other country or in third countries may not employ the terms 'single carrier' or 'through service' or terms of similar import, and shall state that such service is by connecting flights, even when for operational reasons a single aircraft is used. The flight number assigned to services between the US and Canada may not be the same as that assigned to flights beyond the home country of the airline performing the service." These examples show the concern of the US to extend as much as possible its power over the own traffic market for negotiating and trading purposes and at the same time multiply its efforts to restrict foreign carriers as much as possible to their own traffic market to ensure that the foreign carrier carries a minimum of traffic which cannot be called his own! To this end restrictive regulations are extended to include limitations

[25] Cf. Order E-25017, served April 21, 1967 and on Petition for Clarification Order E-25392, served July 10, 1967, and Order 68-9-62, served Sept. 16, 1968, Docket 19252, Opinion p. 6, note 4, and p. 7, note 5, and Permit as amended, condition (1). Cf. also Order E-26146, Dec. 18, 1967, Martin's Permit para (2), Docket 18016.

[26] N.B. Sixth freedom charter authority has been granted by the CAB and was granted to Caledonian, for the carriage of European-originated charter groups. Cf. Caledonian amended permit para's (5), (6), and (7) and condition (1).

on the sales and sales promotional activities of foreign carriers. Governments, as a rule, are very careful not to prejudice their negotiating and bargaining position: Some States in refusing to grant fifth or sixth freedom traffic rights argue that such grants may prejudice their position vis-à-vis the third State involved: allowing a fifth-freedom operator on the segment concerned reduces the value of the traffic rights which the State may wish to negotiate with the third State in return for traffic rights for its own carrier. John H. Crooker mentioned an example: "The Portuguese have permitted five carriers to compete with PANAM and TWA and in return for these authorizations, the Portuguese have received valuable operating rights elsewhere from the Swiss, the French, the Spanish and the Italians. They have traded on the liberal air transportation policy of the US in order to obtain rights from other governments – and the rights they have traded are the rights to compete with US flag carriers." Crooker steps lightly over the fact that the Portuguese allowed those five fifth-freedom carriers to compete with Portuguese carriers as well and that the US may have obtained valuable operating rights for its own carriers by granting fifth freedom rights to those five carriers who operate into the US via Portugal.[27]

Nevertheless there are countries who argue that granting the fifth freedom can only be considered after negotiations with the third State involved have been held. This attitude again is the result of a policy which aims at a 50/50 division of traffic between third and fourth freedom carriers on each of the routes to and from their territories.

For years the CAB objected, for this reason, to the excessive carriage of sixth freedom traffic by certain European carriers: This sixth freedom traffic was held to be the main reason why PANAM and other US carriers had such low percentage shares of the third and fourth freedom market as compared with, for instance, the Netherlands, Scandinavia, Switzerland and Belgium.

The Department of Transportation recently commented as follows: "While this may have been at least partially accurate in the piston engine era, the argument appears to us to have been a dubious one ever since the advent of direct jet service to points throughout Europe." [28]

The Edwards Report remarks regretfully that the share of British operators in the US/UK market declined from 37.8% in 1961/62 to

[27] Cf. John H. Crooker, then Chairman of the USCAB in an Address before the International Aviation Club, Washington D.C. June 9, 1969.

[28] Cf. East Coast Points – Europe Service Investigation, Docket 19255, August 8, 1969, p. 3, Note 1.

30.9% in 1966/67. Note, however, that the fifth-freedom operators' share declined from 12.4% to 9.5% over the same period.[29]

The answer to this problem is sought in the UK and the US in double or multiple designation, that is, by proposing to designate more than one carrier for the routes concerned.[30]

Although a certain balance between third and fourth freedom carriers with similar products and roughly equivalent capacity and frequency may be considered not wholly unreasonable, this must not mean that the whole third and fourth freedom market should be divided among third and fourth freedom carriers. Allowance will have to be made for the carriage of a certain percentage of this traffic by fifth freedom carriers.[31]

After having indicated what traffic of primary and secondary entitlement is in defining a traffic market, we should now go on to discover the extent to which a carrier is entitled to carry traffic of secondary entitlement. In other words, what percentage of its traffic on a given route should be primary? [32] It is impossible to give a general answer. Each individual case must be viewed on its own merits, the answer depending on the circumstances in which the route is operated by all the carriers.

The question is important. A route exchange opens a market to the designated carriers. The definition of the various freedom categories into which traffic is placed determines the capacity which the carriers may operate on the route, the type of aircraft and the frequency of service.[33]

Under the present system of bilateralism, the exchange of traffic rights (the rights to commercially operate specified routes to a specified extent) is governed by the principle of reciprocity: The party granting the rights allows the other party as many as it wishes to have itself, in the territory

[29] Cf. Edwards Report p. 91.

[30] Cf. Loy and Cherington before the International Aviation Club in Washington in April and May 1969. (*Aviation Daily,* April 25, 1969 and May 16, 1969). Cf. also the Edwards Report, pp. 89 ff.

[31] Even the South American countries, for example, allow 25% of their intra-continental traffic to be carried by fifth freedom carriers.

[32] Cf. Carl Nilsson, in *American Aviation,* Sept. 1967: "The freedom of the air is not expanding. On the contrary. Restrictions seem to have become the order of the day. As an example, we can mention that SAS' fifth freedom traffic, which 10 years ago was 22%, has now declined to 10%. We estimate that this trend will continue." These percentages refer to SAS's total traffic; percentages vary from route to route.

[33] Cf. e.g. US CAB Docket 15073 served Nov. 5, 1965. Order E-22851, p. 3: "As an additional protection (besides a reporting requirement) against undue reliance upon fifth freedom traffic DLH's permit will be subject to the condition that flights serving points south of New York shall originate or terminate at a point in Germany. This condition is designed to ensure that the service is, in fact, a through service from Germany by prohibiting practices that would be inconsistent with such a service: no use of equipment south of New York having capacity greater than that of equipment used between Germany and New York, no scheduling of undue layovers (overnighting), no use of different flight numbers, etc.

of the other party. If one of the parties cannot compete effectively on a route, the extent of its operations will determine the extent of operations of the other party. It goes without saying that this practice is not conducive to providing the public with the most extensive service possible.[34]

The principle of reciprocity is interpreted by comparing the revenues derived by each of the designated carriers from the operation of the routes which have been exchanged; the least developed, least efficient or the least interested carrier determines the extent of the operations of the carriers of the other parties.

We have mentioned the compromise solution of the US-Scandinavian agreement to show which traffic could be considered primary, and what could be a definition of true origin and ultimate destination. This compromise solution between a "have" and a "have-not" may be an important achievement from an air-political point of view, at least in the present circumstances.

A far more practical and realistic, less arbitrary and less artificial approach, however, would be to take, as a yardstick for the provision of capacity on a given route, the amount of traffic actually on board the aircraft on each of the segments of the route. If, over a longer period of time, the amount of traffic over third and fourth freedom segments were substantially less than the amount of traffic on fifth freedom segments of the same route, some adjustment might be in order, depending on the circumstances on the fifth freedom segments in question.

This solution would be workable only under a multilateral approach to civil aviation regulation.

Under the present bilateral system, fifth freedom traffic embarked and disembarked in the territory of the State wishing to control the traffic could be distinguished from the rest of the traffic (third, fourth and fifth freedom traffic to and from points other than the points in the territory of the controlling State) on board of the aircraft on the segment concerned.

If traffic to and from the points at the other end of the segments concerned, which embarks or disembarks in the territory of the controlling State, exceeds the rest of the traffic *on board,* a limitation could be imposed on the number of passengers to be picked up and set down at the

[34] Cf. Thomas K. Taylor, speaking about a policy of restrictionism, states: "Its paternalistic protectionism has emphasized the economic position of the operator of the service and has been somewhat less concerned with the wellbeing of the consumer."
"Economic and political considerations affecting international air transport," speech, delivered at Geneva, Oct. 1966 XLV Convention, International Institute of Communication.

point in the territory of the controlling State traveling on the segments concerned.

If a carrier can fill its planes by attracting traffic for the points on its routes, it obviously fills a need and contributes to the economic justification of its operations.

The difficulty remains, however, of how to determine whether a route and its intermediate points and points beyond should be granted to an airline in the first place. Should, for instance, the value of the market between the territory of the one party and intermediate points and points on the route beyond that territory be greater than the fifth freedom market between the territory of the other party and the intermediate points and points beyond?

Frank E. Loy points out that "mirror reciprocity" or "double tracking" which is visual reciprocity (an exchange of routes with the same description and "including an equal number of intermediate points and points beyond or by having an equal number of similar looking routes for each country"), does not represent an 'exchange of real values'," mainly "because of the inclusion of fifth and sixth freedom potential markets".[35]

Where potential sixth freedom markets are concerned, we cannot share Loy's views, because of the special characteristics sixth freedom markets have.

Loy, however, wants to keep the two concepts apart: "What we are looking for is the value (in terms of 'access to market') which a carrier obtains from an agreement and this value is either there or not, regardless of the freedom category of the passenger."

Now, to us this is mere semantics: The freedom category denotes the technical way in which a market is served, exploited and developed. For the sixth freedom this is via the homeland of the transporting carrier and therefore it is of direct importance as a connotation of access to a market.

When Loy states that a market is not a route but a city he should add that the technique of civil aviation regulation for a system of bilateral route exchanges cannot do without the freedom classification to indicate *how* a market is served and developed by a given carrier. Thus a market is a route or route segment (freedom category) in the first place. As long as countries continue to exchange routes bilaterally, this will be true.

Under Loy's interpretation of a market as a city, an exchange of rights should not specify the routes but simply trade a city for a city or one city for two cities, etc., excluding or including *all* fifth freedom traffic.

[35] Frank E. Loy (USA) McGill University, November 1967, "Bilateral Air Transport Agreements: Some problems of finding a fair route exchange" pp. 8, 13/14.

In essence Loy objects to "holding out" transportation services between points which have not expressly been granted in the bilateral agreement.

This view leads to the absurd consequence that airlines should no longer be allowed to advertise or sell air transportation on a single ticket all over the world or even over their own network.

V. ROUTE SPECIFICATION

These and similar considerations have been conducive to the ever more prevailing system of spelling out routes in detail, listing all points which may be served commercially in connection with the territory of the party granting the routes.

If in a route description the intermediate points and the points beyond have not been specified but it is simply stated that services may be operated on a route from A via intermediate points to B and from there to points beyond and vice versa, some States hold that further agreement between the parties is necessary before the airline can actually serve intermediate points and points beyond at its choice.

Such (subjective) interpretation, of course, is not in keeping with the intention of the parties at the time of the conclusion of the agreement, but finds its justification in today's changing approach to the problem of route descriptions in bilateral agreements.

This system severely limits the flexibility of the airlines. Unless their Governments include in the route description a sufficient number of intermediate points and points beyond to allow for switches to meet changing operational, schedule and traffic requirements, airlines will be unable to schedule their services wisely.

Unfortunately this system of specifying all the points which may be served has led to the interpretation, in a number of cases, that points not specified in the route description may not be included in the services even when no traffic rights are exercised between such point and the territory of the party granting the route. The CAB requires a special permit [36] for the inclusion of a point beyond the US not mentioned in the route description of the bilateral agreement or the permit (if no bilateral is in force) even if such point is being served without traffic being embarked in that

[36] Section 1108(b) of the Federal Aviation Act of 1958 requires (with the exception of any operation authorized by a Section 402 permit) that a permit be obtained from the CAB for any navigation of foreign civil aircraft in the USA.

See further new Part 216 of the CAB's Economic Regulations.

point for disembarkation in the US or traffic being disembarked in that point which has been embarked in the US.[37]

Thus a carrier who wishes to combine his service across the North Atlantic to Mexico City with his service to New York for obvious reasons of economy of operation, must apply for a special permit in case Mexico City is not mentioned as a point beyond New York on his route.

If an "unauthorized" point on a route is served, a distinction may be made between a case where carriage of traffic to and from such unauthorized point across the territory of the country which has granted the route is involved (as in our example) and a case where such carriage takes place wholly outside the territory of that country.

Claiming jurisdiction over carriage in the first case is a more obvious possibility than in the second. But even in the first case, if the country granting the route and the country of the airline operating the route are parties to the Air Services Transit Agreement of 1944, it is questionable whether the fact that an authorized traffic stop is made in the one country on a route on which traffic is carried in transit to an "unauthorized" point beyond that country invalidates the rights granted by the Transit Agreement (Art. 1 Sec. 1 (2)).

One could very well argue that an airline of a country which is party to the Transit Agreement is allowed to operate in transit (with or without making a technical stop) via the territories of the other parties to the agreement and that this right in no way is affected by the grant of a route to be operated for commercial purposes to or via the territory of another party to the agreement. In other words the granting of traffic rights on a specified route should be interpreted as a filling in with commercial rights of a number of, as a rule closely defined, route segments to and from the country granting the rights, of all possible routes which could be operated via that country under the Transit Agreement.

[37] Cf. US CAB Order E-23446, which authorizes DLH to combine on the same aircraft traffic moving in air transportation over the Germany-USA-Chile route with traffic between Germany and Colombia although Bogotá is not a point on that route, because "Bogotá is clearly within the path of the route granted DLH." DLH sought neither traffic rights between New York and Bogotá nor stopovers in New York. The CAB denied an Iberia Petition in 1966 asking for reconsideration of its 1965 refusal of a permit to operate Spanish registered aircraft in scheduled service between New York and Mexico City. The CAB argued that nothing in the existing air agreement contemplated the combination of transit and traffic rights to provide a service of the type proposed. The rights of overflying and making technical stops are provided separately (in the multilateral Air Services Transit Agreement of 1944) and cover totally different types of operation, according to the CAB.

Cf. also DLH Permit Order E-26515 approved March 15, 1968, allowing DLH to add Bogotá and La Paz as additional intermediate points on a route between Germany and points in South America via New York.

As a matter of fact, an exchange of traffic rights is not an exchange of routes but rather an exchange of third, fourth an fifth freedom rights between specified points. Therefore if a country which is party to the Transit Agreement grants a terminal route to a carrier of another party to that agreement, this does not necessarily exclude the carrier from extending that route to points beyond the country so long as no traffic rights are exercised between the country and those points. Of course the right to extend such a route may be expressly excluded during the bargaining between the countries concerned. After all, the right to operate commercially across a country can be of substantial value both to the carrier concerned and the country granting the right. When signing the Transit Agreement, however, the parties renounced that right as a bargaining point between them. Excluding the combination of transit rights and traffic rights gives a new interpretation to the Transit Agreement.

It is noteworthy that the CAB on July 27, 1967, started proceedings to resolve the question of whether or not special authority is required for serving an unauthorized point (for combining two different routes), or, as the CAB put it, "the commingling of blind sector traffic by foreign air carriers".[38] Quoting North Atlantic service to New York via Montreal as an example, the CAB calls the Europe-Montreal traffic the "blind sector traffic", Montreal being the unauthorized intermediate point. (Note that Montreal-New York is a true blind sector, as no fifth freedom traffic rights between these two points would be allowed).[39] It should be clear that the

[38] Cf. proposed rulemaking EDR-121 for a new Part 216 of the Economic Regulations based on the jurisdiction of the CAB under Sec. 1108(b), to require special authorization for "revenue traffic carried by a foreign air carrier on a flight operating in air transportation, which is enplaned at one foreign point and replaned at another foreign point, where at least one of such points is not named as a terminal or intermediate point in the carrier's applicable foreign air carrier permit." Part 216 was adopted by Rule ER-525, January 15, 1968, effective Febr. 19, 1968. The CAB made no distinction between traffic carried across the US and "extra-territorial" traffic. The wording makes it questionable whether the Regulation would apply to a foreign carrier wishing to combine its services to different US points authorized to be served on separate routes. It seems, however, that special Sec. 402 authorization from the CAB will be required in that case.

[39] Cf. Doc. 8185, ECAC/4-1, App. 3, p. 82, subpara (v). "A blind sector occurs between two points on a route when an airline is prohibited, on one or more of its services, from carrying traffic coming from one of these points and going to the other." This ECAC definition may give the impression that on a "blind sector," the aircraft of the airline concerned would be prohibited from carrying any traffic. This is the case only if a positioning flight is made, the carrier ferrying its aircraft empty from one point to another point to start a different service. On a blind sector, the traffic already on board may of course be carried (transit traffic). Whether traffic making a stopover in one or both points may be carried is a matter of interpretation. As far as the CAB is concerned, stopover rights are automatically given, unless it is specifically stated that they are not. Cf. e.g. Docket 18154, BOAC, served September 6, 1967: no stopovers permitted at Chicago on the West Coast route; cabotage rights cannot be given: if trip

blind sector traffic is traffic which is not "moving in foreign air transportation" as far as the US is concerned,[40] because it is carried wholly and solely between two foreign points.

As in the first case of transit operations, however, it could be argued that in the case of extra-territorial operations, a Sec. 1108(b) permit is required as far as the foreign air carrier would enter the US via a different air route not contemplated by the applicable Sec. 402 permit, but in that case anything more than a perfunctory approval would be inconsistent with the Sec. 402 authorization.[41] In practice the CAB has asserted its jurisdiction over such blind sector operations by requiring an authorization under Sec. 1108(b).

In adopting Part 216 the CAB argued that "where operations between two foreign points are conducted in the course of a flight operating to and from the US, there can be little question that the international principle of exclusive sovereignty over the air space above a nation's territory permits regulation of all aspects of that flight, including deviation from the authorized route for the purpose of carriage of unauthorized traffic which is itself not moving to or from the US." [42] Note that here the CAB speaks of a deviation from the authorized route, while the question is whether or not one actually can speak of an authorized route, excluding points which are being served without exercizing traffic rights as far as the country granting the route is concerned. In our opinion one cannot. Moreover the CAB speaks of unauthorized traffic. The CAB has no jurisdiction over traffic not moving to or from the US, probably meant "unauthorized combination of traffic on a different route with the traffic on the route to the US." A further argument of the CAB *e contrario* was that since routes are often spelled out in detail in route exchanges and blind sector operations are sometimes specifically named in bilateral agreements, the regulatory jurisdiction over blind sector operations is implicit.

originates inside the country – no stopovers are permitted; if trip originates outside the country there is no cabotage and stopovers are permitted.

[40] Sec. 1108(b) covers navigation in the US and (with Part 375) traffic not moving in air transportation e.g. non-revenue traffic, emergency and other such traffic, and therefore would seem not to be applicable here.

[41] The Board's jurisdiction under Sec. 402 is limited to air transportation and the carriage of traffic between foreign points, not being air transportation, is beyond such jurisdiction. The CAB's jurisdiction under Sec. 1108(b) is limited by its terms to the navigation of foreign aircraft in the US. Expressly excluded from the CAB's jurisdiction under this Section are operations pursuant to a permit under Sec. 402.

[42] Cf. Part 216 of the CAB's Economic Regulation, p. 4. N.B. The regulation is also applicable to foreign carriers. It excludes "the carriage of authorized 'beyond homeland' traffic." Part 216.1. Note ... This wording implies that sixth freedom traffic may be specifically authorized in a carrier's permit, something which is not usually done, as the sixth freedom normally is not covered and therefore freely authorized under bilateral agreements.

Undoubtedly the most important reason why the CAB adopted new requirements for the carriage of blind sector traffic by foreign carriers was the wish to make the possibility to improve the economics of the operations to and via the US by combining two different routes subject to negotiations on the exchange of traffic rights between governments.[43]

It would seem that the CAB, in adopting this new regulation and especially in using this argumentation, goes against the long standing fundamental US concept that a carrier, once operating authority has been granted, should have reasonable opportunity to develop the route and should not be subject to unilateral limitations of frequency or capacity.[44]

The combination of routes indeed enables a carrier to increase the frequency and capacity of service on the route on which an unauthorized point is included. But, as the CAB puts it, all aspects of flights to and via the US can be made subject to its regulations by virtue of the sovereignty over the air space above its territory.

The position taken by the CAB certainly is an about-face if we recall earlier CAB decisions and analyze the CAB argumentation for its change of policy.[45] It certainly is an attack on the economics of airlines operation.

It is moreover rather difficult to interpret existing bilateral agreements to exclude blind sector operations, which as a matter of fact are allowed as a matter of course, with a few exceptions which mainly concern transit

[43] Cf. also Memorandum of PANAM in opposition to the application of KLM for Statement of Authorization pursuant to Part 216, April 3, 1968, pp. 9 ff. The grant of blind sector permission is a decision which is essentially of a "horse-trading" nature according to PANAM. "There is no public policy favoring freedom of blind sector operations. The US aviation policy has properly tended to discourage either the acquisition or the grant of such partial rights, preferring to see the international air transport system develop on a pattern of full traffic rights where these can be justified." (p. 11). One could reason that this US policy to grant full traffic rights *a fortiori* allows what PANAM calls partial rights (blind sector permission). It should be noted, however, that in the Exchange of Notes between the governments of the US and the UK, May 27, 1966, the US inserted traffic restrictions applicable to the routes of the designated air carriers of the UK by not granting traffic rights between Jamaica and Miami on a route between British Honduras or the Cayman Islands to Miami; nor between Okinawa and Japan on a route from Hong Kong to Japan. Treaty Series No. 43, 1966, Washington, May 27, 1966. More recently, in an Exchange of Notes between US and France on April 5, 1960, as "collateral understanding," blind sector rights were exchanged *expressis verbis*.

[44] Cf. CAB member Whitney Gillilland: "The role of the CAB in licensing foreign air carriers." 3rd Inter American Law Conference, University of Miami Law Center, March 22-24, 1966.

[45] Cf. cases cited by G. Nathan Calkins Jr. in *Acquisition of operating authority by foreign air carriers: the role of the CAB, White House and Department of State*. pp. 82 and ff. Mr. Calkins criticizes the change of policy of the CAB (in 1960) and the application of Sec. 1108(b) extra-territorially to counter the threat of unequal competition, the foreign carrier being able to mount more frequencies by combining the traffic of two different routes. *Journal of Air Law and Commerce,* Spring issue 1965. It should be noted that the CAB itself emphasizes that this regulation does not represent a new or changed policy of the Board. ER-525 p. 7.

operations. The provision in bilateral agreements that a designated carrier may operate services via points not mentioned in the route description without exercising traffic rights in such points as far as the territory of the other party is concerned is of a declaratory nature. Such changes in the routing of services may be effected unilaterally, although the authorities of the other party should be informed beforehand.[46]

Although under bilateral air agreements the CAB normally has not the power to require that schedules of foreign carriers be filed for approval, nor the power to require foreign carriers to file traffic data with the Board, the CAB may impose conditions to theses effects in unilateral permits where no agreement exists.[47]

A number of foreign carriers protested against the proposed rule making,[48] while an ECAC group of experts concluded that the problem of commingling blind sector traffic could find no solution outside the framework of bilateral negotiations.[49]

The CAB granted special authorization pursuant to Part 216 to SAS, AF and DLH,[50] cancelling at the same time Section 1108(b) permits under which the commingling was authorized, on flights in air transportation between Scandinavia and France and Germany, and Alaska, of

[46] Note, however, that in the Canada-Trinidad/Tobago bilateral agreement of August 1969, express authorization is given for transportation of traffic between *carrier's* country and specified intermediate points on the agreed routes.

[47] Cf. the "Show Cause" Order E-25823, served Oct. 13, 1967, Docket 19103, directing Alitalia to show cause why the Board should not, subject to the approval of the President, amend Alitalia's permit so as to incorporate interalia the requirement to file for approval all schedules which are or will be operated by Alitalia, including applications to conduct on-route charter flights. Italy had denounced the US-Italian air agreement which consequently had terminated on a year's notice on May 31, 1967, to be replaced by unilateral permits. The Italian government had restricted the frequencies of the US carriers providing all-cargo aircraft schedules in the US-Italian market.

US carriers were operating on an ad hoc basis of unilateral operating rights granted by the Italian government, under which the filing of schedules was required. The Show Cause Order intended to vest in the US Government authority over Alitalia comparable to that possessed by the Italian Government over US carriers.

[48] Cf. especially comments of Swissair, Sept. 25, 1967, Docket 18837 on EDR-121.

[49] Cf. ECAC/CBS Report, 6/12/67, p. 7. The CAB argument that commingling could significantly increase the frequency and capacity of services, was countered by some experts by pointing at the possibility under Bermuda type agreements to control capacity *ex post facto*. It was further noted that in a number of bilaterals the right to include new points on a given route (without the right to carry local traffic between such point and the territory of the other party) is expressly mentioned as not requiring separate negotiations.

Cf. also letter from the President of ECAC to the Chairman of the CAB, February 16, 1968, App. I ECAC/DGCA-Report 15/2/68: "... the meeting concurred in the opinion that a national regulation could in no way affect existing rights, except as provided in procedures laid down in the international agreements, bilateral or otherwise. The CAB regulation which has been introduced unilaterally in the US consequently cannot as such be binding on foreign governments."

[50] Cf. Orders E-26741/42/43, May 2, 1968.

through transit traffic carried between these countries and Japan. SAS's Section 402 permit, authorizing Alaska stopover traffic on scheduled flights between Scandinavia and Japan, had already inherently granted the right to SAS to commingle transit traffic carried between Scandinavia and Japan with the Alaska stopover traffic. This was not the case with the Section 402 permits authorizing turnaround Alaska service, reason why a Part 216 authorization, as mentioned above, was required.

VI. EQUAL OPPORTUNITY

Coming back to the exchange of routes and eliminating the sixth freedom traffic controversy, it would seem that in bilateral negotiations the parties should exchange the same routes (mirror reciprocity), giving their designated air carriers an equal opportunity to compete.

Obviously this system would seem to be to the detriment of the bigger States having more than one important city to trade. Moreover, peripheral States would have difficulty in obtaining routes (and fifth freedom traffic rights) from more centrally located States to points beyond, unless they would threaten to restrict the carriage of sixth freedom traffic to their country by the designated air carriers of such States.

In practice the US, for instance, exchanges a route to New York for a route to each of the capitals of Europe in separate bilateral negotiations with each of them. Faced with the possibility of a single European carrier (a "Europair" or an "Air Union") the US was concerned about the implication of having to negotiate with a combination of States and thus having to trade for a route to each of the capitals of the participating European States a route to a different US city.[51]

The US gateway system limits the carriers of foreign States to a specified limited number of US cities as the gateways to the whole of the USA.[52]

In our view each route exchanged should be open to the designated carriers of both parties so that if a US carrier operates a route from Detroit to Paris in addition to its New York-Paris route, the French carrier should be allowed to operate Paris-Detroit as well as the Paris-New York route.[53]

[51] Cf. also M. Jacques Boitreaud: "L'Europe doit être organisée pour faire face dans les négociations de droits de trafic, aux pays massifs comme les USA et l'URSS." *La Vie des Transports,* page 7, March 4, 1967.

[52] On November 17, 1967 the CAB decided to reopen the Transatlantic Route Renewal Case by setting down for hearing the East Coast Points – Europe Service Investigation, Docket 19255, to determine the need for direct services by US carriers between East Coast cities and Europe without reference to New York, the principal funnel for connecting traffic and through flights to and from other points.

[53] See, however, Jamaica-US bilateral air agreement, October 2, 1969, when the US exchanged routes for US carriers from ten US points to Jamaica and beyond for routes for Jamaican carriers from Jamaica to five US points and beyond.

In principle, however, route exchanges are based on a system of a State's offering a route to a grateway point on its territory for a route to a gateway point on the territory of the other party. In exchanging a gateway point in its own territory for a gateway point in the territory of the other party the revenues which may be obtained or are being obtained by the carriers of the contracting parties from the operation of the route concerned are sometimes taken as a basis for determining the balance of the rights to be exchanged, or which have been exchanged.[54] The economic equivalence of the rights exchanged is measured in terms of the benefits derived from the use of the rights.

The US in this way translates the principle of equal opportunity for the carriers of both parties by putting the opportunities on a level with the benefits derived from them. As a consequence the balance depends entirely on the use made of the rights by the carriers and the carrier of one party by not using the opportunities granted to it to the full, could hold back the expansion of the operations of the carrier of the other party.[55]

To determine the balance (the economic equivalence) of new rights to be exchanged, the value of the points is put on the scale. In this respect the competitive position of the carrier to which the point is granted vis-à-vis other carriers already operating to, from or via that point may be such that the value of a big traffic center will not exceed in value a smaller market served by only a few carriers.

Frank E. Loy argues, that "the accident of geography is critical in determining the value of the routes a country grants or gets".[56]

Loy, furthermore, thinks the place where a passenger pays for his ticket (origin?) is more important than his destination.[57]

A US passenger may get to his destination even if no US carrier serves that destination. He may be brought to a place close to his destination and continue on some other airline. To the US, the exchange of rights with the

[54] Cf. also M. A. Bradley (Canada) in his report to the International Chamber of Commerce, Commission on Air Transport, ICC Doc. 310/223, April 244, 1968: "The actual and potential revenues which will accrue to the airlines, and the equal opportunity to match the earnings of the airlines of the other party are mentioned as being factors which may determine the balance."

[55] Cf. also J. E. Landry, ATA: "Problems of bilateral arrangements," 1968: "... a fair and equal opportunity does not mean an artificial division such as a 50/50 split of the market involved. There is to be no holding of the promotion and development of a market to the capabilities and desires of a lowest denominator."

[56] Cf. Frank E. Loy: "Bilateral air transport agreements: Some problems of finding a fair route exchange." Mc.Gill University, November 1967.

[57] Cf. also the Comments by John H. Spencer, p. 86/87 in *The Freedom of the Air,* 1968, Sijthoff, Leyden. For a large traffic generating country like the US such a geopolitical theory is not surprising, though hardly justifiable.

country concerned (the country of the destination in our example) would have little value because of the accident of geography.

In this interpretation fair exchange would not allow for an equal opportunity for carriers of countries who happen to have an unfavorable geographical position.

If Loy would have said that the value of a market to some or even a large extent depends on the geography of the country, nobody would deny the truth of such statement. But Loy, on the basis of William James's pragmatism, as the example above shows, argues that the US should make use of the accident of geography wherever a country cannot *control* its market effectively because of its geographical position. It seems rather unfair to determine the value of a market in this way while, moreover, no justice is done to the passenger who is forced to travel via an indirect routing with a change of aircraft.

Pragmatism interpreted in a nationalist way does not seem to offer a solution to the problem of international air transportation.

The value of a point further depends on the availability of feeder services to and from that point. Such feeder services enhance the value of the access to that route for the carrier operating these feeder services as well.[58] Here we touch again on the sixth freedom problem.

It may be seen that the aspects mentioned here can affect the evaluation of the opportunities granted under an exchange of routes and traffic rights in bilateral negotiations, or in other words, an equal opportunity is not always an equal benefit. The use which can be made of an opportunity depends on circumstances which may be such that the opportunity is of theoretical benefit only. This could be the case, for instance, if the designated carrier of one of the parties had no equipment available to operate the routes granted or to effectively compete on those routes.

We suggest that the principle of equal opportunity be interpreted to mean equal access *in practice* to the same markets. A market, furthermore, is not a static phenomenon which is there or not; and a market therefore cannot be defined, by virtue of the legal concept of national sovereignty, as a market controlled effectively by a State, but must be interpreted more pragmatically as a market as it exists and could be developed further

[58] Cf. J. E. Landry, *idem*: "The US is uniquely a terminal market. So a given foreign carrier gets access to a far greater sixth freedom market in a route exchange than does a US carrier. Because of schedule convenience the foreign carrier will capture the great bulk of the third and fourth freedom as well." This is the reason why the US "does not subscribe to the concept of mirror reciprocity in its route exchanges – i.e. trading routes with the same, but reversed, description."

through the efforts (penetration) of the carrier or carriers operating routes to, from and via it.[59]

Route grants or route exchanges are normally based upon the wish to arrive at or maintain a balance of rights between the parties. Today this means not a balance of opportunities but an actual balance of benefits. Therefore the amount of service may depend on the extent to which the least interested or least successful carrier derives benefits from the operation of the routes which have been exchanged.

We have already mentioned the principle of reciprocity and the difficulties in determining the balance, at the same time doubting the wisdom of an approach based on these principles. A route grant in essence is a franchise enabling a carrier to earn money. It depends on the ability and the effort of the carrier, however, to make a success of the operation. In case of an imbalance of benefits, one should not resort to some sort of penalty or payment for traffic rights which a carrier wishes to exercise in excess of the rights exercised by the other party.

The operation of air services is not purely a matter of carriers and governments. It is primarily a facility the public requires. To determine whether a route grant is in the public interest a Government should therefore take into account not only the interests of the national carriers, the national economy and the like but also and perhaps in the first place, the interests of the traveling and the shipping public. This is not the present approach.

Civil aviation is a business nowadays. It is exactly for that reason that the emphasis of government control over international civil aviation should shift to the interests of the traveling public and that means to the freedom of the airlines to determine themselves the volume of their service and the choice of their routes, as the best guarantee of serving the public in the most efficient way. An airline renders a service. It should be paid for that. If it can make a profit on a route it pays its own way. If it makes an excessive profit, it should lower fares. If it does not make a profit and the service is in the public interest, it should be subsidized. It is wrong to make an airline pay for the right to operate a route as an indirect subsidy to the national carrier of the country granting the right. To force an airline into a pool with the national carrier is equally wrong. The task of government

[59] Note, for instance, that international US air carriers, through equipment interchange agreements with domestic US air carriers, are able to mount additional frequencies supported by traffic to and from US points not specified in the bilateral air agreement. Foreign air carriers, as a rule, are not permitted to enter into such interchange agreements.

should be, not to let the carrier pay for the right to compete, but to control the competition to safeguard the interests of the public.

Better than a system of calculated protectionism for the exchange of traffic rights based on the use by a State of its power to control a piece of the international air traffic market would be a system of "calculated idealism", a de-nationalization of the air traffic market as a basis for air traffic regulation.

Such regulation on a broader basis would fall outside the controversy of liberalization vs. protectionism.

Instead of concentrating on a carrier's rightful (percentage) share of its own market (the traffic to and from its homeland), the concern would be the relative position in world aviation of the flag carriers of each State as calculated in tonkilometers flown and tonkilometers carried, network, etc.

If, for instance, a country's position in world aviation were in conformity with its share of world trade, a system which is sometimes proposed, it would be incongruous to obtain this position by claiming the right to carry at least 50% of one's own traffic. It would be necessary to take the global picture of international air services into consideration.[60]

A less conservative approach than the "national" approach, that is a more idealistic approach on the basis of what each nation can do in international air transportation rather than what each nation has (the right to do), would stimulate the traffic in the interest of all, and ensure an adequate relative position for each national air carrier.

[60] Cf. also Carl Nilsson, then President of SAS, in *American Aviation*, September 1967, p. 57: "... our share of world aviation is in conformity with our traffic potentials. Denmark, Norway and Sweden have about 4.9% of the world trade. SAS has a 1.8% share of the world traffic." Under the present system, SAS would have little chance to increase its share of the world traffic.

Cf. on the other hand, Paul W. Cherington: "The US proportion of the world passenger market was only 22.8% in 1968." *Aviation Daily*, May 16, 1969. The US share of world trade was 19.8%.

CHAPTER THREE

I. NON-SCHEDULED AND SCHEDULED AIR CARRIERS

To try and control international civil aviation on the basis of a State's own traffic and a system of an exchange of rights determined by reciprocity and a balance of benefits offers no guarantees of adequate service and a sound airline industry.

A route request should be granted unless there are serious reasons not to grant it. As it is, routes are granted only if there is a benefit to the country, that is, to its national carrier, for instance if the grants are necessary to obtain or maintain certain rights from the country of the airline requesting the route. Very seldom are international routes granted on the sole basis of traffic requirements.

In some cases routes are granted for reasons other than those based on the civil aviation relationship between both countries, for political reasons or to compensate for advantages obtained in other fields (trade balance). It is true, however, that official US policy confines civil aviation negotiations to purely civil aviation factors and treats other (economic and political) data as not truly relevant.

The present system of bilateral control of the scheduled international air traffic market is inadequate to meet the growing need for mass air travel in time, by providing for fast, frequent and economical scheduled services to all destinations. This has led to the enormous development in recent years of non-scheduled services using affinity group and inclusive tour charters, the latter especially in Europe. Inclusive tour charters for tourist traffic are operated on a systematic and all-but-scheduled basis.

Inclusive tour facilities offered by charter carriers, moreover, are making inroads on the air travel market of businessmen as ever more non-tourist travelers avail themselves of the cheaper fares intended for tourists. This development invalidates the distinction in government regulations between scheduled and non-scheduled service.

The spectacular development of non-scheduled traffic and non-scheduled carriers gives increasing importance to the problem of diversion, or the distinction between scheduled and non-scheduled air transportation.

Each mode of air transportation has its own particular products and air transport regulations should delimit the offering of these products on the market.

The problem, however, is complicated, since, for regulatory purposes, a distinction must be made not only between non-scheduled and scheduled services but between scheduled and non-scheduled carriers as well. The latter distinction must supplement and perhaps even replace the distinction made in Articles 5 and 6 of the Chicago Convention, which has become more academic than practical as most States now require prior permission for both scheduled and non-scheduled services.

In the US the distinction based on type of carrier for regulatory purposes is more important than one based on type of service, though the type of service offered determines the type of carrier. In any case regulations should not be based on the distinction between scheduled and non-scheduled traffic, as such a distinction can only be an artificial one.

As a matter of fact there are different kinds of scheduled and non-scheduled services: regular services for the carriage of passengers, luggage, cargo and mail; regular services for the carriage of cargo, either on all-cargo aircraft or on combi aircraft; non-scheduled services performed as charter flights for affinity groups, for own use of the charter or for inclusive tours; non-scheduled all-cargo flights, etc.

There are different kinds of carriers as well: regular carriers, all-cargo carriers, non-scheduled or irregular carriers or supplemental carriers, and others.

The US CAB goes on to define, based on the criterion of holding out, a common carrier as one that holds itself out as ready and willing to undertake for hire the transportation of passengers and property from place to place and so invites the patronage of the public who wishes to use its services; and a private carrier for hire as one that agrees to carry such traffic only in special cases.[1]

Contrary to regular carriers, irregular carriers are not permitted by the CAB as a rule to hold out their services to the general public or operate regular services, either alone or in combination with others, or to operate such services except on a very limited scale. These carriers were originally called large irregular carriers, later non-scheduled carriers and today supplemental carriers.

[1] Cf. CAB Reports, Cumulative Index-Digest 1955-60, page 278, and page 407.

The service performed by irregular carriers is supposed to be supplemental to that of the certified system (route carrier service) and intended to accommodate sudden unforeseeable demands and fluctuating needs; between any two points the service must be irregular and infrequent.[2]

It would be too simple a solution, however, to authorize charter carriers to perform "non-scheduled services" without specifying further what kind of non-scheduled service is meant, and to what extent and in which markets it may be performed.

On the other hand, a scheduled carrier could (and perhaps should) be authorized, as far as its own government is concerned, to operate any kind of service. This, in practice, would be limited to the kinds of service other governments would care to authorize it to perform in the various geographical on-route and off-route markets.

Then, for each government, the main distinction which would remain would be the one between designated (regular) carriers and other carriers. This distinction would be a licensing matter for the government of the State of which the air carriers are nationals.

It would not be the same as a distinction between on-route and off-route carriers, since on-route carriers are also off-route carriers, but would mean only that carriers not licensed and designated to operate regular services (mostly under bilateral air agreements) are precluded by their governments from operating them. In other words, both scheduled and non-scheduled carriers would have the same position with regard to the operation of international air services, except that designated carriers would have the exclusive right to operate regular air services.

Charter carriers would thus not be secondary or supplemental or complementary carriers, for their market would not be seen as supplemental to the scheduled market, and regular carriers would be regular only insofar as they are the ones which are designated to operate scheduled services.

This approach is not discriminatory in favor of designated carriers because nothing precludes a charter carrier from being a designated carrier as well. The decision would be a policy matter of the government concerned, and the criterion to be applied would be whether and to what extent competition, in particular between scheduled and charter carriers, should be allowed.[3]

[2] Cf. Part 291, Sec. 1, ER CAB. Sec 101.33, 200.8 and 401(d) (3). Note that supplementals require a certificate under Sec. 401(d) (3), as distinct from exemption authority. Scheduled air carriers require a certificate of public convenience and necessity under Sec. 401(d) (1) and (2) of the Federal Aviation Act of 1958, as amended.

[3] Cf. also Paul W. Cherington in a speech before the International Aviation Club in Washington, May 1969, where he advocates "multiple designation" because "... ad-

Our conclusion is based on the view that the market (traffic) cannot be divided into a charter market and a scheduled market and so charter carriers cannot be prevented from carrying scheduled traffic. There is no such thing as 'scheduled' traffic; any definition of scheduled and charter traffic based on types of passenger and cargo would be arbitrary.

Charter carriers, however, can be prevented from operating scheduled services in certain markets by being designated neither under bilateral agreements nor as beneficiaries of unilateral route permits.

The question remaining is how to determine whether or not charter carriers are in fact operating scheduled services under charter permits both on routes operated by designated carriers and in other markets.

Here a definition of what constitutes a scheduled service should give the answer.[4]

It should be noted, however, that a definition of scheduled services cannot simultaneously be a definition of the traffic carried on such services as scheduled traffic.

A scheduled service is an instrument, a means of carrying traffic. A non-scheduled service is another means to carry what might be the same traffic. Government regulations, therefore, should try to specify the product which a carrier is allowed to offer to the public.

If this product is a scheduled service, the carrier should become a designated carrier; if it is a charter then it must be taken into account that the same kind of traffic may very possibly be carried as moves on scheduled services: through the intermediary of a travel agent or tour operator the same product may, in fact, be offered to the public, as, for instance, resale of individual seats by the tour operator and agent on a more-or-less regular flight schedule.

The result of efforts made by the ICAO Council in 1952 to define sched-

ditional competition may do a great deal of good in the way of putting our existing international carriers on their mettle"; and in the Edwards Report, British Air Transport in the Seventies, H.M.S.O. May 1969: "We believe that double designation is desirable on the London-New York route, given a competitor who is fully equipped to hold his own in the 'big league'." (BUA and Caledonian next to BOAC?)

Cf. also "Civil Aviation Policy", UK Board of Trade, November 1969, para's 10, 125 and 36: "The main scheduled carriers will engage increasingly in charter operation, either directly or through subsidiaries. Conversely, the scope for specialist non-scheduled carriers will increase through changes in pricing policies and in the character of services needed on particular routes."

[4] Cf. e.g. CAB Docket 20384, served March 7, 1969. Aerotransportes entre Rios S.R.L. (Argentine), Opinion p. 2, Note 1: "To delineate the bounds of the non-scheduled air transportation authority being granted, the definition of 'scheduled international air service' made by the Council of ICAO for the purpose of clarifying articles 5 and 6 of the Convention is considered applicable."

uled services in order to distinguish them from non-scheduled services did not find wide application.[5]

IATA "defines" a charter and considers the rest of the operations of the scheduled (IATA) carriers as scheduled services for the application of its fares and rates Resolutions.[6]

The Netherlands, in a Ministerial Decree of April 26, 1960 governing non-scheduled flights, referred to the ICAO definition, but has not done so since in subsequent Decrees on the subject.[7] The 1965 Decree mentioned as criterion for commercial non-scheduled flights whether or not the opportunity to travel had been brought to the notice of the general public. If not, no prior permission was required. The Decree stipulated a number of conditions, including a fare condition, for the operation into, from and via the Netherlands of inclusive tour charter flights by foreign carriers, without the necessity to obtain prior approval. The fare condition is an indication that IT charters are permitted to trespass in activities of scheduled services, be it on conditions comparable to those applicable to scheduled services.

In the 1966 and 1967 Decrees the criteria were changed to define commercial non-scheduled flights which may be freely operated: flights for the carriage of goods or animals for remuneration which are not advertised or otherwise made public, own-use charter flights, inclusive tour charter flights meeting minimum fare requirements, affinity charters.

Under the 1967 Decree non-scheduled flights which are freely permitted are actually own-use, affinity charter flights and inclusive tour charter flights, and flights for the carriage of freight and animals only, while other non-scheduled flights are permitted only as single flights. The Multilateral Agreement on Commercial Rights in Non-Scheduled International Air Services within Europe of April 30, 1956, allows each carrier one such single flight per month between the same two centers of traffic. Non-scheduled flights are made subject to the general condition that scheduled services must not be affected.

While prior to 1960 non-scheduled passenger flights were permitted by the Netherlands on the condition that fares would at least be equal to IATA fares, such flights are no longer freely permitted because of the difficulty in defining the non-scheduled character of such flights. For non-scheduled cargo flights the sole criterion applied by the Dutch aeronautical authorities apparently was the prohibition of their public advertising.

[5] Cf. ICAO Document C-WP/1123 and 7278-C/841 of May 10, 1952.

[6] Cf. Resolution 045.

[7] Cf. Decrees of September 27, 1965, July 25, 1966, October 30, 1967 and February 17, 1969.

A complete change of policy was finally embodied in the new Decree of February 17, 1969, by which prior permission is required for all commercial non-scheduled flights, except for all-cargo non-scheduled flights and flights within Europe performed by *Netherlands'* air carriers for the carriage of IT passengers at a fare not lower than 60% of the lowest comparable IATA return fare (the economy class fare, excluding group fares and IT basing fares [8] and fares for special categories such as students, seamen and the like) and except for the categories of the non-scheduled flights performed by *foreign* carriers, covered by the Multilateral Agreement of 1956.

The definition of a Netherlands air carrier is based on the substantial ownership and effective control concept.

A basic change is that the 1969 Regulation is applicable to carriers instead of to aircraft, as stipulated in Article 5 of the Chicago Convention. This change interalia allows for bona fide sub-charters. On the other hand mala fide use of Dutch aircraft can be prevented since permission is granted to a carrier and not to the aircraft performing the non-scheduled flight.

Also the Decree is applicable not only to foreign air carriers but to Netherlands air carriers as well.[9]

Although the new Decree intended to make tighter control of non-scheduled operations from, to and via the Netherlands possible, it did not give criteria for the approval or disapproval of non-scheduled flights, except for IT charters in Europe, which are free if the price of the tour is higher than a certain minimum. A measure of freedom for non-scheduled flights, especially IT charters, seemed reasonable as far as Europe was concerned in view of the fact that IATA carriers are able to compete there on comparable terms.[10]

If charter carriers are accepted as competitors of scheduled carriers, the same conditions should apply with regard to the product they offer to the public, short of the possibility for charter carriers to offer scheduled services and present themselves as designated carriers with published time tables, fares, and rates and conditions on specified routes.

If this were done, there would be no point in allowing charter carriers to operate on the routes regularly served by designated carriers. Charter

[8] This is the fare at which capacity is offered by the airline to the charterer, agent or tour operator.

[9] Cf. Decree of February 17, 1969, especially articles 3, 9 and 11.

[10] N.B. Although IATA allows IT charters by its members in Europe and Africa, non-IATA carrier competition has increased to such an extent that KLM in Geneva in 1969 proposed to abolish the minimum tour price set by IATA to prevent competition between scheduled and charter operations of IATA carriers. (Cf. IATA Resolution 045, para 8, (a), (iv).)

carriers should then be allowed to compete only in the off-route markets of designated carriers.

But if they are not accepted as competitors, their products should be essentially different from the scheduled product.

Should regulations to these effects prove feasible it might be desirable or even necessary to conclude bilateral agreements governing charter operations, that is, the operations of charter carriers, and the charter operations of scheduled carriers which might then be designated as charter carriers as well.[11]

An essentially different product would create a separate market or at least presuppose the possibility to create such a separate market.

Since it is practically impossible to break the market down into different categories of passenger traffic for regulatory purposes, the purpose of such separate special bilaterals covering charter operations can only serve to establish a limit to the penetration of the market by charter operations both geographically and in terms of product, by limiting the area which they would be allowed to serve as well as the quantity and the kind (or quality) of their services.

A different and fresh approach to the problem of distinguishing between scheduled and non-scheduled services is made in the Report of the Edwards Committee,[12] where it is stated, correctly, that the distinction makes little or no sense.[13]

The essential feature of scheduled services, according to the Report, is the collective demand for such services, bringing with it a public service obligation [14] that justifies some degree of protection. The degree of the obligations of the operator, which in turn is a reflection of differences in public demand for different kinds of air services, would be a criterion for distinguishing between different types of operations for regulatory purposes. In addition to the collective demand, there is a clear demand for cheap whole-aircraft-load travel, and this type of service places a lesser degree of obligation upon the operator.

This new approach concentrates on the analysis of the air transport market to provide the distinction on which to base government regulations for assigning the necessary degree of protection to different types of service

[11] We will revert to this problem later. The US Government in 1969 initiated discussions on the conclusion of special bilateral arrangements concerning the operations of charter carriers, in order to give the US supplementals a more stable basis for their international operations.

[12] Cf. "British Air Transport in the Seventies", May 1969, page 57 ff.

[13] Idem the Director-General of IATA, Mr. Knut Hammerskjöld in his address at the Opening Session of the 25th Annual General Meeting at Amsterdam, October, 1969.

so that "the customer will be able to buy what he wants at the minimum economic price compatible with safety."

In our opinion, however, it is not the task of the government to try and regulate air transport by trying to distinguish between differences in public demand (collective or otherwise) and on the basis thereof to impose upon the carriers a certain degree of public service obligation in return for a degree of protection.

It is up to the airlines to determine how public demand can best be met and which type of service should be offered. The operator chooses a certain type of service which is expected to yield a profit. The government merely observes the types of service offered and ensures orderly development and fair and orderly competition, competition being the most effective way by which the traveling public can be assured of getting what it wants.

To regulate competition in a fair and orderly manner merely distinguishing between scheduled and non-scheduled service is wholly insufficient.

To regulate competition effectively governments should recognize the differences among products airlines offer. The protection which the airlines need is the regulation of each type of service so that equal conditions apply to all operators offering one type of service catering to one market. The demand determines the type of service offered. At the same time the type of service influences demand, since traffic moves at the lowest fares. Therefore, it is not the type of demand, collective or for whole-aircraft-load travel, which constitutes a valid distinction for regulatory measures, but rather the type of service and its relationship to the market.

An airline offers service for profit. It is not entitled to protection because its service happens to be public and the government wishes to place a public-service obligation on the operator.

Demand exists only insofar as there is a product (or a service) to meet it and to the extent the public wants to use that product (or service).

Although price is an integral part of the product, the extent to which the product (or service) is actually used, is influenced by it.

In other words, willingness and ability to buy at the purchase price determine the quantitative demand.

It is not the task of governments to influence qualitative demand though they may influence quantitative demand by regulating prices. Therefore

[14] "By 'collective' here we mean, not that it is required by everyone at the same time, but that a significant proportion of the community could be expected to take the view that it should be available if they wish to use it." Edwards Report p. 57.

Cf. also the US concept of "common carrier service".

governments should not take the qualitative demand as a basis for regulations but only the products as they are offered on the market: regulations should protect qualitative demand from being abused by producers.

One who engages in producing takes it upon himself to serve the public at a profit to himself, but he should not use the public to make a profit. Offering a product on the market calls for responsible, honest management and an honest business approach. It is the task of government to ensure them.

Thus demand is definable only in terms of the product which actually meets it: demand, as far as it concerns governments, is *"ex post producto."*

What we have said about the regulation of the place and the role of non-scheduled carriers applies similarly to all-cargo carriers, both scheduled and non-scheduled.

II. ALL-CARGO SERVICES

There is a tendency among various States to consider the operation of all-cargo services as an activity not covered by standard bilateral air agreements. Although mention is made of the operation of "air services for the carriage of passengers, cargo and mail", this is interpreted to mean mixed passenger/cargo/mail services.

Thus a conflict arose between Italy and the USA which had to be solved by arbitration. The tribunal was requested to decide the following question: "Does the air transport agreement between the USA and Italy of February 6, 1948, as amended, grant the right to a designated airline of either party to operate scheduled flights carrying cargo only?" [15] While Article 96(a) of the Chicago Convention reads: "Air service means any scheduled service performed by aircraft for the public transport of passengers, mail *or* cargo," Section III of the US-Italy bilateral air agreement spoke of "passengers, cargo *and* mail".

It was rightly argued by the tribunal that "and" and "or" are often used as equivalents, and therefore are interchangeable. Both the objective of the agreement and the intention of the parties led to the conclusion that the operation of all-cargo services was covered by the agreement.

In practice, however, the arbitral decision does not correspond with the

[15] Cf. US Treaties and other International Acts Series 5624. Compromise signed at Rome, June 30, 1964, and Advisory Opinion of the Arbitral Tribunal, Geneva, July 17, 1965, giving an affirmative reply to the question.

reality of the increasing number of States wishing to deal separately with all-cargo services.[16]

It is entirely appropriate to distinguish between mixed passenger-cargo-mail services and all-cargo services, each type having its own economic, commercial and operational characteristics. This, however, is a distinction which was not usual until recently. It is therefore incorrect to try and interpret existing agreements concerning the operation of international scheduled air services as not including authorization for the operation of all-cargo services.

On the other hand, the capacity provisions of bilateral agreements automatically apply to the operation of all-cargo services as well, for they can be used to determine, on the basis of traffic requirements, the extent to which such services may be operated on the routes specified in the agreement.

As a clear distinction can be made between mixed passenged services and all-cargo services, it is questionable whether international civil aviation regulation should apply the standard criteria for the authorization of scheduled air services (routing, frequency, capacity on the basis of third, fourth and fifth freedom traffic requirements and reciprocity) to the operation of all-cargo services.

There is still another new type of combi service, which is passenger service plus palletized cargo accommodation. If different criteria were to be applied to these combi services, the question could arise whether the aircraft, being used simultaneously partly for passengers and partly for cargo, should be treated as a passenger service, an all-cargo service or both, or be made subject to another set of rules.

In actual practice States will wish to apply the same criteria to all-cargo and combi services as they apply to mixed passenger services, that is, they will concern themselves with competitive impact on the services of their national carriers. Although it is difficult to deny formally the right to operate all-cargo services or combi services under the existing type of bilateral air agreement, the terms of these agreements often allow for an interpretation which can severely restrict or even make impossible the operation of all-cargo or combi services.

There will probably be a growing need to agree on a more flexible

[16] Cf. Also ITA Bulletin No. 18, May 1, 1967 and ITA study, "Traffic rights and Air Freight growth," 1967, No. 67/3-E. The Tribunal did in fact conclude with the statement that: "It is not for the tribunal to pronounce on the question of whether the disputed agreement and the other agreements based on the Bermuda agreement still constitute an appropriate, fair and equitable solution, in view of the development of civil aviation and the growing importance of all-cargo services. This question has not been submitted to the tribunal; it is a question for governments."

regime for cargo services. Pending general acceptance of the need for a separate set of rules for all-cargo and combi services, and in order to avoid any doubt as to the possibility of operating all-cargo and combi services under the provisions of bilateral agreements, a solution would be to include, preferably in the Annex to the agreement, a clause permitting the designated airlines to operate the agreed services "with any type of aircraft and with any configuration they may choose." This would allow the operation of aircraft with a mixed passenger/cargo/mail, a combi or an all-cargo configuration. An additional provision might then be required to the effect that the utilization of the capacity thus provided for the carriage of traffic to and from the territory of the other contracting party shall remain subject to the Bermuda or similar capacity clauses of the agreement.[17]

But when specific routes are requested by one or both parties for the operation of all-cargo services the negotiation of a separate cargo route schedule might be required. Certain advantages would accrue as all-cargo routes might be granted more easily. In an Amendment to the Belgium / West-German air agreement, all-cargo services were mentioned in addition to the mixed passenger services (on which freight and mail is carried in the belly of the aircraft as far as space is available in addition to the space occupied by the luggage of the passengers) authorized in the agreement.[18]

Air cargo is expected to grow at a higher rate than air passenger traffic, and in the near future it will require a highly specialized ground-handling organization. This may be beyond the capabilities of the airlines themselves, and international transportation by air on all-cargo services might have to become subject tc forms of cooperation among carriers which are different and separate from cooperative arrangements for mixed passenger services. While the freight carried on mixed passenger services makes a substantial contribution to their economic operation now (which will be even more true for the new wide-bodied type of jet aircraft, such as the Boeing 747 and DC-10) the growth of air cargo may mitigate the competitive impact of all-cargo services on mixed passenger services and allow for separate cooperative agreements.[19]

[17] Cf. e.g. Agreement between the USA and Denmark, effected by Exchange of Notes at Washington D.C. on June 7, 1966, Annex A. Cf. also US-Japan Agreement, 1965 and 1969.

[18] Amendment of November 29, 1966.

[19] The necessity for freighter capacity is clearly shown on the North Atlantic where, in 1958, 33% of total air cargo traffic was carried by freighter aircraft. This share grew in the summer of 1966 to 50%. In 1968 the percentage rose to 58.2%. (175,100 tons) The Edwards Report gives a less optimistic forecast for the further development of all-cargo operations (at least for UK airlines): "... despite a very substantial growth in the volume of freight moving by air, the scope for operations with all-cargo aircraft

In this light, and given the fact that the air cargo market is a different market altogether, a special regulatory regime (separate bilateral agreements for all-cargo services) may prove to be not only desirable but unavoidable.

A separate regime for air cargo would make all-cargo services possible between specified points. To this end it would be necessary to define closely services offered in the air cargo market as a separate field of activity not covered by the usual restrictions of existing bilateral agreements.[20]

It might then be necessary to define types of air cargo services in order to protect the carriage of cargo on mixed passenger services.

In 1954 the ECAC adopted a Recommendation (4) requesting Governments to allow indirect routings for intra-European all-cargo services and in 1959 a Recommendation (40) to try and free the carriage of freight on mixed services from the 5th freedom restrictions imposed in bilateral (mixed passenger service) agreements.

For the economic operation of all-cargo services it is especially important to permit indirect routings, the commingling of cargo traffic or the combination of different cargo services.

In an Exchange of Notes between the US and France, on May 29, 1969, a collateral understanding on all-cargo services was reached, not only allowing the commingling of cargo traffic on different all-cargo services (US carriers were granted the right to serve points in the UK and West Germany – countries not specified in the route schedule of the air agreement – on all-cargo services to points in France, though they did not have traffic rights between such points and France); but also granting complete flexibility in the order of points served (in France, the UK and West Germany); and moreover granting the right to transship cargo between these all-cargo services and between these services and combination (mixed passenger) aircraft services without regard to flight numbers. French carriers were granted similar privileges on routes to the US.

These provisions recognize the need for different and separate arrangements to enable the economic operation and further development of air cargo services (directional imbalance of cargo traffic).

In fact it is the growing protectionist interpretation of existing bilateral

will continue to be relatively small in the next decade." (p. 113) We believe that all-cargo aircraft operations will continue to grow, certainly after 1973, when the impact of the introduction of the wide-bodied aircraft will have been neutralized by traffic growth.

[20] N.B. The implementation of the Bermuda capacity provisions is based on statistics giving the origin and destination of the traffic. The initial and ultimate destinations of cargo traffic as a rule are not readily available and normally on-line origin and destination statistics constitute the basis for determining the capacity of the all-cargo services

agreements and the restrictive attitude of governments, inspired by their national airlines, which makes it increasingly necessary to go into detail on the operation of international commercial air services when drafting new regulations. This, in turn, brings about the further diversification of international civil aviation regulation, the need to spell out the activities airlines are allowed to engage in.

We may, in the end, have separate rules for passenger, cargo and mail transportation on mixed services, for all-cargo and combi services, for charters by route carriers and by charter carriers, for blocked-space charters, for services operated with leased aircraft, etc.

Thus States will create a network of ever more detailed regulations which will further complicate the development of the carriage of traffic over the ever more sophisticated network of air services.

If it becomes necessary to negotiate the right to flexibility in operating international air services the further development of international civil aviation will be stifled. Carriers will see their chances to obtain and maintain profitable operations diminish and their economic growth thwarted.

III. INCLUSIVE TOUR TRAFFIC

Inclusive tour traffic, as a separate phenomenon, saw its first spectacular development in Europe. Success may be due to the increase in numbers of people able to travel (more leisure time, better wages) who are still inexperienced and wish to place themselves in experienced hands. Moreover lower fares and lower overall prices made the IT product immediately very popular. The air transportation part of the package has become increasingly of secondary importance. IT holidays are produced and offered to the public by tour operators, who are wholesalers. Travel agents act as retailers. Air carriers have little influence on the composition of the end product offered to the public.

Both the CAB and IATA agree that, as far as IT charter flights are concerned, the airline should not engage in the operation of the tour, since the charter (and the charter price) would then be a fiction.[21]

The fact that the operation is conducted on a charter basis is an important criterion for regulatory purposes. When other transportation interests participate in airline ownership, as was the case with the German charter carrier Sudflug, which was wholly owned by two tour operators, the airline was considered to be chartering to itself, or indirectly engaged in the pro-

which the designated airlines will be entitled to operate under the Bermuda provisions.

[21] Cf. also e.g. Canada ATC Rule No. 1969-A-4, eff. Aug. 31, 1969, art. 1 (g): "An air carrier is not eligible to act directly or indirectly as a tour operator."

duction, sale and operation of the inclusive tours transported on its "chartered" aircraft.[22]

Such relationships "blur the distinction between charter and individually-ticketed operations, because the charter is a fiction." [23]

International non-scheduled charter flights, especially inclusive tour (I T) [24] flights performed by charter carriers, have become an attraction for holiday traffic mainly because their fares are lower than those of scheduled services. Charter carriers have thus helped develop the social traffic (low-income groups).

Apart from its lower fare, an IT packaged holiday relieves the traveler of financial worries during his holiday. As a result governments were inclined to adopt a liberal policy on such charter flights as they developed in Europe, realizing that the growth of tourism to their country would be of general benefit to the national economy ("multiplier effect" of tourism).

Governments are willing to close their eyes to the possible adverse effects which charter flights by the charter carriers may have on regular services in general and on the services of their own scheduled air carriers in particular (no capacity restrictions, half-hearted fare limitations). The result is that scheduled carriers, in the absence of strict (enforcement of the) rules governing the operations of charter carriers have had to consider ways and means of protecting themselves against price competition and have been forced to either lower fares on their line services, or find ways to operate charter flights themselves outside IATA control.

Experience shows that traffic moves at the lowest available fares. Therefore, the fare competition offered by charter carriers cannot be ignored by scheduled carriers. This is especially true where governments allow charter carriers to operate in the same markets as those served by scheduled carriers.

However, charter regulations normally stipulate that "charterworthy traffic" is subject to certain conditions: the passengers to be transported must have a certain affinity; the group must travel together and stay together during the whole trip, or, in the case of an IT charter, must comply with a number of conditions designed to set this traffic apart from scheduled passenger traffic, such as precluding the use of the tour for point-to-point travel.

[22] Cf. CAB Docket 17205, Order E-24697, decided Dec. 1, '66.

[23] Cf. Ibid., Dissenting Opinions; In 1968 Südflug was taken over by Lufthansa.

[24] Inclusive tour means a circle or round-trip tour which combines air transportation and a land arrangement (accommodation and surface transportation) subject to conditions. For affinity, see IATA Res. 045, para 4 (b). See also Appendix II.

The difficulty, however, appears to be the definition of traffic that should travel on line services, with scheduled carriers.

In practice, scheduled carriers, now that this holiday traffic has been created, cannot live without it, because it constitutes their growth potential. On the other hand, if the scheduled carriers are forced to offer fares as low as those of charter carriers, the average yield per passenger transported threatens to become so low that profitability of scheduled operations can no longer be expected.

Governments must choose, therefore, between accepting charter carriers as competitors of scheduled carriers (so that scheduled carriers have to find new ways to meet their competition), or finding new criteria to separate charter-carrier markets from scheduled-carrier markets.

The question may be raised here if and in how far on-route and off-route criteria can be used to delimit the fields of activity of scheduled and charter carriers.

In Canada, for instance, designated (scheduled) carriers are free to operate, in addition to scheduled flights, on-route charter flights, but are restricted in the performance of off-route charter flights.

Charter carriers, on the other hand, have only a secondary right to operate charters on routes regularly served by designated route carriers.

In Scandinavia charter carriers are restricted in the operation of charter flights over routes which are operated regularly by scheduled carriers, at least as far as intercontinental flights are concerned.[25]

In the USA the performance of off-route charter flights by foreign route carriers is regulated by the Economic Regulations of the Board, Part 212 and subject to prior permission. This Part does not authorize the performance of off-route IT charter flights. Foreign route carriers, however, do not need special authority to conduct on-route charter flights (including IT charters if chartered to foreign tour operators).[26]

The problem cannot be solved, however, on the basis of this distinction alone, if at all.

In addition to the on-route/off-route distinction, market development is of major importance.

[25] Cf. e.g. Danish Charter Rules Nov. 1, 1967.

[26] Cf. Südflug, Order E-24697, Jan. 31, 1967: "... as a matter of policy the Board has decided not to exercise jurisdiction over foreign tour operators to the extent they organize IT's abroad for transportation to the US."

Cf. also Docket 20618, NACA Motion, Dec. 27, 1968; the (NACA) supplementals argued that the foreign route carriers needed special authority to conduct on-route IT charter flights, (Part 378 not being applicable to foreign route carriers, see further) and held that the CAB waiver of jurisdiction could only apply to foreign *charter* carriers.

This is especially true of IT charter flights, which constitute, in a way, regular traffic.

IT traffic can move on scheduled services just as well as on charter flights and would do so except that non-IATA (charter) carriers can offer lower minimum tour prices to the public.

The IT market is too big to exclude scheduled carriers from a major portion by authorizing them to compete in the IT market only insofar as operations on their scheduled routes are concerned. The IT charter market, by its very nature, is not a route market, it is a holiday market with its own specific market characteristics.

The problem is therefore essentially a matter of deciding where and to what extent non-scheduled carriers should be allowed to compete with scheduled carriers in the IT market and not whether, where and to what extent scheduled carriers should participate in the IT market in competition with charter carriers.

The same is true of the affinity charter market. Since it is very difficult to control, in practice, the existence of affinity, the problems for governments become those of deciding which and to what extent carriers should be allowed to operate such charters, and avoiding any discrimination among carriers as to the conditions under which they are authorized to operate.

As a matter of fact, the market cannot be broken down into different categories of passengers (IT, affinity, scheduled or non-scheduled), at least not for the purpose of regulating the competition between scheduled and non-scheduled carriers.[27]

For the purpose of regulation, a better yardstick would be the kind of service each carrier is allowed to offer the public, how much service and where. This could then be the criterion for defining a carrier as a charter or a route carrier.

Three aspects of IT development required particular attention: First, if carried by irregular (charter) carriers, this form of charter carriage should not divert traffic from scheduled carriers but truly supplement scheduled services. Second, conditions as far as government policy is

[27] Cf. also ECAC/ITCR-Report of 22/5/69: Framework for a common policy on IT charter flights on the North Atlantic, March 1969. The report cites as the two main principles:

a) There is only one travel market, no part of which is reserved for a particular type of operation and scheduled airlines must have full access to the IT market; and

b) when carriers specializing in non-scheduled flights operate IT flights over the North Atlantic, their role is complementary to that of scheduled carriers.

Cf. also Rec. No. 7 and 8 concerning ITC operations and Rec. No. 9 concerning affinity charters on the North Atlantic. ECAC 1968-'69, Doc 8841, INT. S/1 and 8842, INT. S/2.

concerned, should be equal for all air carriers participating in this traffic. Third, the public should be protected against misleading advertisements promising all-in holidays and suggesting first rate means of transportation if the price advertised did not cover the whole package and out-of-date equipment operated by an obscure carrier were used.[28]

It may be noted in this respect that under Sec. 101 (33), of the Federal Aviation Act of 1958 as amended, supplemental air transportation is defined as "charter trips in air transportation . . . to supplement the scheduled service . . ." Inclusive tours and split charters may be regarded as being within the scope of charter service but special restrictions have to be imposed on such services, to prevent diversion and make these flights conform to the demands of Sec. 101 (33).[29]

On Sept. 27, 1966 the President of the US approved the issuance to a number of US supplemental carriers of certificates to operate foreign charter service, including inclusive tour flights to various parts of the world, thereby reversing a 1963 decision denying this type of service in order to avoid diversion from scheduled carriers.[30]

In a Court proceeding, the Supreme Court, in May 1968, upheld a decision of the Second Circuit Court of Appeals of July, 1967, ruling that granting IT charter authority to supplemental carriers did not fall within the jurisdiction of the CAB under the Act.[31] The decision came as a relief

[28] The International Chamber of Commerce, with Headquarters in Paris, which is the international voice of the users of air transportation, in its Brochure published in 1962 under the title, "International Tourism and Economic Development," advocated inclusive tours as a way to promote tourism. At its bi-annual Congress, held at Montreal in May 1967, the ICC dealt with the protection of the public by including in the "International Code of Standards of Advertising Practice" provisions on IT travel advertising. As to the safety aspects of charter carrier operations, cf. also the Netherlands' R.T.L. (Air Navigation Orders) as amended on May 7, 1968 (Statute Book 240) instituting the requirement of an operational permit for air carriers. (art. 104).

[29] Cf. JALC Winter 1967, pp. 179 ff. Eugene G. Sayre on "Statutory interpretation, inclusive tours".

[30] Cf. Part 378 of the Board's Special Regulations, "Inclusive tours by supplemental air carriers, certain foreign air carriers and tour operators". While Part 295 covers transatlantic supplemental air transportation in general, Part 378 governs inclusive tour operations by US supplemental carriers and US tour operators and certain foreign air carriers for all markets throughout the world, giving at the same time safeguards against diversion.

Cf. Docket 11908 et al. reopened Transatlantic Charter Investigation (all-expense tour phase), decided March 11, 1966, served Sept. 30, 1966, p. 7. The inclusive tour authority was given by Orders Nos. E-24237/8/9/40/1/2, served Sept. 1966. The Order E-24240 of Sept. 30, 1966 applied to the transatlantic market.

[31] While the District of Columbia Circuit Court of Appeals ruled in July 1966 that the term "charter trips" has no fixed meaning and that it is left to the CAB to "evolve a definition to conform to the changing needs of the aircraft industry," the Court of Appeals for the Second Circuit in July 1967 decided that the notion of "charter" excludes solicitation and the sale of individual tickets, whether or not such selling is done through the medium of a traval agent who has first chartered the aircraft. The first decision applied to IT charters in domestic service, the second to IT charters in inter-

to many European countries who feared a serious diversion of traffic from their scheduled carriers to IT charter flights.[32]

The Supreme Court's decision, however, invited an amendment of the Federal Aviation Act of 1958 to remove any doubts as to the CAB's authority to permit supplemental carriers to conduct inclusive tour charters. The amendment was enacted on September 26, 1968.[33]

The CAB's change of policy on supplemental air carriers, authorizing them to operate IT charter flights, resulted from circumstances which had changed since 1963, when there was a downward trend in US flag carrier participation in the North Atlantic market. In 1966 the basic financial and operational soundness of the scheduled operators PANAM and TWA could no longer be questioned. Moreover the CAB argued that all traffic carried by supplementals would be newly generated (which is not necessarily the same as supplemental).[34]

In adopting Part 378 the CAB's argument was not very consistent: on the one hand it accepted a diversion from the scheduled carriers, on the other hand it anticipated entirely new traffic. As for the resulting fare competition, the CAB stated that scheduled carriers can meet it with promotional fares.[35]

national service. The Supreme Court Ruling did not affect the decision with regard to IT charter authority in domestic service.

[32] Cf. also a Press Release of the IATA Dublin Group, April 21, 1969, concerning US supplementals: "At a time when the scheduled airlines are directing their financial, technological and planning resources to move in the phase of mass transportation and will have adequate capacity to meet anticipated traffic demands [a changed pattern in the present system regulating North Atlantic air commerce] would not only imperil the orderly economic development of the airlines, but the interests of the European public economy as a whole."

[33] Cf. Bill S.3566, enacted as Public Law 90-514, September 1968. It may be noted that the Supreme Court was equally divided, thereby affirming the Second Circuit Court's decision. Apart from solving the question of the Board's statutory authority, an important consequence of this Law is the possibility for supplemental carriers to carry individually ticketed members of the general public in competition with scheduled operators.

[34] The question may be asked whether this traffic could not be generated just as well by scheduled carriers. Here we touch upon the main problem of the "division of labor" between regular and irregular carriers.

[35] Cf. the IATA Conference held at Rome, December 1966, where (proposed by PANAM) new Inclusive Tour Group fares (GIT's) for groups of 15 persons or more with no affinity, and new affinity group travel discount fares (GTD's) were agreed upon, both categories of fares having come into effect on the first of April 1967, and intended to take the wind out of the sails of the supplemental carriers.

For the GIT's, the basing fare, which is the fare the travel agent organizing the tour, or the tour operator, pays per passenger to the carrier, and the minimum selling fare, which is the lowest fare the passenger must pay for the transportation plus land arrangements, were set at $ 250 and $ 320 (off-season) and $ 300 and $ 370 (peak-season). These lower fares proved to have a substantial negative effect on the average revenue per ton kilometer sold on the North Atlantic routes of the regular carriers, although overall traffic volumes did increase.

Not only the improved results of regular US carriers, but also the balance of payment argument prompted the CAB to give supplemental carriers additional charter and IT charter authority. Inclusive tours, it was believed, would in fact have a substantial generative effect on foreign travel to the USA, because "foreign travelers are especially sensitive to price and will be attracted by the predetermined cost features of IT's."

It must be understood that IT charters, as distinct from IT travel on line services, are a new and special type of service which cannot easily be assimilated into, nor set apart from, either non-scheduled or scheduled services. As a rule non-scheduled carriers are not permitted to offer scheduled services although scheduled carriers are permitted to offer non-scheduled services.[36] The inclusive tour market encompasses both traffic which once moved on regular services and traffic which is newly generated because of attractive fares and the availability of complete holidays. As scheduled carriers can offer similar types of service to the public (a GIT on the North Atlantic can be considered as a kind of partial IT charter), the IT charter authority at least partly amounts to the admission of new carriers to the scheduled traffic market. According to the CAB, however, the "ITC public" is not the same public as is traveling on regular services.

The CAB stressed that the supplementals, with regard to IT's, are denied the right to engage in "individually-ticketed service".[37]

To prevent the authority from being used as a subterfuge for individually ticketed transportation, the charter tour passenger is subject to the rigidities of a group itinerary circle route. He must be willing to travel and share facilities with strangers and he is confined to a predetermined departure and arrival time.[38]

A further important aspect is the "pricing requirement" designed to prevent undue undercutting of the fares of the regular carriers, and diversion of regular traffic to IT charter services.[39]

[36] Sec. 401 (d) (3) prohibits the issuance of a certificate for supplemental air transportation to the holder of a regular certificate of public convenience and necessity. This presumably precludes the acquisition by a route carrier of a supplemental carrier under Sec. 408 of the Federal Aviation Act as amended.

[37] Cf. Part 378.2 (b) (5) of the Ec. Reg. of the CAB, which requires a minimum of 40 participants if more than one group is carried, with a maximum of 3 groups on one charter with one tour operator.

N.B. Part 295 (2) (b) (2) permits split-charters, so that the carrier can combine two different groups from different charterers on one aircraft.

[38] Cf. Memorandum of Charles S. Murphy, then Chairman of the USCAB, reproduced in ECAC/NSIT/ICIT/2-DP/1, 10/3/67, p. 6. The European Civil Aviation Conference, (its study group for non-scheduled and IT services, under chairmanship of the Portuguese Director-General of Civil Aviation Mr. Veres) had asked CAB to clarify its new regulation for intercontinental IT's of US supplementals and Mr. Murphy complied with this request.

[39] N.B. The individually-ticketed IT charter passenger is subject to separate con-

In February 1969 the IATA Dallas Traffic Conference adopted bulk fares on the North Atlantic with effect from November 1, 1969 ($ 235 in peak season and $ 184 in low season) [40] as a further protective measure against the competition of the supplemental air carriers. The bulk fare concept allows travel agents to book blocks of a minimum of 40 seats eastbound and 20 westbound for resale to the public as a package deal with hotel accomodation. The GIT fares were maintained as well as the affinity group fares (50 persons).

The bulk fare concept (contract bulk inclusive tour, or CBIT) sets different contractual arrangements between the airlines and the travel agents as compared with the IT basing fares (ITX or SIT fares).

Price control of IT charters, however necessary, may not be sufficient to preclude cut-rate competition between scheduled and irregular carriers, which then assumes the form of a rate war in stages. Ultimately this may hurt both scheduled and non-scheduled air carriers beyond repair.[41]

The major problem in avoiding diversion is ensuring that most of the passengers carried by irregular carriers are those who would not have traveled otherwise at the higher fares of regular services.

Affinity charter group traffic is closely regulated in most cases, the regulations intending to set this traffic apart from the general public inter-alia by prohibiting public solicitation.[42]

ditions to prevent undue undercutting of the fares of regular services. The minimum price for ITC passengers has been established by the CAB at 110% of any available individual scheduled fare or at 130% of any CBIT fare charged by a scheduled carrier for the route in question. Cf. Reg. SPR-33, Amendment No. 4 to Part 378, effective November 14, 1969, 378.2 (b) (4).

Cf. also Part 378 A.10: "No BIT or series of tours shall be operated, nor shall any tour operator sell or offer to sell, solicit or advertise such tour or tours, unless there is on file with the Board the form of contract between the tour operator and tour participants, the tour operator's surety bond and . . . [etc.]."

The Board declined to exercise jurisdiction over foreign tour operators with respect to BIT's which originate in a foreign country.

[40] N.B. These fares are not public fares but only transportation prices. The bulk fare concept is a kind of partial IT charter on line services. (cf. Res. 079a)

[41] Note the bankruptcies of such charter carriers as British Eagle, Trans Globe and InterNord, which hurt the international airline industry.

The organization of the supplemental carriers in the US, NACA, protested the bulk fares which the IATA carriers according to the NACA intended to subsidize by eliminating the 5% round trip discount on basic North Atlantic economy and first class fares, which decision was taken in Dallas at the same time. IATA agreed on further reductions coming into effect on March 1, 1970 (Caracas, November 1969) as the Dallas package was not accepted by Alitalia with the result of an "open-rate" situation on the North Atlantic as from November 1, 1969.

[42] Cf. Part 208.3 of the CAB Regulations:

(p) "Solicitation of the general public" means: a solicitation going beyond the bona fide members of an organization (and their immediate families);

(q) "bona fide members" means those members of a charter organization who have not joined the organization merely to participate in the charter as a result of solicitation directed to the general public."

Implementation of these regulations, however, is another matter. For IT charter traffic such a dividing line, both in theory and in practice, is virtually impossible to draw and the carriage of this traffic by non-scheduled carriers should be made subject to conditions equal to those applying to scheduled carriers. To scheduled carriers this charter traffic constitutes an essential part of their market. Its carriage both on their scheduled services and charter flights, enables them to obtain optimum load factors, optimum utilization of their fleets and at the same time offer a wider range of service to their clients, so that their charter services support their regular markets. In other words, the charter market, in the widest sense of the term, and the operation of charter flights, constitute an indispensable part of regular carriers' overall marketing efforts and total operations.

If governments do not effectively prevent diversion to non-scheduled carriers, regular carriers will be forced into price competition with irregular carriers both on their scheduled and charter services. This would dilute their revenues further and might entail the necessity of government subsidies in the end. The least the regular carriers can expect in that case is competition on equal terms enforced by the governments. If this is not done the regular IATA carriers, to compete effectively in the IT travel market, will have to abolish the minimum selling fare.

This would mean abolishing the IATA fare agreement for a substantial part of the regular carriers' traffic, justified only if competition from the irregular carriers in this market would be greater than that among the regular carriers themselves. By thus moving into the field of activity of non-scheduled carriers, regular carriers could show their governments that they are prepared to meet the traffic demands of all the different markets. This would reduce the role of irregular carriers to that of overflow carriers when and where the regular carriers lacked capacity.

By carrying affinity group charter traffic, IT groups, and possibly split-charter and affinity charter traffic on a part-charter basis on regular services, the regular carriers would erase the distinctions between regular and non-scheduled services and between regular and irregular carriers. Irregular carriers moving into the markets of the regular carriers could, in their turn, claim recognition on a far broader basis than the original one justifying their existence.

In consequence governments might authorize or designate carriers, regardless of their regular or irregular status, to serve specific markets, specified both in terms of routes (on-route and off-route) and in terms of kinds and the extent of services to be offered.[43]

[43] Cf. also the US view that "policies concerning charter and scheduled services

IV. NON-INCLUSIVE TOUR (AFFINITY) CHARTER TRAFFIC

Next to inclusive tour charter traffic, affinity group charter traffic is of particular importance. It is noteworthy that the charter share of transatlantic travel in the years 1962-1963-1964 showed a stable growth percentage of 12% per year. The percentage increased to 14.3% in 1965, to 15% in 1966, to 21.3% in 1967. According to a CAB press release of February 1969, the total number of pro rata (as distinct from single entity or own use) charter passengers during the 1968 transatlantic charter season, April 1 through September 30, increased 26% over the 1967 period. The 1969 season shows a 60% increase over the 1968 period.

The US carriers' share of the charter market increased from 31% in 1965 to 42% in 1966 and to 60% in 1967 and 1968. US supplemental carriers carried 44.8% of the charter traffic in 1968. Their percentage share grew at the expense of the regular carriers' share.

As, since 1968, the carriers are required by the CAB to report all transatlantic operations, it was possible for the CAB to give a breakdown into US and European origins: about 62% of the charters originated in the USA.

As the average increase of charter traffic is considerably higher than the average increase of scheduled passenger traffic, the share of charter traffic in relation to total traffic is increasing as well. In the 1967 charter season the percentage was 17%, in 1968 18.9% and in 1969 more than 25%!

The foreign route carriers' share of pro rata charters in the transatlantic market declined from 61% in 1965 to 27% in the 1968 season. The foreign charter carriers' share rose from 4% in 1964 to 15% in 1968.

Two conclusions seem apparent: "non-scheduled" traffic is rapidly becoming as important as scheduled traffic; and US supplemental carriers carry a very large share of the charter market over the Atlantic. On the Atlantic route IT traffic has not yet made its mark.[44]

In addition to the inclusive tour authority,[45] the authority for split-charter transportation is of special interest.[46] Split-charter authority, con-

should be based on the type of service provided without regard to the type of carrier providing the services"; and "... each country should be in a position to determine which of its carriers, scheduled and supplemental, should be permitted to operate international services." ECAC/INT.S/1 Report 18/6/68, p. 22. App. 2 (Doc. 8841, INT. S/1)

[44] The IT authority to US supplementals could not be exercised pending the outcome of court action, and the full impact of the IT facility cannot be expected before 1970. Cf. ECAC/ECO-II/2-WP/3 of September 1969.

[45] Cf. Part 378.

[46] Cf. Part 214 governing foreign charter carrier operations.

While it was decided by the courts that the CAB did not have the right to extend trary to plane-load charter authority, concerns air transportation performed by an air carrier on a time, mileage or trip basis, where half of the aircraft capacity is engaged by a person or a group and the remaining half by another person or group.[47] This definition is a rigid one requiring each group to be comprised of one-half of the capacity of the aircraft. It dates back to 1964.[48]

A more flexible system is given for supplemental air transportation, authorizing in geographic areas other than the transatlantic markets, the carriage of up to three groups on one aircraft, with each group consisting of 40 or more passengers.[49] The CAB will grant to foreign charter carriers privileges similar to those granted to US supplementals for US originating trips combining three groups on one aircraft. However, only one tour operator or charterer will be allowed per aircraft. Foreign originating trips do not come under these provisions as the CAB considers these to be subject to the supervision of the foreign government concerned.

The split-charter product constitutes direct competition with group-fare travel on line services.

With regard to non-IT charter flights operated by foreign scheduled air carriers, the CAB distinguishes between on-route and off-route charter trips. Under foreign air carrier permits (Section 402), authority to conduct charter trips between the points which they are authorized to serve is expressly granted. This is the on-route charter authority which incidentally includes the right to conduct sixth freedom charter flights, provided the operation is conducted via, and lands at, a terminal point mentioned in the foreign air carrier permit, on the way to and from the authorized point in the US.

Another example of conducting a sixth freedom charter operation by converting it into an on-route operation is mentioned in a recent proceeding concerning the open-jaw authority ("a US-Amsterdam eastbound leg coupled with a Paris-US return leg is a common type of a US transatlantic package sold").[50]

the definition of charter to the IT formula, the split-charter formula was recognized as falling within the administrative powers of the CAB.

[47] Cf. Transatlantic Charter Investigation, Order E-20530/1, February 24, 1964, and Order E-20776, April 30, 1964.

[48] Cf. Part 214.2.b.2. and Part 295.2.b.2.

[49] Cf. Part 208, and Order E-23350, March 11, 1966, and E-24237/9, September 30, 1966, Supplemental Air Service Proceeding. N.B. On November 28, 1967 the CAB proposed to amend Parts 214 and 295 to bring them in line with Part 208. These amendments were adopted, Docket 19309, Proposed Rulemaking EDR-129 and Regulation No. ER-531 (Part 295.2.b.2.) and ER-532 (Part 214.2.b.2.) March 26, 1968.

In July 1969 the NACA proposed to lift the limit of three groups per aircraft as long as groups of at least 40 seats are booked. See further under V.

[50] Cf. Martin's Application for amendment of permit, Brief of the Bureau of Oper-

This authority has not yet been granted by the CAB. In a recommendation of the Bureau of Operating Rights of the CAB, granting is recommended, subject to an uplift ratio to maintain a balanced directional flow, on the condition that the charter group remain for 24 hours in the home country of the carrier on its one mandatory stop there, either immediately before or after the performance of a transatlantic leg.

It should be noted that this proceeding concerned the operations of a foreign charter carrier and therefore the on-route part of the flight is defined by the country of which the carrier is a national and not by the route as authorized in the permit.

The off-route charter authority of foreign route carriers to conduct charter trips between points other than those authorized, was included in the foreign air carrier permits by the adoption of Part 212 of the CAB's Economic Regulations.[51] Each off-route operation is made subject to a Statement of Authorization to be issued by the Board.

The basic purpose of this amendment was to grant foreign air carriers off-route charter authority commensurate with reciprocal rights granted by foreign countries to US carriers.[52] The foreign air carriers' charter authority, however, is broader in some instances than that granted US carriers under CAB regulations: US certified route carriers' off-route charter operations are subject to volume, frequency and regularity restrictions imposed by Part 207 of the Board's Economic Regulations (no more than 2% of the revenue plane miles operated in scheduled service). Such restrictions do not apply to the off-route charter operations of foreign

ating Rights of the CAB to Examiner E. Robert Seaver, March 28, 1968. The Examiner recommended the grant of authority for Netherlands-originating open-jaw circle tour charters limited to flights serving only Canada and the US, and the denial of US-originated open-jaw charter authority, and the Board followed this recommendation (Dockets 19570 and 19745, served December 24, 1968).

51 Part 212 does not refer to the homeland of the carrier as the terminal point via which the flight should be operated to make it an on-route charter flight. The Board, however, will not permit a foreign carrier to circumvent Part 212 by transferring traffic at some intermediate point on its route to another of its own flights for onward carriage to an off-route destination.

N.B. Foreign air carriers are not permitted to interchange aircraft with crew for off-route operations by charter. They are permitted to do so for on-route operations if both carriers are authorized to operate over the route concerned. They are permitted to interchange aircraft with crew by lease agreement for off-route operations, and on-route operations even if the lessor is not authorized to operate on the route concerned. Such interline charters and leases are cooperative arrangements and will be discussed in the following chapter on lease agreements (proposed Part 218 of the CAB's Economic Regulations).

52 Cf. e.g. Lufthansa amendment to foreign air carrier permit, Docket 17782, Order E-24685, approved January 25, 1967: "The holder hereof shall be authorized to engage in charter trips in foreign air transportation, subject to the terms, conditions and limitations prescribed by Part 212." (off-route charter authority)

air carriers.[53] The Statement of Authorization of Part 212.4 should not be considered as a license in itself but is merely a "finding by or on behalf of the Board that a given charter proposal meets the requirements of the provisions of the existing Part 212 and the foreign carrier off-route charter permits."

To attach terms, conditions or limitations to the foreign route carrier off-route charter authority, as included in the foreign air carrier permits, would require proper proceedings: notice, public hearing and Presidential approval under Sec. 402(f) of the Federal Aviation Act as amended. This cannot be done through a CAB rule-making proceeding. In actual fact the CAB has never refused, or imposed limitations on, off-route charters by authorized foreign air carriers.

However, in this respect we should mention the Regulation adopted by the CAB on November 22, 1967, through a simple rule-making proceeding,[54] which requires foreign air carriers to file quarterly reports of data concerning type and volume of charter operations to and from the US, "to alleviate further the basic information deficiency concerning civil charters." [55]

This new Regulation constitutes a departure from the policy of the Board to treat on-route and off-route charters separately and differently. Foreign air carriers are required to report the origin and destination of their charter flights, the number and the capacity (number of seats and tons of cargo available), and the itinerary of *all* charters operated to and from the US.

In a way this new Regulation amended the foreign air carrier permits of the foreign carriers operating into the US. The Board, however, argued that obtaining minimal information on the extent of operations under the permits granted comes under the power granted to the CAB in Section 204(a) of the Act.

Moreover, the foreign air carrier permits specifically provide that the

[53] A proposal to that effect engendered such serious opposition by foreign air carriers and governments and by the State Department, that it was dropped. (Cf. PSDR-13a, December 3, 1965). Part 207 intended to offer protection to US supplemental carriers. In 1967, by Amendment 4, effective January 18, Regulation 482, the CAB, however, argued that reasons justifying a liberalization of the restrictions at issue outweigh the economic necessity of protecting the supplementals to the extent currently afforded by Part 207, at least for the short-term future (the Vietnam situation provides the supplementals with a substantial source of revenue). Exemption was granted to PANAM, TWA and NorthWest to promote maximum use of US carriers in air transportation to and from the US.

[54] Cf. Sec. 204(a) containing the general rule-making provision.

[55] Cf. Regulation No. ER-519 effective January 1968, Reporting Data pertaining to Civil Aircraft Charters Performed by Foreign air carriers. Part 217 of the CAB Economic Regulations.

Board may from time to time prescribe reasonable terms, conditions and limitations required by the public interest. Note here that the investigation of the terms, conditions and limitations of foreign air carrier permits, instituted in January 1961,[56] is still pending before the Board, partly as a result of heavy opposition on the part of foreign governments and foreign carriers and the more than reasonable doubt of CAB's jurisdiction to amend the permits of foreign carriers through a rule-making proceeding.[57] At this point the Canadian Rule 1969-A-1, effective February 1, 1969, concerning international non-scheduled charter commercial air services, merits attention.

This Rule deals with entity (own-use) charters (the whole charter is paid by one person for his own account), pro rata (affinity) charters (the passengers pay a share of the transportation costs).

While the 1968 Rule allowed split-charters of not more than two groups of not less than 40 persons on one aircraft, the 1969 Rule allows not more than three pro rata affinity groups of not less than 40 persons on one aircraft and all the persons to be transported must board the aircraft at the same point and deplane at the same point.

Rule 1969 makes a distinction between on-route third and fourth freedom charters by scheduled carriers and off-route charters operated in third and fourth freedom by these carriers. For off-route charters in fourth freedom a ratio is established of five fourth freedom charters for every four third freedom charters operated into Canada by the carrier in the previous operating year (called basic entitlement), while one fourth freedom flight will be authorized for every third freedom flight applied for in the current calendar year in excess of the number of third freedom flights used in calculating the basic entitlement.

The Rule establishes equal primary rights for both Canadian and foreign designated (route) carriers to operate on-route charter flights between the two countries, on routes authorized in a bilateral agreement concluded with Canada.[58] Foreign designated carriers have a priority lower than Canadian route and charter carriers to operate off-route charter flights originating in Canada but higher than foreign carriers of third countries (to which the transportation is fifth freedom carriage). New is the express distinction made between on-route and off-route charter flights, off-route

[56] Cf. CAB Docket 12063, proposed Part 213.

[57] The collection of information on on-route (and off-route) charters of foreign carriers gains special significance if we think of the intention of the Board to review its policy on the on-route charter authority of foreign regular carriers.

[58] N.B. It may be seen that this system is unfavorable for route carriers with only few routes.

charter flights being flights operated by foreign designated carriers between points other than those which they have been authorized to serve, and flights operated by foreign carriers other than the designated carriers. This special concern with charter flights originating in Canada and basic entitlement underlines the priority given to third freedom transportation.[59]

When we review developments in the field of charter traffic, we note that the split-charter concept is a step towards erasing the dividing line between charter flights and line services, by allowing group-fare travel on charter services. The CBIT on the other hand is a step towards erasing the dividing line between IT charter flights and line services by allowing IT group travel on line services.

It is just as difficult to determine which traffic is charterworthy, by setting affinity requirements for group charters in order to put such traffic apart from the general public which is earmarked to travel on line services, as it is to divide the market into passenger traffic categories. In theory, affinity requirements look like a common-sense solution to the problem of charter flights, giving members of organizations of limited membership with a purpose other than travel the possibility of traveling together at lower fares by chartering aircraft capacity, or the possibility of traveling at lower fares by going together on a charter flight. The question is only which is more important, traveling together or traveling at a lower fare?

A charter fare is a rebate granted when a block of seats is bought by the same person at one time. Such a rebate (wholesale price) is normal business practice. Why should this be valid for charter flights only if the buyer is an organization fulfilling certain conditions? The reasons are: to prevent individually-ticketed service by resale at low prices, to protect the fare structure of the line services, to prevent competition between charter flights and the line services of IATA carriers.

In the face of increasing competition by charter carriers, however, IATA carriers have been forced to take a fresh look at the problem. They want to be able to compete with non-IATA carriers on equal terms.

Since it appears that affinity requirements are very difficult to enforce by governments who have adopted the IATA system for the operations of non-IATA carriers, Robert S. Burnstein [60] suggested abolishing them so that the charter carriers could "offer group charter fares directly to the public without the need for organizational affiliation to be eligible for the lower fares."

[59] See also Rule No. 1969-A-3, amending App. C. to Rule No. 1969-A-1, dated June 17, 1969.

[60] Cf. *Travel Weekly*, March 4, 1969.

Burnstein also suggested placing affinity charter flights on the same basis as IT charters. The travel agent or tour operator thus would become responsible for charter development.

There is a lot of merit in these suggestions. The Netherlands abolished the membership limit of charter-worthy organizations in 1969. Further steps to abolish affinity requirements seem indicated. Affinity requirements from a market point of view are artificial conditions designed to reduce the market available to charter flights.

From the point of view of government regulation an adequate technique of regulation should not try to regulate the market, or, in other words, define who is charterworthy, but rather should try and define what a charter is. Pending such definition, however, affinity remains essential.

Chartering is a device for offering a cheaper product to the public. The device, and not the public who may make use of it, should be regulated. A charter is a construction offering a specific, low-fare product. The question is, what kind of construction justifies the quotation of a lower fare?

Of course the public that wishes to make use of the device should be considered. It should not, however, be regulated.

In addition to regulating the charter as a device, the air carrier should be regulated as an instrument for transporting traffic, the use of which is limited, at least if that is what the government concerned wants.

A solution to the problem of the regulation of charter flights should not try to set charterworthy traffic apart from the general public, but concentrate instead on defining a charter as a device for transporting air traffic at a lower fare and regulating the competition of charter carriers by keeping the offering of the charterproduct on the market separate from the offering of the scheduled product.

The charter itself offers a guarantee against undue undercutting of regular fares because it places the responsibility for the entire operation on the charterer, travel agent or tour operator. Charter traffic furthermore is group-fare traffic and therefore a minimum size of the groups which may make use of this facility should be specified when defining charter as a special low fare device for air transportation. Charter flights, by excluding individually-ticketed traffic, need not interfere unduly with regular services.

The charter carriers, then, are those specializing in this kind of air transportation. The own-use charter, the affinity charter and the group IT charter should all be subject to the charter definition.

This solution does not imply that regular carriers would not be able to offer the same charter product to the public, in addition to their regular product.

V. TRAFFIC RIGHTS FOR CHARTER CARRIERS

Regular international flights normally are authorized on a bilateral basis and non-scheduled flights by unilateral government regulations. In a number of exceptions, non-scheduled flights are authorized by bilateral or even multilateral agreement.

Regarding the right to overfly and make technical landings in the territory of another State on non-scheduled flights, Article 5 of the Chicago Convention on non-scheduled flights may be compared with the multilateral "International Air Services Transport Agreement" of 1944 for scheduled services, which extends to Member States the first and second freedoms of the air, subject to certain conditions.

Article 5 does not expressly authorize the imposition of the condition of prior permission. Nevertheless as a rule States require prior permission for commercial non-scheduled flights performed by foreign aircraft or foreign air carriers.

Under the distinction made by the CAB, foreign operators require authorization from the Board in the form of a foreign aircraft permit (navigation within the USA)[61] for operations which do not constitute air transportation – if they are not common carrier operations. For common carrier operations a foreign air carrier permit is required.[62]

The certificates of US supplemental carriers state that the operations of the supplementals shall at all times be conducted in accordance with all treaties and agreements between the US and other countries. As a rule, the agreements with other countries do not cover supplemental operations, and landing rights must be secured for the supplementals outside the existing system of the bilateral agreements.

Negotiations on these traffic rights may be conducted on the basis of reciprocity if the foreign country concerned has a non-scheduled carrier operating into the USA.

Otherwise such negotiations may entail the necessity for the US to trade new route authority for the foreign route carriers, in return for traffic rights for US supplementals, or at least charter authority for the foreign route carriers if US route carriers are not operating charter flights to the country concerned.

While non-scheduled flights come under Article 5 of the Chicago Convention, IT charter flights pose a special problem, since these flights have

[61] Cf. Part 375.1 and 375.24.
[62] Cf. Sec. 402, Fed. Av. Act.

a number of characteristics which may lead to the conclusion that they should be dealt with as scheduled flights, which fall under Article 6 of the Convention.

For the purpose of regulation the problem is of prime importance: non-scheduled flights are mostly charter flights and part of these are IT charter flights. From the point of view of reciprocity what is being traded should be clear. In other words, do the flights fall under Article 5 or Article 6 of the Chicago Convention? If they come under Article 5 they can be dealt with separately from regular services. If not, they affect the trade of traffic rights laid down in the bilateral air agreements.

Gazdik argues that the question can be answered by determining whether or not IT charter flights should be considered public transport. Public transport, he states, is closely linked with the definition of scheduled air service in Article 96 (a) of the Convention. Furthermore Article 6 of the Convention provides the framework within which public air transport is to be carried out in the form of scheduled services. Article 5, however, does not extend the freedoms of the air to public transport. Therefore, according to Gazdik, "it is doubtful whether any public transport can be performed under this article." [63]

IT charter flights, he then argues, involve the holding out of transportation to the public for a single price per person. Therefore, IT charters are public transport.

Suggesting that the dividing line be drawn between Articles 5 and 6 to separate public transport from bona fide charters, Gazdik concludes that "any ambiguity can be eliminated by adopting the ICAO defintion of 1952." IT charters would then come under Article 6 and bilateral air agreements (the requirement of designation of the carrier, specification of the routes, rate control, capacity and frequency control etc.) would be applicable.

The simplicity of this solution is alluring, but a bit of a tour de force.

First of all, Article 5 of the Convention adopts the criterion of "non-scheduled", which is not necessarily the same as "non-public transport", or charter flights. Single flights, for instance, may be performed under Article 5 even if they are open to the public. On the other hand, Article 6 may indeed concern public transport, although the ICAO defintion merely states that each flight should be open to use by members of the

[63] Cf. "Are I.T.C. scheduled or non-scheduled services?" in *The Freedom of the Air*, edited by Edward McWhinney and Martin A. Bradley. 1968 A. W. Sijthoff, Leyden. pp. 114 ff.

public.[64] This is so, however, only insofar as such transport is offered in the form of scheduled air services and the possibility of public transport in forms other than scheduled services is left open.

Second, in the case of IT charter flights, it is not the carrier but the tour operator or the travel agent (the charterer) who holds out to the public by resale of individual seats. It would be difficult to bring the tour operators under bilaterals.[65]

Third, scheduled services are difficult to define, and the ICAO definition may not help in all cases. One could, for instance, easily think of non-scheduled (without regularity or published time table) IT charter flights, notwithstanding the fact that they may be open to individual members of the public.

On the other hand, on special occasions like sports events, fairs, conventions, etc. series of special flights are performed, sometimes as charter flights but open to the general public, whose regularity is published in a time table valid during a short period. Are such series of charter flights regular services or non-scheduled services? [66]

The regulatory problem of charters is not so much a matter of whether they are public transport or not, but rather that they offer as far as the public is concerned the possibility of a lower fare than is available on regular services.[67] The charter can justify its lower fare as a wholesale (bulk) fare, applicable to the sale to the public of blocks of seats subject to other conditions than those offered on scheduled services, or a package (IT) fare.

What we need is a clear definition of the charter product (rather than the charterworthy traffic), for regulatory purposes, together with a definition of IT package tour and perhaps the introduction on a more general scale of the US concept of indirect air carrier, especially for tour operators as producers of a certain kind of air transportation by resale.[68] Introduction of a licensing requirement for indirect air carriers seems necessary

[64] Gazdik apparently reads the definition as involving public sollicitation on a regular basis (time table) to *individual* members of the public, although this is not mentioned in the definition *expressis verbis*.

[65] Cf. the US regulatory problem of the air freight forwarder (consolidator), which is considered to be an indirect air carrier and as such requires a special licence under the Federal Aviation Act of 1958.

[66] N.B. As a matter of fact, a major portion of scheduled air travel in a way is special event travel!

[67] A lower fare can also be justified in the case of a lower-quality product (economy fare, slower and obsolete aircraft).

[68] Compare for instance, the international air freight forwarder who in the US is recognized by the Act as air carrier (indirect air carrier). Cf. Ec. Reg. 297.22. Cf. also CAB Order 69-4-138, April 30, 1969, stating that the tour operator under the IATA CBIT Resolution is an indirect air carrier. Also, Part 378 grants indirect air carrier authority to tour operators.

or at least desirable in order to be able to exercise control over travel agents and tour operators who, in fact, may act as carriers by chartering or leasing capacity with crew for resale to the public by consolidation in competition with direct air carriers.[69]

Next to the criterion that the entire capacity of the aircraft must be hired, additional criteria for the definition of the charter product for regulatory purposes under Article 5 of the Chicago Convention could be:

a) hiring by someone other than a direct air carrier;

b) performing the flights (the transportation) for the exclusive commercial responsibility of the charterer for his own use, or for the use of a group which he represents;

c) reselling individual seats by the charterer, subject to
   i) fare limitations,
   ii) the prohibition of one-way transportation,[70]
   iii) the resale being effected on the basis of an all-expense paid tour of a minimum duration (IT charters),
   iv) the charterer being a recognized travel agent or tour operator;

d) reselling of blocks of a minimum number of seats to groups of passengers, subject to
   i) fare limitations (lower minimum fares),
   ii) the groups being identifiable as such,[71]
   iii) the charterer being licensed as an indirect air carrier, permitting

[69] In practice tour operators and travel agents work closely together to establish their charter program, but there is a need for some control over the tour operators and travel agents to prevent mala fide practices (operation as indirect air carriers rather than as agents).

[70] Cf. Austrian Rule, Febr. 1, 1970 (North Atlantic charter flights): "(g) one-way tickets must not be issued, passengers must be transported both ways within the same group."

[71] Public solicitation with a view to forming groups should not be permitted as this would make it impossible to identify a group as such. Cf. also Order 69-5-124, May 27, 1969 p. 4; "Charters may not be formed as a result of solicitation to the general public." N.B. Charter transportation is group travel. There must be a community of interest among the group beyond the transportation itself. To identify groups from the general public the affinity concept is used. (Cf. Res. 045, IATA). Cf. also ECAC Recommendation No. 9, para 6: "that States use the most appropriate method to exercise control over the means employed by charterers to make up the load of affinity charter flights in the case of groups either national or foreign."

Cf. also Canadian Rule 1969-A-1 and Amendment 1969-A-3, June 17, 1969 on entity and pro rata charters, which permit no more than three groups of at least 40 persons on one and the same pro rata charter; and Rule 1969-A-4, August 31, 1969, on IT's with chartered aircraft, allowing no more than three IT groups on one charter flight of one and the same tour operator.

N.B. IATA does not authorize more than one group per aircraft for affinity group charters. IT charters are authorized within Traffic Conference 2 (Europe and Africa). No affinity is required for groups of IT passengers.

consolidation of different groups into a whole planeload to be carried in one aircraft (split charters).

For cargo charters similar principles could apply.

The NACA, in July 1969, proposed loosening the affinity requirements of the CAB's Economic Regulations (Parts 208 and 295). A number of US trunkline carriers strongly objected, arguing interalia that the "redefinition of affinity proposed by the supplemental carriers would destroy the integrity of the charter concept and corrupt the distinction between group and individually ticketed travel." [72]

The economic condition of the scheduled carriers in 1969 was not as healthy as in 1965 when the Board found that the scheduled carriers could bear whatever diversion would result from expanding the definition of charter. The Board, at the time, authorized split charters on the North Atlantic. NACA proposed to lift the three-group limitation and permit the carriage of an unlimited number of groups so long as each group engaged at least 40 seats.

In the cargo field there are no split charters in international air transportation.

IATA does not permit split charters at the moment. The introduction of the wide-bodied jet aircraft may lead to changes in this respect.

Defining charter by trying to set group travel apart from the general public poses serious problems of enforcement. It would seem that to the extent affinity requirements cannot properly be enforced, fare limitations become necessary.

As the main objective of a charter defintion is the protection of the viability of the scheduled services or rather the scheduled carriers (whose "right to fly is granted in conjunction with the duty to fly in order that service is available to all and at all times" [72]), the problem, in essence, is the certification of charter carriers and the extent to which their competition with the scheduled carriers is accepted (fare competition). Supplemental air transportation does not exist. As far as it would exist, it would constitute an insufficient basis for economic airline operation.

In general we feel that the criterion of holding out to the general public, or open to the general public, could be replaced by a distinction between the various products (instruments of competition) which are offered to the public by direct and indirect air carriers.

Returning to the problem of traffic rights for charter carriers and

[72] Cf. Docket 21255, Supplemental Answer of Certain Trunkline Carriers to a Joint Petition of Certain Supplemental Air Carriers for Institution of Rulemaking Proceeding, November 3, 1969, p. 44. For IT groups, see however, SPDR-18, 30/3/70.

charter flights by regular air carriers, the first question is whether or not a government wishes to license charter carriers in addition to (charter operations performed by) the national scheduled carriers and if so on which basis and to what extent. The second question would be whether a government wishes to allow foreign charter operations by foreign route carriers or by foreign charter carriers into its territory, and if so on which basis and to what extent.

Finally the question arises whether a government wishes to regulate charter operations by unilateral, bilateral or even multilateral agreement.

Governments are still experimenting with unilateral regulations concerning charter operations, and in Europe efforts are being made to arrive at a common policy along the lines of IATA Resolution 045.[73]

Most States license charter carriers in addition to their regular carriers but this is not to say that charter operations by regular carriers and the operations of charter carriers should or do receive separate treatment. Nevertheless since most regular carriers are bound by the provisions of IATA Resolution 045 governing charter flights, charter carriers have more freedom of operation, as far as fare requirements or rules for affinity, etc., are concerned, where government regulations are more liberal than the IATA Resolution.

In order to regulate competition between regular IATA carriers and irregular non-IATA carriers (charter carriers), and especially between US supplemental air carriers and regular European air carriers, the ECAC considered imposing a fare condition, a frequency (flight volume) restriction and a reciprocity requirement in national regulations. IATA itself tries to prevent undue competition between the regular and charter operations of its member carriers (Resolution 045). It is the governments' task to prevent undue competition between charter carriers and both regular and charter operations of scheduled air carriers.

As opposed to scheduled services, charter operations are dealt with by governments on a more incidental basis under unilateral State regulations. The CAB, however, issues charter permits to charter carriers authorizing the operation of charter flights to and from the US, subject to conditions and limitations, for three- to five-year periods. Most other States grant permits to carriers for individual or series of charter flights.

To regulate charter operations by charter carriers in the form of bilateral agreements between States would establish these carriers and their operations on a basis comparable to that of regular carriers and could thereby

[73] Cf. ECAC Recommendations No 7, (1) and Rec. No 8, (3) and Rec. No 9, (3), 1969. Doc. 8841, INT. S/1 and 8842, INT. S/2.

change the supplemental character of charter transportation. This might be wise, for it is doubtful if charter operations should be treated as supplemental to the operations of regular carriers. Charter operations, however, could very well be defined as a different product with an independent right to exist, and then it would be entirely adequate to conclude separate bilateral air charter agreements. Such agreements should apply to charter operations as such (i.e., of both charter and regular carriers). We will revert to this problem later.

The US government, with a view to establishing more firmly the operations of US supplemental carriers, has shown interest in the conclusion of bilateral charter *carrier* agreements.[74] If put into practice, such a policy would be bound to affect the charter operations, or at least the off-route charter operations, of regular air carriers.

Charles S. Murphy, at the time Chairman of the CAB, stated, "I anticipate that we will follow liberal policies with respect to authorizations for US and foreign air carriers to bring charter groups into the USA because of the economic and social benefits of increasing the flow of visitors to the US. With regard to charters originating in the US, I anticipate that we will be mindful of considerations of reciprocity as well as suitable measures to prevent undue impingement upon scheduled services. In particular we will give attention to the need for provisions to prevent an excessive imbalance in the directional flow of charter traffic as between charter groups originating within the US and inbound charter groups." [75] For the US the directional balance argument served to ease the balance of payments problem.

Here a clear distinction is made between the carriage of outbound traffic originating in the US, and inbound traffic, the latter receiving a more liberal treatment.

Thus, in addition to the problems of defining charter and IT charter service, licensing charter carriers and indirect air carriers as well as regular carriers, balancing the interests of scheduled services and charter flights (including IT charters), there is the problem of distinguishing between inbound and outbound traffic.

The distinction between inbound and outbound traffic influences reci-

[74] Cf. Frank Loy in a speech before the International Aviation Club in Washington DC. April 24, 1969.

[75] Cf. Memorandum, reproduced in ECAC/NSIT/ICIT/2-DP/1 of 10-3-'67 and Report of 17-3-'67. See further the answer to a request by the ECAC for clarification received from the Chairman of the CAB, dated 6 July, 1967, EC/9/21-0118 of 11/7/'67 and Doc. 8841, ECAC/INT. S/1, App. 2, 1968.

procity: Third freedom charters would embody the entitlement to operate fourth freedom charters.[76]

In this connection a suggestion made by Prof. John H. Spencer to the effect that the third freedom traffic perhaps constitutes "the one ineluctable parameter of route structure negotiation" demonstrates a similar line of thinking, be it for more fundamental reasons: traffic generation reflects the "full gamut of population, economic, commercial, service-efficiency, tourism and passenger-nationalistic preference pressures and potentials." (Though tourism and nationalistic pressures are equally reflected by fourth freedom traffic)[77] While Prof. Spencer's suggestion applies to bilateral route structure negotiation, the directional balance argument concerns charter operations. All the same the underlying reasoning merits attention as it involves an important principle.

It is an arbitrary decision to attach a greater value to the traffic-generating capacity than to the traffic-attracting capacity of a country. Traffic is a two-way street and the international route network has not developed to a point where one-way streets have become necessary to avoid traffic congestion.

Prof. Spencer's suggestion was also made as a contribution to the solution of the fifth freedom problem and as such it may be valuable as a purely technical formula for arriving at an adequate system of allocating route structure rights. That his suggestion may be more realistic and equitable, as he argues, is doubtful, except perhaps for big traffic-generating countries.

The reciprocity requirement would entail the granting of permits in return for equivalent permits being their image, in other words, the rights granted should be mirrored by the rights received. This would mean that a permit granted by a European country to a US carrier to transport charter (IT) traffic from the US to that country, should be compensated by a permit granted by the US to a carrier of that country to transport charter (IT) traffic from its country to the US, which is, in effect, an exchange of third freedom charters.

Similarly fourth freedom charter rights could also be exchanged.

Here we see a difference between regular traffic and charter traffic, inasmuch as the directional balance argument determines reciprocity for the

[76] Cf. the "basic entitlement" of the Canadian Rule 1969, A-1 of Febr. 1, 1969: Third freedom [off-route] charter flights operated from its own country to Canada in the preceding operating year, [. . .] will establish the basic entitlement for fourth freedom charter flights for the next calendar year from [off-route] points in Canada, in the ratio of five fourth freedom charter flights for every four third freedom charter flights.

[77] Cf. *The Freedom of the Air*, p. 86/87.

operation of charters, something which it never could do for scheduled services which are operated on the basis of route exchanges and not on the basis of individual flights per direction. A route must be used both ways to make commercial operation of the services over it possible.[78] Charter flights are operated on the basis of the profitability of each individual flight (empty leg problem).

The US CAB grants charter permits to foreign air carriers for periods of three or five years, sometimes limiting the number of charter flights to be performed under them.[79] Moreover it attaches certain conditions, such as the requirement that the flights must be carried out between the homeland of the carrier and the US and that a certain ratio should be maintained between US-originating charter trips and charter trips to the US (the directional balance argument). Direct cross trade (fifth freedom) operations between the US and third countries usually are allowed if they concern traffic to the US.[80]

Thus, while it is possible to distinguish charter operations according to the place where traffic originates, because of the specific character of charters, it may be difficult to base an exchange of charter authorizations on the directional balance criterion. Some countries are primarily traffic-generating as far as charter operations are concerned, others are traffic-attracting areas (for tourism). A directional balance in these cases is virtually impossible. It would also be virtually impossible to divide charter operations more or less equally between carriers of the two countries without forcing the market.

Our conclusion, therefore, is that the directional balance criterion is impracticable both for scheduled services and for charter operations. Moreover, the traffic-generating potential of a country, while constituting a firm basis for the operation of charter flights, cannot be taken as the sole or main criterion for the allocation of route structure rights for scheduled air services, a route being by nature a two-way street. Nevertheless the traffic-generating potential of a country may be used as an adequate

[78] It is sometimes argued that the origin of the traffic is a factor to determine the capacity which route carriers are entitled to operate: for instance if more country A originating passengers travel on a route between country A and country B than country B originating passengers travel on that route to country A, carriers of country A are entitled to operate more capacity on that route than carriers of country B.

[79] Cf. Transavia, N.V. Docket 18588, Order E-26136, served Dec. 19, 1967; Caledonian Airways, Docket 16372, Order E-25017, served April 21, 1967; Martin's, Docket 18016, served Dec. 21, 1967. In the case of Martin's the CAB granted planeload cargo charter authority limited to ten one-way flights in any calender year.

[80] Cf. Caledonian Airways Ltd., CAB Press Release December 21, 1967, CAB 67-171. p. 2 and Martin's Permit, Dockets 19570 and 19745, Served Dec. 24, 1968, condition (2), (ii).

technique of regulation in determining route structure rights to be allocated to scheduled air carriers. It could not be a way to establish entitlement to the carriage of traffic on a route, without taking into account the traffic-attracting potential of the country as well as the potential of the country as a gateway to other destinations.

Reciprocity for charter operations, furthermore, can be based only on the principle of equal opportunity.

A result of the directional balance argument is that a frequency limitation may be imposed on charter flights by relating the number of charters in fourth freedom to the number of third freedom charters which a carrier operates to a country.[81] As we have already pointed out such a system is inadequate if it concerns countries one of which is predominantly traffic-generating and the other traffic-attracting.

Within the ECAC thought has been given to a frequency limitation of IT charter flights by US supplementals to Europe in the form of a percentage (1%) of the number of all scheduled flights performed per month in the preceding year to the gateway concerned.[82]

The percentage limitation of charter flights, relating the percentage to the scheduled service performed, is already being applied in the US with regard to off-route charters. This is done by limiting the total off-route revenue mileage of US route carriers in relation to their total annual on-route revenue mileage. It is not certain if this limitation also applies to US-carrier IT charter flights. Foreign air carriers are not authorized to perform off-route IT charter flights.[83]

[81] Cf. Canada Rule No. 30/67, May 19, 1967, para 10, c. and Rule 1969-A-1 of February 1, 1969.

[82] Cf. the NATCAPIT group of experts of the ECAC, Report of 21/2/69, and ECAC/ITCR-Report of 22/5/69. In the latter Report a limitation to a proportion of transatlantic flights is recommended so that the volume of this charter traffic (by both US and European charter carriers) does not impair the services provided by scheduled carriers. The limitation suggested in the Report is 1% of the transatlantic flights performed to the State concerned in the previous year, to be calculated per month, or 60 such charter flights. With regard to a fare limitation for North Atlantic IT charter flights, the IATA bulk fare would seem to be the appropriate yardstick. Note that Japan imposed a limitation on the number of charter flights by US supplemental carriers (46 in 1968 to be increased in subsequent years).

[83] Cf. Part 212 of the CAB Regulations concerning off-route charter operations. This Part was amended in 1969 (ER-570) by adding a requirement that records of names and addresses of passengers on pro rata charter flights in foreign air transportation, both on-route and off-route, should be maintained to prevent individually-ticketed services in the guise of charter services.

N.B. IATA does not allow IT charter flights over the North Atlantic, but instead adopted the bulk-fare concept as a part-IT charter possibility on the North Atlantic as from November 1, 1969. In September, however, Alitalia broke the agreement, contending that the bulk-fare did not go far enough to meet the supplementals' competition. Alitalia wanted an *individual* fare sufficiently low to compete with the charter flights of the US supplementals.

Limiting the frequency of charter flights, apart from considerations based on reciprocity, implies the recognition of charter flights as serving essentially the same markets as regular services and intends to limit competition quantitatively.

As for the fare condition, it is clearly intended to limit competition qualitatively. While tariffs of charter flights are free, although in the US carriers are required to comply with tariffs setting forth specific rates for charter flights, as published by them, IT's on charter flights are usually bound to a minimum selling price for an individual IT.

IATA allows its member airlines to sell IT's only at prices at least equal to the lowest applicable regular fare on scheduled services.

Government regulations for ITC flights of charter carriers mostly require higher minimums.[84] In Europe, however, IT's on charter flights are offered to the public at ever lower fares, often as camping tours.

As a result, the Netherlands' non-scheduled regulations have successively lowered the minimum selling fare of IT's on charter flights. Under the 1969 Regulation this fare has been set at 60% of the lowest applicable IATA fare for IT charter flights which may be freely performed within Europe.

To control fares in the US, the prospectuses of IT's must be filed. In Europe forms giving all details of the IT operation must be filled in.[85]

It should be noted that the condition of a minimum selling price cannot prevent price competition between regular and charter carriers since the prices at which the carriers offer capacity to the tour operators are not regulated (ITX fares).

Minimum fare requirements for charter flights may become superfluous if the product can be closely defined, that is if the possibility of one-way transportation is excluded for IT and split-charter traffic and passengers on such charter flights are required to travel together both outbound and on their return journeys etc.

The efforts of the European States who are members of ECAC to harmonize their regulations governing non-scheduled and especially IT charter flights were aimed at restricting such flights by US supplemental air carriers (and European charter carriers) to protect European scheduled air carriers.

[84] Cf. e.g. Canada (115%) and the US (110%, and 130% of CBIT fares).

[85] Cf. Part 378.18. After January 1, 1969, the Statement of Authorization *prior* to solicitation was no longer required.

Cf. also Annex to Recommendations Nos. 7 and 8, ECAC/ITCR-Report, 1969 and ECAC/INT.S/2-Report, 12/7/69, pp. 20 ff.

The aeronautical authorities agreed to adopt an attitude of severe restraint with regard to US supplemental transatlantic operations.[86]

They argued that "if there is an ITC market on the North Atlantic, the scheduled carriers should meet that demand," that "ITC operations by US supplementals or European non-scheduled carriers should remain complimentary to the operation of the scheduled carriers," that "a control should be exercised on the frequency of ITC operations between various parts or areas" and "tariff problems should be closely examined" as well as that there was a "need to ensure that a group participating in an IT remain together throughout the whole trip," and a need to determine "to what extent ITC operations re frequency and availibility to the general public are scheduled or non-scheduled under the ICAO Definition" (of 1952).[87] It should be noted, however, that the criterion of regularity of the ICAO defintion (recognizably systematic series) no longer is appropriate for regulatory purposes. The criterion is the penetration of the market by the operations concerned, for which the flight volume may constitute an adequate yardstick.

The need for a common European policy was made clear in the ECAC report [88] by arguing that "Europe should be considered from the tourist point of view as a single entity and that its political divisions should in no way become a source of fresh advantages for the supplemental carriers

[86] Cf. ICAO Assembly, Buenos Aires 1968, DGCA Report re-amendment of the Federal Aviation Act confirming the ITC authority granted to the US supplementals, 5/9/68.

[87] Cf. the two reports, one of the CAB in ECAC/NATCAPIT/1-WP/1 of 7/2/69 and the other of ECAC in NATCAPIT/1-Report 21/2/69. The US report emphasized the public and economic benefits to be realized from the development of IT charters, while the ECAC report feared a considerably diversionary impact of an uncontrolled opening of the ITC market to the supplementals.

[88] NATCAPIT/1-Report 21/2/'69, p. 23.

Cf. also ECAC/INT. S/2-Report 12/7/'69, Recommendation No. 8: Capacity and Frequency Control for ITC Operations across the North Atlantic and Other Conditions:

"1. that, in case in which charter IT's on the North Atlantic are permitted, they should be limited to a proportion of transatlantic scheduled flights so that the volume of such charter traffic does not impair the services provided by scheduled carriers;

2. that authorizations given by one State should not unduly affect the policy followed by other States and that any State should feel free to impose more stringent criteria than another State, and that the implementation of this recommendation shall not in any way prevent States that are not prepared to authorize IT charters on the North Atlantic to or from their territory to continue this policy;

3. that, in so far as such IT charter traffic has multidestination characteristics, European civil aviation administrations receiving applications should, when considering them, consult with the administration of those countries where a stop is to take place on the air journey, and inform those countries to be visited by surface means or by scheduled air transport services"; In Recommendation No. 7 conditions were laid down for "Tariff Control for ITC Operations across the North Atlantic," based on IATA conditions, while Recommendation No. 9 aims at establishing a "common policy on the control of affinity charters."

or of disadvantages for the scheduled carriers." Tours cover more than one country, and this indeed raises the necessity for agreement among the countries concerned.

Although the characteristics of the IT passenger are different from those of the normal passenger on scheduled services in a number of respects and although the introduction of the IT facility brought new business to the airlines, it is clear that the IT passenger represents a portion of the market of the scheduled carriers and that the IT charter flights cover a market which the scheduled carriers need for their continued growth and which therefore is the very market of the scheduled carriers.

Perhaps the fact that the IT charter passenger in practice is sold individually is the main problem. To solve this problem by assimilating IT charter flights with scheduled services and bringing them under the regulation of scheduled services (mainly bilateral agreements), however, would be difficult.[89]

The issue makes the problem of the definition of scheduled air service (ICAO in 1952) topical again.[90]

The ITA, in the short annotation mentioned above, regrets that in the ICAO definition the criterion of an operation "irrespective of payload" was left out, because this criterion would have set regular services clearly apart from both ITC and affinity charter flights. The criterion is not a valid one, scheduled services not always, and non-scheduled services sometimes, being operated "irrespective of payload".

It would be wrong to try and fit this new mode of transportation into the existing patterns of international civil aviation regulation. As the ITA rightly states, an IT is not a flight, not a transportation service. It is a journey. In other words, it is a different product.

The European air traffic market lags far behind the US domestic air traffic market. The intra-European air network shows many deficiencies in schedules, frequencies and direct connections offered by the airlines. The traveling public, however, suffers in silence. It is only the International Chamber of Commerce in Paris which represents the voice of the user of air transport. But the user himself is passive where it concerns his "right" to travel in the way he chooses.

In practice it has been found that generally an increase of air service frequencies between two given points generates new traffic. Not always,

[89] A solution advocated by Portugal.

[90] Cf. also ITA Bulletin No. 46, December 11, 1967, pp. 1429 ff.: "The IT is not a mere transport operation like the regular service and a (group) charter, but the group IT and the charter flight have in common the maximum utilization of the aircraft used."

however, does a carrier have the right type of aircraft available to operate a route with a high frequency which is necessary to make the operation economic. Normally moreover, the smaller the aircraft the less economic the operation. To operate at high frequency with a larger aircraft may lead, on the other hand, to low load factors, and this is no solution either. Only when the traffic is there, does a high-frequency operation with a large-capacity aircraft make the operation economic.[91]

Unfortunately the development of charter traffic in many cases, and especially in Europe, removes the possibility for scheduled airlines to obtain the most economic operation of their routes and at the same time offer the best product to the public.

The solution to this problem lies either with the protection of the scheduled carriers on the routes operated by them or with the decision of the scheduled airlines to compete with the irregular carriers by offering similar low-fare service. It is not surprising that many governments prefer the latter solution because it releases them from the obligation to restrict the non-scheduled carriers which would deprive the public of the possibility to travel at very low fares, while at the same time it forces the scheduled carriers to offer their services to the public at lower fares. But it is only when traffic substantially increases as a result of such a rate war, that the financial position of the scheduled carriers is not seriously affected to the detriment of the public which relies on the uninterrupted service of the scheduled carriers.

We need, for the purpose of the exchange of traffic rights, a new distinction between the different kinds of carriers and their services, in addition to distinctions between the various products offered to the public, which should be closely defined in order to prevent undue competition.

For the purpose of the exchange of traffic rights, the technique of the exchange should be taken into account looking for the most adequate distinction between the various kinds of services.

One of the principal recommendations of the Report of the Committee of Inquiry into (British) Civil Air Transport in the Seventies, under the chairmanship of Sir Roland Edwards,[92] concerned the need to re-appraise the traditional distinction between scheduled and non-scheduled services: "the terms should be redefined in the light of recent developments in the inclusive tour and holiday charter field."

In our opinion the distinction between scheduled and non-scheduled

[91] Cf. "Discussion of Airline Load Factors and Capacity," M. Brenner: ". . . the industry must deal with indivisible units of capacity i.e. plane-loads of seat-miles."
[92] *British Air Transport in the Seventies,* May 2, 1969.

services for regulatory purposes should be replaced by the distinction between operations authorized under bilateral air agreements on specified routes and operations on routes not specified in bilateral agreements. Operations on specified routes should not be limited to scheduled services, but should include any type of service by the designated airlines.

This distinction would not automatically exclude charter carriers from operating on routes specified in air agreements. Charter carriers could very well be designated to operate certain specified routes. If they were, they would become a route carrier on those routes. The distinction between charter carrier and regular carrier in such case would be erased on the specified routes concerned. On the other hand, regular carriers could very well be authorized to operate certain types of service on routes other than those specified in bilateral air agreements. They would then become a charter carrier in addition to being a route carrier.

The main reasons for this new distinction are that a route carrier, if it is to survive on a specified route, must be able to carry any kind of traffic on that route, where it is supposed to compete effectively, and that a carrier must be able to compete in any category of traffic on that route in order to expand in conformity with traffic developments.

What should be decided is where and the extent to which irregular carriers should be authorized to participate in affinity charter and IT traffic, and not where and the extent to which regular carriers should be authorized to operate affinity and IT charter flights in addition to their regular services.

If irregular carriers do generate new traffic and do not rely for their business on traffic diverted by lower prices from scheduled airlines,[93] a sympathetic attitude of the governments would seem justified and even desirable.

The CAB, however, in authorizing the supplemental carriers to conduct IT charter operations, hoped to have these carriers develop US inbound traffic as a means of alleviating balance-of-payment problems. This of course was a purely nationalistic and opportunistic objective and it did not answer two fundamental and interrelated questions:

1. Can the international air traffic market support an increased number of carriers; in other words, is there room for irregular as well as regular carriers?

[93] Cf. the conditions imposed by the CAB: all-expense tours must really be IT's, must consist of groups, must quote minimum fares . . . etc.

Cf. also Rec. 7 and 8 concerning IT charter flights, cited above and Rec. 9 concerning a "Common Policy on the Control of Affinity Charters": "Whereas regulations concerning inclusive tour flights – which are open to the general public – may have the

2. If so, can the industry bear the increased downward pressure on fares as a result of the competition of irregular carriers in the scheduled international air traffic market?

In a Report made by the aeronautical authorities, Members of the ECAC, in February 1968, fear of overcapacity on the North Atlantic route in the 1970's was expressed, because there was no confidence that the traffic would grow fast enough to enable the economic use of the capacity already planned for these routes by flag carriers.

An additional form of competition introduced by way of inclusive tour charter carriers therefore seemed highly unfortunate.[94]

"The European countries," the ECAC felt, "must have regard for the stability and financial soundness of their national carriers. It is on these airlines that the European countries must depend for the provision of basic public service. These airlines are making provision for the growing demand of the market." [95]

It is not without foundation that the scheduled airlines fear an erosion of the scheduled market because of the diversion of (scheduled) traffic to ITC operations and IT traffic to fictitious affinity charters of charter carriers. Affinity charters operated by scheduled airlines are affected, as well, by diversion to ITC operations and fictitious affinity charters. And even the individual passenger who travels for business purposes is finding it cheaper to travel on an ITC basis and to buy his ticket through a tour operator.

As a matter of fact, it is not primarily a question of erosion (diversion) but rather of the dilution (lower fares) of the scheduled market through the activities of non-IATA charter carriers, which threatens the scheduled airline industry. It is for this reason that CAB regulations are designed "to assure that passage is not sold to an individual in such a manner as to become the equivalent of individually-ticketed service, which carriers of the charter class are prohibited by law from offering." Not only individually-ticketed passengers on charter flights but also split-charters compete with (group travel on) line services because a number of small organizations forming different groups could easily charter an aircraft.

Caledonian Airways (Prestwick) Ltd. and Sudflug were the first European non-scheduled carriers authorized by the CAB to operate IT charter flights to and from the US.

effect of displacing part of the traffic involved into the field of charters by associations or groups presenting a merely fictitious affinity."

[94] Cf. also the Press Release of the IATA Dublin Group of April 21, 1969, cited in the previous chapter.

[95] Cf. ECAC/DGCA Report, February 15, 1968.

In the Caledonian case the CAB relied on the conditions imposed by the British Government, which were substantially those imposed by IATA for Europe. Caledonian was granted the authority to perform IT charter flights between the UK and the US, provided such charters originated in the UK. In 1967 this authority was extended to include authority to perform IT charter operations originating in the US and destined for the UK.[96] At the same time Caledonian was authorized to perform passenger charters originating not only in the UK but in a number of specified countries on the European continent and destined for the US as well.

It should be remembered that charter operations, as a rule, do not come under bilateral air agreements which normally govern only scheduled services. The policy adopted by foreign governments with regard to the charter operations of US air carriers may therefore influence US policy with regard to both off-route and on-route charter operations by foreign air carriers to and from the US.[97]

Here again the distinction can be made between charter operations conducted by scheduled air carriers designated under bilateral air agreements and charters operated by irregular, charter or supplemental air carriers.[98]

The principle of reciprocity could be applied either by allowing charter operations, regardless of the carrier conducting these operations, or by granting reciprocal rights separately to regular and irregular carriers. In other words, if a foreign charter carrier obtained a permit from the CAB, could the US government claim the admission of a US supplemental carrier by the foreign country concerned or should permission to the regular designated carrier of the US for conducting charter flights to that foreign country be accepted as an adequate and appropriate reciprocity?

Much would depend on how governments evaluated the role of irregular air carriers.

[96] Cf. Docket 16372, Order E-25017, April 19, 1967, which provides that ITC flights originating in the US should be governed by Part 378.

[97] Of late the CAB has had reservations about the on-route charter authority of foreign regular air carriers, until now included in Section 402 permits; the Board has decided to re-examine its policy on this matter. Cf. e.g. CAB Order No. E-24295 (amending the routes of JAL), Docket 17106, September 22, 1966, Opinion p. 2; and CAB Order E-24571, approved December 23, 1966, Olympic Airways.

[98] N.B. While on-route charter flights by regular carriers come under Sec. 402 permits, off-route charter authority of foreign route carriers is included in Sec. 402 permits (and governed) by Part 212 of the Board's Economic Regulations; charter transportation, including IT transportation, by foreign air carriers engaged in charter transportation only (foreign non-scheduled, irregular or charter carriers) are governed by Parts 214, 203 and 211 of the Board's Economic Regulations. Part 214 is the complement of Part 295 governing transatlantic passenger charters by US supplemental air carriers (as distinct from route carriers).

An indication of US policy in this matter can be given by analyzing the CAB charter rulings in the Condor and Martin's cases, both involving non-scheduled foreign air carriers.[99]

Condor is fully owned by the regular foreign air carrier Lufthansa, and the regular foreign air carrier KLM has a 25% stock interest in Martin's.

The cases posed the problem of the control relationship between two foreign carriers, here between regular and irregular carriers of the same nationality.

The US policy laid down in these decisions not only dealt with permissible and prohibited relationships between carriers, to which we will revert later, but at the same time is an example of the authority which the CAB is prepared to grant foreign regular and irregular air carriers for the conduct of charter operations to and from the US.

The CAB, in essence, considered that US policies [100] should not be imposed on a foreign government if this would prevent that government from conducting its international air transportation services in the way it chose and made no distriction between a privately-owned irregular carrier and an irregular carrier controlled by a scheduled carrier or one that was a member of IATA.[101] If a foreign government licenses regular and irregular carriers to conduct charter operations, even if the irregular carrier is affiliated to or owned by the regular carrier, the CAB will not interfere.[102]

The CAB thus did not add any divestiture requirement to the permits of Condor and Martin.

While, as far as the CAB is concerned, charter operations may be conducted by foreign regular and irregular carriers, whether or not they are affiliated, one CAB Board member in his dissent in the Condor case, stated that Lufthansa could now provide, under the off-route regulations of the Board, essentially all of the services for which authority was sought for Condor (duplicative authority). Because of the relationship between Lufthansa and Condor no competition could exist between the carriers. That, he concluded, is not the way to do business in the USA.[103]

[99] Cf. Orders E-26146, Docket 17233 and E-26147, Docket 18016, served December 21, 1967.

[100] The policy of the Federal Aviation Act would prohibit such relationships of ownership and control between US scheduled and supplemental carriers (Sec. 401 (d) (3) and Sec. 408). Such limitations derive from US anti-trust laws. The Act does not extend this policy to foreign carriers.

[101] Cf. Order E-26146. Opinion, p. 4.

[102] N.B. Considerations of reciprocity weighed heavily in favor of CAB's taking such an attitude! Neither Western Germany nor the Netherlands limit US operations to their countries unduly. Cf. Order E-26146, Opinion p. 5.

[103] Cf. CAB 67-171, 382-6031, December 21, 1967, Press Release.

However, the CAB imposed conditions designed to give reasonable assurance that the operations would be conducted independently of Lufthansa and KLM, and that there would be "no holding out of any identity or relationship between them".

From these rulings appears that the CAB is prepared to extend charter rights to foreign air carriers, both regular and irregular if both scheduled and supplemental US carriers receive liberal treatment in that country. In other words, reciprocity is not interpreted as a carrier for a carrier.

It is up to each government to determine the instrumentality for conducting its international air transport operations, scheduled and non-scheduled, but the CAB insists upon ensuring that the separate identity of each carrier be preserved.[104]

The extent to which regular international air services and international charter flights may be operated, however, is subject to a bilateral and unilateral system of regulation. Finally, by whom such international operations may be conducted, and in what manner, is in the first instance the sovereign decision of the State of the carriers concerned.[105]

New regulations proposed by the US CAB governing inter-airline charter or lease-with-crew arrangements among foreign air carriers [106] should be mentioned here. Arrangements for interchange of equipment between foreign carriers to conduct on-route operations will require a CAB license subject to Presidential approval, under these regulations. Freedom to operate on-route charter flights with aircraft chartered or wet leased from another foreign air carrier, therefore, will be affected as well.

Off-route charter flights by foreign air carriers with chartered or wet leased aircraft are permitted by the CAB only in case of emergency.

The new regulation to which we will revert in the following chapter, if adopted, can frustrate the efforts of foreign carriers to obtain maximum utilization of their aircraft.

We have already mentioned a number of aspects of the non-scheduled

[104] Cf. a recent CAB case, CMA SA, Docket 209200, served August 29, 1969, when CMA proposed that the Mexican government grant authorizations to US supplementals for charter flights, and PANAM stated that US traffic rights for foreign scheduled services should not be traded for foreign landing rights for US supplementals. The Board, however, argued that CMA's permit permits unlimited on-route charters, and therefore landing rights for US supplementals were particularly relevant to the Board's grant of on-route charter rights.

[105] In bilateral agreements it is usually stipulated that the substantial ownership and effective control of the designated carriers should be vested in nationals of the party designating the carriers.

[106] Cf. Docket 21080, EDR 166, Juni 12, 1969. (Proposed new Part 218 of the Board's Economic Regulations)

problem. We have looked into the market and the difficulty of distinguishing between various categories of traffic; the IT facility, the fear of diversion and the need for equal conditions for charter carriers and regular carriers operating in the charter field; all-cargo operations; the distinctions made among various carriers; the definition of (non-)scheduled service; the on-route/off-route distinction; the collective-demand aspect and possible criteria for the charter product; the directional-balance aspect; the reciprocity aspect; the criterion of regularity; the need for tariff and volume restrictions; IATA group and bulk fares; the non-IT charter product; the affinity problem; split-charters; the problem of individually-ticketed service; and the exchange of traffic rights for charter operations.

With regard to the last aspect, and in particular to the regulation of non-scheduled services, the starting point must be the realization that charter traffic is here to stay, no longer in a secondary or supplementary role but in a position of value equal to 'regular' traffic. The recognition of this fact will enable adequate regulation of the charter product.

While in Europe a multilateral agreement was concluded covering certain very limited categories of non-scheduled flights within Europe [107], and European countries are seeking a more-or-less common policy of severe restraint with regard to the North Atlantic charter operations of charter carriers, there is a growing need to establish more firmly the policy to be followed in the field of international charter operations, including IT charters.

The State's usual unilateral regulation of non-scheduled services should be amended by multilateral agreement on the role of, and the extent of freedom to be given under government regulation to, charter services.[108]

Strictly speaking, authority for charter operations could be exchanged together with scheduled authority and included in the same bilateral agreement, leaving it to the parties to the agreement to designate the carriers entitled to exercise the rights granted.[109]

On the other hand, the States could enter into special bilateral agreements (the exchange of three- or five-year charter carrier permits) governing the operations of designated charter carriers, or true bilateral charter agreements.

Finally, multilateral agreement could be negotiated replacing Article 5 of the Chicago Convention of 1944.

[107] "Multilateral Agreement on Commercial Rights in Non-Scheduled International Air Services within Europe," April 30, 1965.

[108] Cf. the efforts within the framework of the ECAC.

[109] Cf. on-route charter authority which, as a rule, is included by the CAB in the Sec. 402 permits.

As we believe that charter traffic cannot properly be separated from regular traffic, we would advocate the inclusion of charter authority in existing bilateral air agreements, leaving it to the States to decide which carriers will be designated to exercise these charter rights. This, however, need not necessarily happen: Charter services are a special device and a separate product for transporting international air traffic, and they could very well be regulated by separate bilateral arrangements or multilateral agreement. A separate regime for charter services, regardless of whether the carrier performing the service is regular or charter, probably would best correspond with the growing independence of the charter product in the international air traffic market.

The problem of regulating the competition between regular services and charter services and between regular carriers and charter carriers would then have to be solved by clear definition of charter service on the one hand, and the government decision on which regular and charter carriers to designate for the performance of charter services, on the other. The principle of multiple designation, therefore, would have to be included in separate bilateral agreements concerning charter services.

Regular carriers, in a number of cases, have established affiliate non-IATA charter carriers to operate charter services outside the framework of the IATA[110] and it might be useful for the sake of flexibility to make it possible for such affiliate carriers to operate charter services with aircraft owned by the mother company and vice-versa (interchangeability of aircraft).

By the same token the alternative solution of a separate bilateral or multilateral regime for charter services by designated charter carriers only should not be based on the principle that regular air carriers should no longer be authorized to operate charter services as well as regular services. Since regular carriers are bound to IATA resolutions it might be necessary to include not only the definition of the charter product, together with volume and group and IT charter limitations, in separate bilateral or multilateral arrangements, but also tariff restrictions, in order to regulate competition with the regular product (the activities of regular air carriers in the charter field and the carriage of group traffic on line services).

The same would go for non-scheduled all-cargo (charter) flights: orderly competition could be assured by prohibiting individually waybilled cargo services and consolidation on one flight, except for indirect air carriers (international air freight forwarders); in other words, by permitting only own-use charter traffic and incidental cargo flights, which, by serving

[110] Cf. for instance Condor.

a special interest, do not compete with the regular product and thus do not affect regular all-cargo services.

With regard to the exchange of charter rights the main problem is to prevent possible adverse effects of such exchange on scheduled carriers and to protect the interests of the weaker party, which could be achieved by clearly distinguishing the charter product from the regular product and ensuring an equal opportunity for the carriers of the countries exchanging charter rights.

The formula for an exchange of charter rights, however, should not be the "equal exchange of economic benefits", as this formula clearly hampers the further development of the traffic, but rather, on the basis of what we have said before, the promotion of traffic through adequate regulation of the offer of capacity according to the various products. It may be necessary to keep a certain balance in the number of producers (carriers) in order to enable each carrier to obtain a share of the market in conformity with its possibilities and ability. To try and force traffic to travel on the services of the national carriers through protectionist and restrictive measures is not the way to promote the national carriers or the development of the traffic to, via and from one's country as this method in practice does not work and the public chooses its own way to travel and may turn to other routings.

We have mentioned charter carriers affiliated to regular carriers which are used to compete in the non-IATA charter field. We have seen, however, that the CAB would like to apply limitations upon inter-carrier relationships. Such limitations are based, in the first place, upon US anti-trust laws.[111]

A further consideration, however, is preventing a carrier from enjoying traffic rights which it has not been granted by the CAB. Such indirect benefits may be detrimental to the interests of US carriers and therefore not in the public interest, as not having been expressly authorized by the CAB. The question is whether, and if so to what extent, US jurisdiction extends to the control of such relationships.

In the Condor and Martin's Cases, the relationships were between carriers of the same nationality and the CAB did not want to require Lufthansa and KLM to divest themselves of control of the irregular carriers, in order not to go against the policies of their governments. The control relationship being between carriers of the same nationality, the CAB could

[111] These limitations are embodied in Sec. 399.82 of the CAB's Economic Regulations re "passing off of carrier identity by affiliation between carriers" (added by Amendment No. 8, effective November 29, 1965).

argue further that no significant detrimental effects upon the US traveling public or US carriers would result if there were assurances that operations would be conducted independently.

In the following Chapter we will go more deeply into the problem of affiliation between carriers of different nationality.

Affiliation may exist between a US carrier and a foreign carrier operating into the US or between two foreign carriers one or both operating into the US. In the second case two different intergovernmental bilateral relationships are involved, which may create the problem referred to above, where the CAB has not expressly granted the benefits which may result from the affiliation.

Furthermore affiliation between carriers, according to the CAB, may lead to unfair and deceptive practices or unfair methods of competition.[112]

In this respect we may observe that today the choice between freedom and protection seems irrelevant. What is relevant is the "how" and the extent of control by governments. This can be illustrated by attitudes (i.c. of the CAB) towards the various forms of relationships among carriers. A relationship between a regular and an irregular air carrier may be felt to erase the distinction between scheduled and non-scheduled authority as granted to each of the related carriers, and this may affect the government's control (CAB) over the operations of each carrier.

A relationship between two regular air carriers of the same nationality may confuse the division of labor as intended by the government under the separate authorizations granted them. A relationship between a national regular or irregular carrier and a foreign regular or irregular carrier may entail advantages both for the national and the foreign carrier which escape government control and may lead to a situation which was neither intended nor desired by the government.[113]

In the same way a relationship between two foreign carriers may confuse and frustrate the regulatory system of the government who authorized each of them individually to operate into its territory.[114] A relationship between a foreign regular and a foreign irregular carrier of different nationality would complicate the situation even further.

A relationship between two foreign carriers of the same nationality,

[112] Cf. CAB, Policy Statements, Part 399.82. (d) and Sec. 411, Fed. Av. Act.

[113] US carriers are subject to the requirements of Sec. 408 and 412 of the Act in regard to any relationship with foreign air carriers. Prompt approval is possible under the terms of these Sections or by exemption under Sec. 416.

[114] A foreign air carrier permit "should not be regarded as a 'rentable asset', enabling the holder rather than the CAB to determine who shall operate air services to the US." (Cf. PANAM, Brief to Examiner in ALM Application, March 25, 1968, pp. 51/2. Docket 18595).

either two regular carriers or a regular and an irregular carrier may, however, create fewer problems inasmuch as the authorization to operate into a country is usually granted to a State and is therefore dependent on the nationality of the airlines rather than on their individual identity and identification. Here the problem may be limited to the distinction made between scheduled and non-scheduled carriers.

Less far-reaching relationships, such as blocked-space and pool arrangements, pose fewer problems.

In the next chapter we will devote special attention to lease agreements of aircraft with or without crew because the use of each other's aircraft may develop into one of the most important ways for smaller carriers to provide competitive service and bigger carriers to arrive at economic utilization of their aircraft, something which, with the drop in yield – because of increasingly lower fares and rates – is of critical significance in lowering the cost-price of airline operations.

Applicable Economic Regulations of the CAB

Part 200	Definitions and instructions.
Part 203	Terms, conditions and limitations of certificates of public convenience and necessity; foreign air transportation.
Part 207	Charter trips and special services.
Part 208	Terms, conditions and limitations of certificates to engage in supplemental air transportation.
Part 211	Applications for permits to foreign air carriers.
Part 212	Charter trips by foreign air carriers.
Part 214	Terms, conditions and limitations of foreign air carrier permits authorizing charter transportation only.
Part 215	Names of air carriers and foreign air carriers.
Part 216	Commingling of blind sector traffic by foreign air carriers.
Part 217	Reporting data pertaining to civil aircraft charters performed by foreign air carriers.
Part 218	Lease by foreign air carrier or other foreign persons of aircraft with crew. (Proposed June 13, 1969, EDR-166, Docket 21080).
Part 221	Construction, publication, filing and posting of tariffs of air carriers and foreign air carriers.
Part 295	Transatlantic supplemental air transportation.
Part 297	Classification and exemption of international air freight forwarders.

Special Regulations

Part 375 Navigation of foreign civil aircraft within the US.

Part 378 Inclusive tours by supplemental air carriers, certain foreign air carriers, and tour operators.

Part 378a Bulk Inclusive Tours by Tour Operators.

Policy Statements

Part 399 Statements of general policy.

On June 4, 1970, a new Part 213 of the CAB's Economic Regulations became effective after approval by the President of the Board's Order 70-6-33 in the 1961 Foreign Air Carrier Permit Terms Investigation (Docket 12063).

Part 213 permits the CAB to retaliate against foreign air carriers whose governments restrict the schedules of US international air carriers.[115] Part 213 gives the CAB the power to require foreign air carriers to file their schedules for approval and to direct foreign air carriers to file traffic data covering their operations to the US. Disapproval of schedules will be subject to Presidential disapproval.

The adoption of this new Part was prompted by the need for powers to combat foreign governmental restrictionism and the wish "to provide increased incentives for foreign governments to refrain from unilateral restrictionism."

Part 213 is entitled: Terms, Conditions and Limitations of Foreign Air Carrier Permits.

[115] Such retaliation will be directed against predetermination of capacity and frequencies under Bermuda-type air agreements. In the case of countries which do not have a bilateral agreement with the US, the Regulation gives the CAB the power to take retaliatory action "in the public interest." No retaliation seems possible against foreign route carriers whose governments restrict the operations of US supplemental air carriers, as these operations do not come under bilateral air agreements.

CHAPTER FOUR

I. COOPERATIVE ARRANGEMENTS

In the face of the tremendous growth of the international air traffic market and rapid technological developments, the anachronism of national policies and the absence of a truly international policy are likely to create ever more conflicts. International air carriers have great difficulty planning their development and their fleet requirements because it is impossible to assess the extent to which they will be able to implement their plans in view of the prevailing national policies of the States. The airlines do not know whether they shall be able to exercise the necessary traffic rights and, if so, on what conditions and at what cost.

As it is, each individual State adopts an air policy which, in its opinion, is best suited for its particular situation and for promoting the interests of its national carriers which operate international routes. In practice this leads to conflicts with other States trying to defend their own particular interests. Often a State finds that its air policy does not yield the desired results because it cannot agree with other States on the most suitable approach to the international regulation of international air transport. If there is no agreement, no State can attain the objectives of its national policy.

Until now the "Bermuda" principles have served as the internationally agreed compromise in international civil aviation regulation. Increasingly, however, these principles are abandoned in practice. Predetermination of capacity, a practice which the Bermuda system condemned, is taking on importance. This means that competition, as a regulatory device, is being replaced by a system of closely apportioned entry into each other's markets.

This is not to say that the Bermuda principles offered an ideal solution.

They did offer, however, an indispensable internationally accepted common basis for international civil aviation regulation.[1]

A consequence of the present situation is that in many cases possibilities for economical operation become marginal at best. As a remedy carriers turn to cooperation, both as a means of obtaining (being able to exercise) the required traffic rights and as the best possible alternative to air-political restrictions which would otherwise be imposed on their operations and, indirectly, on their sales activities. In other words, in some cases traffic rights can be obtained only on the condition of cooperation with the national carrier.

More and more governments make a provision in bilateral agreements that the exercise of the rights exchanged shall be subject to an agreement between the designated air carriers of both parties concerning the conditions of their operation of air services on the agreed routes.[2]

On the other hand, by combining their efforts, carriers may reduce costs and improve the efficiency of their operations, and thus offset the disadvantages of not having independent freedom of action.

Such cooperative arrangements in most cases level off the differences between weak and strong carriers, large and small, rich and poor, because they replace restrictions which would have been imposed on the operations of the stronger (foreign) carrier by the government of the weaker carrier to neutralize the differences in strength between carriers operating the same or similar routes.

Such cooperative agreements aim at sharing traffic (traffic revenue). This is an indirect way of predetermining capacity, or the amount of revenue to be derived from the exercise of traffic rights.[3]

A number of other factors and circumstances is conducive to cooper-

[1] Cf. also Stuart Tipton: *The success story of civil aviation* June 23, 1966: "I believe the tide is running strongly against restrictive philosophies in international aviation and in favour of reaffirmation of the Bermuda-type exchange of economic opportunities without advance limits on capacity."

[2] Cf. for instance France-India bilateral air agreement, *Journal Officiel* Sept. 7, 1969, art. 4 C and D as amended by Exchange of Notes on October 30, 1961.

[3] In ECAC discussions on liberalization, an antithesis developed and still exists between liberalization and cooperation: the advocates of cooperation held that cooperation should come first which would obviate the need for liberalization. The advocates of liberalization stressed that liberalization should come first in order to enable the carriers to decide freely whether or not and how to cooperate.

Cf. also John C. Mc.Carroll: "The Bermuda capacity clauses in the jet age," *JALC* Spring 1963, p. 119 ff. "When frequency restrictions are imposed (on the stronger carrier), the service available to the public is held at a level which will permit the least efficient carrier concerned to operate. Therefore the need for prior approval of any schedule increase or of the use of improved equipment will probably cause the supply of services to lag behind demand rather than preceding and perhaps developing demand."

ation: in case of excess capacity, especially in the off-season, cooperation avoids low average load factors; it achieves optimum schedule coordination; it solves spares and maintenance problems which is especially important to carriers with small fleets.[4]

With the development of mass air transportation by wide-bodied jet aircraft and in view of the enormous investments required for these aircraft and their operation, the views of the majority of governments and airlines are bound to turn from present concepts of international air-transportation regulation and operation based on nationally defined interests, national resources and national instruments, towards ways and means to resolve conflicting national interests and supplement national resources through various forms of communal airline operation management.

During the 15th Session of the Assembly of the ICAO Economic Commission, the US, together with Colombia and the UAR, proposed to study the economic implications of cooperative arrangements. This proposal, considering that cooperative agreements become increasingly frequent and varied, suggested a study of the economic factors involved, especially in "pools", blocked-space arrangements and multi-flag airlines. It was noted that the legal aspects of this question were already being studied by ICAO.[5]

Apart from legal problems which seem surmountable, the political, economic and operational aspects of such forms of cooperation may lead to adjustments of the national aviation policies of the States of the carriers concerned and the States which are confronted by operations to their territory of aircraft under a cooperative agreement: the latter States may wish to prevent a third party from indirectly exercising, through some cooperative arrangement, rights not granted to it, and they may wish to prevent an undue adverse effect on the competitive position of their own national carriers; they may further wish to have a clear picture as to which party is responsible for the safety of the operation of the aircraft concerned.[6]

The proposal of Colombia, the UAR and the US lists for study the

[4] Cf. Stephen Wheatcroft in his very clear analysis: *Air Transport Policy*. 1964, pp. 99 ff.

[5] Cf. ICAO Doc. A15-P/1, p. 57 April 1966.

For the legal aspects see René Mankiewicz, *JALC,* Autumn 1965, pp. 304-310: "Aircraft operated by international operating agencies"; and ICAO Doc. 8572 A15-P/1 p. 105.

[6] Cf. Wassenbergh, *Netherlands International Law Review,* Year 1963, Issue 3, p. 275 ff.: "Interchange of aircraft on International Routes and the Philippine-UK conflict."

advantages and disadvantages to States, airlines and the public of cooperative agreements between airlines; the reasons for their existence; the effect on competition and fares; their duration; their effect on market development; the trend of such arrangements in the light of economic and technoligical developments.

The Assembly of ICAO, however, decided first to try and obtain more information about existing cooperative arrangements of the kind envisaged by Article 77 of the Chicago Convention (international operating agencies or joint air transport operating organizations or pools).

We have suggested that for the weaker airlines, the smaller countries, the "have-nots" in civil aviation, cooperative arrangements may make it possible to achieve more successful airline operations, or even simply to mount an operation with modern equipment.[7]

We have also stated that cooperative agreements may enable an airline to expand in a market where the lack of traffic rights does not permit such expansion. In the first case the cooperation may be seen as a form of aid to a developing country, in the second case, as a means of breaking through protectionist policy.[8]

Examples of the first category are multi-national cooperation among a number of French-speaking African States in the airline "Air Afrique" [9], with French assistance; cooperation between PANAM and Air Afrique on a route between Africa and the US and a similar arrangement between PANAM and Nigerian Airways; and the more recent agreement between Sabena and Austrian Airlines on the operation of the route between Vienna and New York.

Examples of the second category are pool agreements between European airlines and the Brazilian airline Varig, cooperation between KLM, IBERIA and VIASA on the mid-Atlantic route, cooperation be-

[7] Cf. also Frank Loy: "The impact of supersonic transport on the political and practical aspects of international air transportation," 2nd Annual International Congress of Aeronautical Technology, Hot Springs, Arkansas, 1967, in which he remarks that blocked-space agreements allow "have-nots" to participate in air transportation with modern equipment. See also *ITA Bulletin* No. 14, April 3, 1967, pp. 441 ff.

[8] Cf. Jorge Perez y Bouras, Director General of Aeronaves de Mexico, and IATA President at the AGM, Nov. 1966: "Larger carriers should respect the rights of others by operating only the frequencies that are justified. If development of regional carriers is hindered by fifth freedom exercised by larger carriers then there should be a reasonable reduction in these rights." Also at the AGM of IATA, Manila, Dec. 1967, the plea for better understanding between large and small carriers was repeated by Perez y Bouras and B. Toda, President of PAL.

[9] The Association possesses the nationality of each of its Contracting States. Its aircraft are registered in the Ivory Coast and therefore have the nationality of that country.

tween BOAC and a number of Commonwealth carriers, cooperation between BEA and a great number of European carriers.

When these cooperative arrangements are approached by the partners in a businesslike way, as a means of improving efficiency and reducing costs, and no arguments based on questions of air-political strength are used, they can work substantially to the benefit of international air services. If, however, the cooperative arrangement is used to limit the capacity of the commercially stronger carrier and secure high load factors for the weaker partner, they hamper the development of international civil aviation.

An interchange agreement involves the use of the same aircraft over the routes of two carriers to provide a one-plane through service.[10] A leasing agreement involves the use by a carrier of an aircraft owned by somebody else. A pool agreement involves the pooling of revenues derived from operations on a common route, the revenue share each partner obtains being dependent upon its production share. A joint venture involves the operation of a service or services whose costs, capacity and revenues are shared on a 50/50 basis.

In pooling services each partner maintains its own identity and operates its own services. In a joint venture the identity of the partners is less evident. Services are operated jointly, partners must agree on all aspects of the operation and there is little or no opportunity for independent decision. Frequencies and capacity, schedules and type of aircraft are all subject to mutual acceptance.

Under a pool agreement partners have more freedom, although available air-political rights determine the production of each of the partners and therefore the revenues each will derive from the pool. If traffic rights are available, each partner may increase production, the revenues fall in the pool and the costs are entirely for the account of the carrier concerned.

A joint venture is an integrated operation, whereby both partners have the right to 50% of the capacity of each flight, and the identification of the carrier is of secondary importance.

The CAB takes a dim view of joint ventures because the CAB thinks that they make it possible for each of the partners to obtain route authority not granted under bilateral air agreements, the partners operating on each other's behalf, or at least to derive revenues from rights not available to them. Moreover, the CAB insists upon a clear identification of the

[10] Cf. for instance the NorthWest/PANAM interchange service Minneapolis/St Paul – Detroit (NorthWest) – Detroit – London (PANAM), approved by the CAB (Sec. 408 and 412 and Sec. 102), Docket 19472, Order 69-2-126 of February 25, 1969.

carrier who is responsible for the operation so as to avoid confusing the traveling public.

In our opinion these fears of the CAB are a bit exaggerated.

A joint venture can concern only a route or routes for which both partners hold the necessary operating authority as granted in bilateral air agreements or unilateral permits. It may be, however, that one of the partners has no traffic rights on certain sectors of the routes concerned. Traffic on these sectors in that case can only be carried by the partner enjoying the rights concerned. The revenues derived from that traffic remain outside the common account. The traffic carried on such sectors is identified as to carrier by the flight coupon. The public can be informed by means of a pamphlet explaining who is in operational control of the flight and who is responsible for the operation.

The common use of aircraft, as in the case of a joint venture, is a valuable means to rationalize airline operations. The protection of the traveling public should not be used as an argument of convenience to protect the national carriers.

As it is, the public can only benefit from joint ventures. The safety aspects and the responsibility and liability aspects of a joint venture can easily be covered.

Pool agreements are commercial agreements, in many cases designed to compensate for the exercise of traffic rights by a foreign airline, in excess of the economic benefits derived from the reciprocal rights by the national carrier. The desire of national carriers to obtain their share of available traffic underlies the existence of a great number of pool agreements in Europe and elsewhere.

Sometimes pool agreements are concluded because traffic demand on a route cannot sustain competitive service. Pooling services then helps to minimize losses.

Pool partners agree to schedule the services to be operated in pool in consultation with each other, to sell each other's services as if they were their own, in short to identify themselves with their partners.

There are of course different kinds of pools, sometimes with built-in limitations:

Revenue sharing can be limited by the ceiling of the capacity brought into the pool, such as when partners use different types of aircraft, in order to keep the carrier operating the smaller aircraft from obtaining an unreasonable advantage from the pool.

Revenue sharing can be based on the ton-kilometer production of each of the partners, and adjustments made, through a system of coefficients, if one of the partners operates an aircraft less suited to the route concerned (for instance, if an aircraft is too big for the traffic demands of the route, or the route concerned is operated by one of the partners as a segment of a longer route and its services therefore are only partially used for the traffic on the pooled route).

Revenue sharing may be limited by agreeing to limit payments made under the pool (for instance by setting a ceiling so that no payment is due for traffic carried below the ceiling, or by fixing a percentage of the revenues brought into the pool by the weaker partner as a maximum for the payments due by the stronger partner).

Pool agreements should be made to stimulate both partners to optimum sales efforts; there should be no distinction in sales efforts between the services of one partner and the other.

Although higher revenues obtained by one partner may result in higher payment to the other partner, the amount which may be kept by the first partner is proportionally higher as well. A true pool agreement always excludes competition between partners.

Pool agreements as a rule are looked upon favorably by governments as they tend to rationalize the schedules of the partners on the routes pooled and thus improve the economy of operations. Moreover, pool agreements offer a solution to air political problems.

On the other hand pool agreements, by eliminating competition between the partners, may result in poorer on-board service. The desire for optimum financial results may lead to capacity limitations aimed at higher load factors. Both results are to the detriment of the traveling public.[11]

Pooling services may have a competitive impact on third carriers operating the same routes.

In its policy statement [12] the US therefore stipulated that pool agree-

[11] Cf. Thomas K. Taylor, Vice President of TWA: "Economic and political considerations affecting international air transport." Instituto Internazionale delle Communicazioni, XIV International Convention Geneva, Oct. 1966: "Protective restrictionism takes many forms. One of the more common types is the pooling of traffic and revenues by two or more carriers. The benefits to the pooling partners are evident. Each avoids the need for competitive numbers of aircraft or frequency of service and each can count on a guaranteed amount of revenue. The only one who suffers is the traveler, for once the stimulus of competition is removed, load factors rise to an excessive level and the quality of service tends to stagnate. The momentum for total market development is lost."

Cf. also Edwards Report, p. 98 (6): "... are often a useful instrument guaranteeing reasonable access (for the British airlines) to routes and traffic, and facilitating the economical operation of international routes. On the other hand ... may ... tend to lower the standards of service offered to the public."

[12] Civil Air Policy, 1963. Pool agreements between US carriers are not authorized

ments should be examined on a case-to-case basis to determine competitive impact, especially with an eye to possible violation of anti-trust laws. Because the US has more than one national carrier, a pool agreement concluded with a foreign airline by one may have an adverse effect on the operations of another. Where a country has only one national carrier, a pool agreement concluded with a foreign carrier as a rule meets with government approval. The government may wish to have a say in the conclusion of an agreement between two foreign carriers to pool operations to its territory, but bilateral air agreements usually do not provide for such an eventuality.

If each carrier has been authorized individually to operate into the territory of the country concerned on the route concerned, there would seem to be no basis in the air agreements to prevent them from operating the route in pool.

Of course a government could argue that since pooling has not been specifically mentioned in the air agreement, it cannot be allowed unless specifically granted.

The Canada-Mexico air agreement of Dec. 21, 1961, (art. III) states:

"1. Both Parties agree that, subject to the provisions of this article, a designated airline of either contracting party may enter into a pooling arrangement for the operation of any of the routes specified in the route schedule of this agreement.

"2. 'Pooling' means any arrangement made by a designated airline with any other airline or airlines of the same or different nationalities for the purpose of operating jointly any of the agreed services and to share amongst themselves the revenues and expenses thereof. [We would call this a joint venture!]

"3. For the purpose of such pooling a designated airline may establish schedules, time-tables, combined or through joint fares and rates, enter into lease, with or without crew, charter and interchange of equipment arrangements.

"4. Any such arrangement by the designated airline of one contracting party must be notified in writing to the other contracting party.

"5. Arrangements referred to in this article are limited to pooling on any of the specified routes:

a) between the designated airlines of the contracting parties;
b) between a designated airline and other airline or airlines of the same contracting party;

by the CAB, nor as a rule are pool agreements between a US carrier and a foreign carrier.

c) between a designated airline and a designated airline or airlines of a third country which is or are authorized by the other contracting party to exercise third and fourth, or third, fourth and fifth freedom traffic rights at the point in the territory of the other contracting party through which the pooled service is to be operated.

"6. Nothing in this article shall prevent the establishment and operation of the other joint operating organizations, international operating agencies or pooling arrangements referred to in articles 77 and 79 of the Chicago Convention."

This article may be interpreted as having a declaratory character, meaning that pooling normally is authorized under bilateral agreements even though not specifically mentioned. Paragraph c) contains a limitation which is a rather obvious one as it is difficult to envisage a pool agreement with a carrier who has not been authorized to operate the route concerned by the country through which the pooled service is operated. A pool agreement can never lead to the exercise of more traffic rights than have been authorized in the first place. Nor can a pool agreement give a carrier actual participation in the operation of a route which it is not authorized to operate. Under a pool agreement the carriers pooling their services retain their individual identity on the route concerned.

One of the first requirements of successful airline cooperation is the availability of reliable traffic statistics. IATA collects traffic satistics, and in Europe the EARB collects statistics enabling its member carriers to follow closely traffic developments on the continent.

The example of the European airlines was followed by a group of Asian carriers, who formed the Orient Airlines Research Bureau (OARB) in September 1966 to stimulate the development of regional Asian traffic. Members are PAL (Philippines), KAL (Korea), CAL (Taiwan), MSA (Malaysia), THAI Airways (Thailand), Garuda (Indonesia), JAL (Japan), Air Vietnam, Cathay Pacific Airways.

The same is true for Africa where the Association of African Airlines (AAFRA) was established during the seventh Conference of African Airlines at Accra on April 4, 1968. Members are Air Afrique (Abidjan), Air Congo (Kinshasa), Air Mali (Bamako), Air Algérie, East African Airways (Nairobi), Ghana Airways, Nigeria Airways, Tunis Air, Sudan Airways, United Arab Airlines and Ethiopian Airlines, Libyan Arab Airlines, Air Malawi, Air Guinée and Zambian Airways.[13]

East European countries cooperate in a kind of pool agreement among their airlines (the 'six pool'). The Arab countries, too, are working toward

[13] Cf. *ITA Bulletin,* May 13, 1968, and *Interavia Air Letter,* 25-2-1970.

close cooperation in the field of civil aviation and airline operation in the form of a Pan Arab Airline.[14]

However, while the availability of reliable statistics is a prerequisite for successful airline cooperation, data on traffic carried by individual airlines are used as a justification by governments for the imposition of capacity and traffic restrictions on an airline in order to limit fifth and sixth freedom carriage, and even in restricting the carriage of third and fourth freedom traffic in order to arrive at a balance between the traffic carried by the designated airlines of the parties to a bilateral agreement.

The USCAB, the US Department of Justice, the Immigration and Naturalization Service (INS) and many national civil aviation administrations collect traffic data. So does ICAO.

Bilateral air agreements sometimes contain a clause stipulating the collection and exchange of traffic statistics to be used for the interpretation of the agreement.

Statistics, therefore, serve conflicting purposes: to restrict the designated airlines under bilateral air agrements and to assess the share of the cooperators on the basis of traffic analysis and traffic forecasts.

On the following pages we shall devote our attention more especially to a form of cooperation among airlines, operational pooling, which results from the need to share equipment and crews so that smaller carriers can acquire or use highly expensive big new aircraft or so that economic utilization of these aircraft is possible. In practice these arrangements contribute to the more flexible, efficient and economic operation of air services. We are referring to aircraft lease agreements among air carriers.

It should be remarked, however, that lease agreements among air carriers not necessarily, and in fact very seldom, involve commercial cooperation between the parties to the lease agreement. The USCAB is inclined to assume that it does, unless proof to the contrary is given.

A wet lease agreement provides for delivery of the leased aircraft with crew to lessee to perform services as specified in the agreement and for redelivery of the aircraft to the lessor after performance of the services.

Lessor usually is responsible for maintenance and servicing of the aircraft except for technical inspection and maintenance en route when the aircraft is in the possession of lessee. These and other ground services, and documentation, flight operations, communications, etc., are the responsibility of lessee.

Lessor is responsible for the airworthiness of the aircraft and for having the aircraft conform to government regulations. Lessor is also responsible

[14] In S-America the SACAA follows the ECAC example.

for the licenses of the crew, their hotel costs, daily allowances and the like. Lessee is responsible for all traffic carried. Lessor holds lessee free and harmless for liability and indemnity connected with aircraft and crew (loss or damage to aircraft, death or injury to crew). Lessee holds lessor free and harmless for lessee's personnel during the time that the aircraft is in the prossession of lessee. Lessee holds lessor free and harmless for traffic carried. Lessor takes care of hull insurance, lessee for public bodily liability and death, public property damage liability and cargo and mail liability insurance. Lease agreements usually stipulate that the aircraft is operated on permits of lessee as the aircraft is commercially operated under the exclusive control of lessee. They are increasingly popular among airlines. The attitude of governments to this form of cooperation, however, is still reserved.

II. AIRCRAFT LEASE AGREEMENTS IN INTERNATIONAL AIR TRANSPORTATION

The regulations governing the operation of international non-scheduled flights as a rule adopt, as main criterion for their applicability, the registration of the aircraft, its nationality. In the regulations governing the operation of *scheduled* flights, however, the important criterion is the nationality of the *carrier* performing the flights.

With the gradual disappearance of the dividing line between non-scheduled and scheduled air transport more attention should be, and is being, paid to the nationality of the *carrier* operating *non-scheduled* flights. This means that the substantial ownership and effective control becomes important for carriers operating non-scheduled flights, as well. The UK, for instance, has entered into agreements covering the operation of non-scheduled flights in which the substantial ownership clause has been incorporated [15]

National charter regulations sometimes even contain the provision that flights may not be performed with aircraft not owned by the contracting charter company unless special permission has been obtained.[16]

On the other hand, States tend to attach increasing importance to the nationality (registration), ownership of and control over the *aircraft* operated by (designated) carriers on *scheduled services,* in addition to the

[15] Cf. also Javier Rubio García-Mina "Iniciación al estudio del mercado de Transporte Aéro" VI B, Note 32, Ingeniería Aeronaútica y Astronaútica de Madrid, Marzo-Abril 1964.

[16] Cf. e.g. Danish charter rules Nov. 1, 1967, para D(c).

substantial ownership of these carriers. This is, among other things, a consequence of the growing practice of carriers to lease or charter aircraft from other airline companies for use on their own services.[17]

The tendency to attach importance to the nationality (registration) and ownership of the *aircraft* used by designated airlines may be of a temporary nature.

The "responsibility for and control over the *operation* of the aircraft", however, remains of particular interest. The nationality and ownership of aircraft will become less important in future, not only in distinguishing between scheduled and non-scheduled air transportation, but in general, as the tendency to "internationalize" the use of aircraft becomes ever more of an economic necessity.[18]

Internationalizing the use of aircraft means that aircraft are used by carriers of different nationalities. This is not the same as "the internationality of aircraft", or their international registration.[19]

Internationality of aircraft would be the right of an institution possessing international personality to claim and exercise quasi-territorial jurisdiction over aircraft independently of any State. Bin Cheng points out that the international registration of aircraft is entirely different from joint registration. While joint registration poses no problem, international registration would not seem possible under the Chicago Convention. Aircraft operated under joint registration would possess the nationality of one or all of the participating States, and independent international persons operating the aircraft would need to become party to the Convention.[20]

As long as the aircraft the use of which is internationalized are registered in a State party to the Convention, and are used by carriers of States

[17] N.B. We are not referring here to the "tax trade-off" lease concept, which provides favorable possibilities for aircraft financing. US leasing companies and institutions especially are becoming more interested in leasing aircraft equipment to airlines. First National City Bank, for instance, has leased a large number of aircraft to US airlines!

[18] Cf. also Jaques Naveau: "La Banalisation des Aéronefs," *Revue Générale de l'Air et de l'Espace,* 1968, No. 2, pp. 136 ff., who traces the legal history of the international interchange of aircraft, and states that "the contract of 'banalisation' constitutes a new legal technique to the extent that it allows a carrier to use its aircraft to exercise traffic rights obtained by others." It should be noted, however, that such carrier not necessarily exercises traffic rights obtained by others but in fact only *indirectly* derives benefits from the exercise of such rights by such others.

[19] Cf. Bin Cheng: "Nationality and registration of aircraft – Art. 77 of the Chicago Convention." *JALC* Autumn 1966, p. 552 ff.

[20] "Internationality of aircraft, operated by international institutions or operating agencies possessing independent international legal personality, is impossible under the Convention because such institutions constitute independent international persons who cannot benefit from the provisions of the Chicago Convention without being parties thereto." Bin Cheng, *op cit.* See for joint registration ICAO Doc. 8722-C/976 of 20/2/68.

parties to the Convention, the registration would not seem to pose any problem. Joint registration would not seem to be necessary. Nor would transfer of the registration from the State of registration of the aircraft to the State of the carrier using the aircraft seem to be required in order to enable the carrier to use aircraft registered in another State. If this were made necessary, the advantages of internationalizing the use of aircraft would be nullified. To create an international register for aircraft used by carriers of different nationality probably would create more problems than it would solve.

States should accept the use by carriers of aircraft of a different nationality (registered in another State) and of aircraft owned by somebody else, at least if the carrier assumes full and exclusive responsibility for commercial operations with that aircraft.

The distinction between "air navigational aspects" and "air transportation aspects" should be kept in mind here: as regards the air navigational aspects, the final responsibility for the international navigation of aircraft lies and remains with the State of registry. The functions under Annex 6 to the Chicago Convention, however, may be delegated by the State of registry to the State of the operator in cases of lease and hire-purchase agreements.[21]

This may apply between State A and State B when an aircraft registered in State A is operated by a flight crew employed by an airline of State B or in case a flight crew of an airline of State A operates an aircraft registered in State B.

In practice, it will not be so much the registration or nationality of the aircraft used by a carrier which will give rise to questions on the part of governments, as the ownership of and more especially the control over the aircraft and the relationship between owner and user, insofar as it involves control over the operation concerned.

Under bilateral agreements the governments of the respective parties designate the national carriers which will be entitled to exercise the rights exchanged. The governments undertake to accept each other's designations and to issue to the designated carriers an operating permit without undue delay. The designated carrier, however, must be sub-

[21] Cf. also ECAC/BANA/2-Report, 26/2/69, and Recommendations Nos 3 and 4. Rec. 3 concerns the facilitation of hire-purchase or long-term lease agreements between persons of different nationalities by enabling the registration of the aircraft on the register of the State of which the operator or user is a national. Rec. 4 concerns the "Delegation of Annex 6 Functions", ECAC/INT. S/2-Report, 12/7/69, p. 6/7. An agreement concerning the delegation of functions under Annex 6 applies between the Dutch and Philippine civil aeronautics administrations (1969), and among the Scandinavian, Swiss and Dutch civil aviation authorities (12/5/69).

stantially owned and effectively controlled by nationals of the party designating the carrier.

The CAB, under US legislation [22], furthermore requires that a recipient of such permission be "fit, willing and able" to provide the services authorized, and that the operations are in the public interest.[23]

The fact that rights are granted in a bilateral agreement makes a "prima facie" case on the question of public interest. The CAB, however, in recommending to the President the issuance of a foreign air carrier permit under Sec. 402, takes account of any possible detrimental effect the granting of the permit may have upon US carriers, as this is considered contrary to the public interest.[24] This, of course, violates bilateral air agreements containing express provisions to resolve such matters in consultation.[25] The CAB, furthermore, may impose conditions in a foreign air carrier permit as far as is "required by the public interest", which means that the CAB must prove that the conditions are necessary to the public interest.[26]

The fitness, willingness and ability of an air carrier to operate the routes granted in the bilateral agreement and assurance that the carrier will not violate ownership and control precepts are two matters which normally should be determined by the government designating the carrier; they should be of no primary concern to the other party. Only if a designated carrier, in practice, relies upon the operational facilities of another carrier to provide long-term services as authorized under the air agreement, may the (fitness,) willingness and ability of the carrier and its ownership and control as required by the air agreement be questioned by the other party.[27]

[22] Federal Aviation Act of 1958 as amended, Sec. 401, (d) and Sec. 402, (b).

[23] "Avalon is fit, willing and able since its organization is adequate and competent, its proposed plan of operation based on its experience is adequate, and its balance sheet shows that it is financially sound and has financial resources to carry out its plan of operation."

The *fitness* test in Sec. 401 (d) concerns the prospects for reliability in conforming to the Act and Regulations (safety requirements, business reliability in dealing with the public). The *willingness* may be determined from the past conduct of the applicant to comply with the Act. The *ability* properly to perform the air transportation applied for is derived from financial status, past experience and management qualifications, in case no going-concern status can be shown. Cf. Cumulative Index-Digest, pp. 1031 ff. 1955-60.

[24] Cf. also PSDR.21, Docket 20029, July 10, 1968, p. 10 of Proposed Rules.

[25] Sec. 1102 of the Act requires the Board to issue a foreign air carrier permit if the applicant satisfies the requirements of the agreement, whether or not in the opinion of the Board such action would be in the public interest.

[26] Cf. Sec. 402(b).

[27] In other words, the Act requires that the lessee should be willing and able to operate the services concerned unassisted.

However, as a rule, bilateral air agreements concluded by the US contain a provision that a designated carrier should be qualified to comply with the applicable laws and regulations of the other party. The provision reads: "... provided that the designated airline or airlines may be required to qualify before the competent authorities of that party, under the laws and regulations normally applied by these authorities, *before* being permitted to engage in the operations contemplated by this agreement".

It should be noted that the relevant standard clause in bilaterals reads differently, inasmuch as reference is made to "... the laws and regulations normally and reasonably applied to the operation of international air services in conformity with the Chicago Convention of 1944." Another article in bilateral agreements gives the parties the right to withhold or revoke an operating authorization, to suspend the exercise of the rights granted or to impose conditions on the exercise of these rights, interalia if the substantial ownership and effective control are not vested in nationals of the other party, or in the case of failure by the designated airline to comply with the laws and regulations of the party granting the rights, (normally referring to those laws and regulations relating to the admission to or departure from its territory of aircraft engaged in international services and of passengers, crew, or cargo).

It is normal procedure for an operating permission to be granted immediately ("without undue delay") if the carrier is qualified to fulfill the conditions of the Chicago Convention and those of substantial ownership and effectieve control. Only *ex post facto* is it possible to withhold an (additional) operating permission, revoke, suspend or to make conditional, existing authorization in the case of non-compliance in practice with the substantial ownership clause, national laws and regulations referred to or the provisions of the agreement itself.

The question here is whether it is possible to impose conditions on the exercise of the rights granted in case the carrier, after having operated exclusively with its own aircraft, starts operating with leased aircraft.

The US goes a step further and introduces its national legislation into the international field of civil aviation operations: if a foreign carrier is dependent for its aircraft and crew upon another carrier with whom it has concluded a wet lease agreement (leasing aircraft and crew), its "fitness and ability", as well as its "effective control" over the operations conducted under the wet lease under US legislation may be questioned by the CAB before an operating permission is issued. One could argue, for instance, that if the value of the leased aircraft exceeded the value of the total fleet owned by the lessee, the lessee can no longer be considered the true beneficiary of the rights granted.[28]

PANAM plainly holds the view that leasing aircraft and crew by a foreign carrier from another carrier is the leasing of the foreign carrier's routes to the other carrier.[29]

The CAB has adopted a policy on wet lease agreements between a *US* air carrier and a foreign air carrier,[30] which focusses on the development of a healthy, competitive *US* air transport industry. As such, this policy is not representative of how wet lease agreements should be approached in general, but nevertheless the considerations of the CAB are interesting because they illustrate a number of aspects of wet lease agreements which are of general importance.

In 1965, the CAB adopted a less restrictive attitude toward wet leasing by foreign air carriers from US supplemental and all-cargo carriers, because of the growing need for these carriers to improve the utilization of their aircraft and to supplement their operating revenue. A number of (negative) criteria to establish wet leases as being in the public interest of the US were listed.[31]

The most significant criterion is that operations under the wet lease must not have a significant adverse competitive impact an any US carrier. The CAB tends to interpret this criterion as meaning that any benefit to a foreign carrier has, by definition, an adverse competitive impact on US carriers.[32]

A case in point is the Order disapproving a wet lease agreement between EL AL Israel Airlines Ltd, and the US supplemental carrier World Air-

[28] In the bilateral air agreement concluded between India and Belgium, April 6, 1967, an interpretation is given of "substantial ownership and effective control" as including the effective control of the management of the designated airline and the substantial ownership and effective control of the greater part of the fleet and the equipment which is used for the operation of the services. (Cf. art. 3, para 4).

[29] PANAM on PSDR - 21, EDR - 140, PDR - 27, October 14, 1968. The Proposed Policy Statement is concerned with the creation of special rules regarding fitness, willingness and ability under Sec. 402(b) of the Act: Part. 399.20(b) (ii) gives a presumption of fitness, etc., in the case of a pre-existing operation. The Act does not define fit, willing and able but the Board has established a number of criteria. PANAM, however, feels that the Board should rule on a case-by-case basis.

[30] Cf. Regulation No. PS-27, Amendment 6 to Part 399, April 16, 1965, which became Part 399.19.

N.B. US carriers are not allowed to wet lease from each other.

[31] Cf. Part 399.19 of the CAB's Economic Regulations.

[32] The managerial freedom which should be given to (foreign) air carriers, requires the approval of a wet lease agreement if it has no demonstrable adverse effect (on US carriers). Such arrangements should not be approved only when the approving authority (the US CAB) considers the arrangement to be to the *advantage* of national (US) carriers.

ways Inc.,[33] where it was argued that "... an inter-carrier arrangement that enhances the competitive advantage of a foreign air carrier to an extent where its market domination adversely affects the US air carrier certificated to serve the same market is not in the public interest." [34]

Another important aspect is that the CAB reserves the right to impose limitations on the permissible duration of wet leasing according to the stage of development of the foreign air carrier lessee.[35]

A wet lease, in the opinion of the CAB, ought to be a transitory proposition.[36]

The CAB feared that otherwise wet leasing arrangements might develop into a device whereby the foreign air carrier remains a shell and, in effect, hires out its permit.[37] We will revert to this aspect in more detail later.

III. AFFILIATION BETWEEN AIR CARRIERS

On May 11, 1965 the CAB proposed an addition to Part 399, Statements of General Policy, about the "passing off" of carrier identity by affiliation between a US air carrier and a foreign air carrier.[38]

The CAB considered that the public holding out of relationships between US air carriers and foreign air carriers may tend to create the impression that the air transportation performed by related carriers is part of a unified transportation system. The impression that air travel is being performed by one carrier when it is in effect being performed by another may constitute an unfair or deceptive practice or an unfair method of competition or may be otherwise contrary to the public interest.[39]

The term "affiliation" (between a US air carrier and a foreign air carriers) is defined by the CAB as follows: [40] "Affiliation" means that one of the

[33] Cf. Docket 19864, Agreement CAB 20259, Order No. E- 26928, 3 to 2 decision, June 17, 1968 (TWA and PANAM opposing approval).

[34] N.B. Here the CAB uses the argument of the existence of an imbalance in favor of EL AL, while no restrictions apply to US carriers in the Israeli market.

[35] In the case of the wet lease agreement between the US air carrier Airlift International and Alitalia, the CAB ruled that an extension of the agreement after the expiration of the two-year period, which the Board had set as a maximum for such cases, would be in the "public interest". Cf. Docket 15081, March 31, 1964. See also Order 70-1-98, Jan. 19, 1970 (Alitalia/TAP).

[36] Cf. e.g. Sec. 399.19 (c) (3): "Where the sole purpose of the wet lease is to enable the foreign air carrier lessee to replace equipment rendered non-operable by an emergency beyond its control (an accident), such wet lease *may* be approved for a period not to exceed six months." Cf. Flying Tiger, Docket 20028, September 19, 1968.

[37] Regulation PS-27 p. 5.

[38] Docket 16151 PSDR 11, May 11, 1965.

[39] Cf. Part 399.82 (a) and PSDR-11. Explanatory Statement and Reg. No. PS-29 adopted October 26, 1965, which became Part 399.82 effective November 29, 1965.

[40] Cf. Part 399.82(b).

carriers, directly or indirectly, has *one* of the following relationships with the other:

a) owns or controls 10% or more of the securities of the other with or without an accompanying power to vote;
b) is in control of the other within the meaning of Sec. 408 of the Federal Aviation Act;
c) has any of the interlocking relationships described in Sec 409 of the Federal Aviation Act;
d) is jointly controlled with the other carrier, directly or indirectly, by a third person;
e) provides general agency service for the other carrier.

The conclusion of a wet lease agreement in itself obviously does not constitute an "affiliation" (between the lessor and the lessee) as defined in the passing off regulation referred to above.

However, CAB's way of thought as demonstrated in this Regulation with respect to the protection of the public (preventing the public from being misled as to the identity of the carrier) may further illustrate the CAB's policy on wet lease agreements, especially as lease arrangements often result from affiliations. Although the policy on wet leases to foreign air carriers as well as the passing off regulation apply only to arrangements between US air carriers and foreign air carriers [41], and the CAB has not adopted a definite policy with regard to wet lease arrangements between two or more foreign air carriers operating to the USA[42], this same way of thought can be found in cases involving foreign air carriers only.

One of the most noteworthy cases in this respect is the Air Jamaica Ltd. Case.[43] The Board considered that "BOAC and BWIA, which propose to perform the operations for Air Jamaica, require additional authority to carry out these lease agreements with Air Jamaica."

Except for the carriage of fifth freedom traffic on flights to and from the homeland of the carrier [44]), the CAB does not authorize air transpor-

[41] In the Air Transport Development Agreement of December 10, 1963, between Air Afrique and PANAM, it is stipulated, interalia, that the lessee (Air Afrique) provides the air transport service through the lease of seats and cargo space for the transportation of baggage, cargo and mail in aircraft operated by lessor (PANAM), pursuant to its published schedules on a route between the US and Africa (a blocked-space agreement). Air Afrique identification is to be affixed to the exterior of the aircraft. All the operations conducted under the agreement shall be subject to lessor's operating practices and procedures. N.B. It is important in these agreements to show clearly who is responsible for air transportation and who is the operator of the service and of the aircraft on the route, as otherwise the public may be deceived.

[42] Cf. however Proposed Rule Making Part 218, EDR-166- Juni 13, 1969, "Lease by foreign air carrier or other foreign person of aircraft with crew." (see further p. 136 ff).

[43] Cf. Docket 15919 et al. decided Jan. 19, 1966, E.23280.

[44] Cf. in shipping the so-called "cross-trade" which is third country traffic. In the

tation between the USA and a foreign country to be performed by the carriers of a third country.[45] Since there were no "significant details" of the Air Jamaica operations left to independent determination by the Jamaican-controlled management, it was considered doubtful whether Air Jamaica could be found fit, willing and able to engage in air transportation as a direct carrier. The Board considered BOAC and BWIA as the carriers who in effect would be engaging in air transportation between Jamaica and the US.

Grounds for waiving the policy on ownership and effective control, so as to be able to grant a permit to Air Jamaica, included in this case, "the reciprocal rights granted to PANAM and Delta, and Jamaica being a friendly and neighboring Caribbean nation which only recently achieved its dependence." Consequently foreign air carrier permits were issued to BOAC, BWIA and Air Jamaica subject to conditions designed to preclude passing off the services of Air Jamaica as services of the affiliated carriers (BOAC and BWIA), or as being part of a unified transportation system.[46] One of the conditions was that no joint public relations activities should be engaged in at points served by both carriers, which might tend to pass off the services of one carrier as the services of the other carrier or as part of a unified system of which each is a part. Another condition was that BOAC (BWIA) aircraft (except substitute aircraft) wet leased to Air Jamaica should carry the livery of Air Jamaica in substitution for that of BOAC (BWIA). Yet another was that the interior of the aircraft wet leased to Air Jamaica should contain a sign showing the foreign air carrier in operational control of the aircraft and the fact that the crews of that carrier were operating the aircraft, etc. The preoccupation of the Board clearly is to prevent the public from being deceived in any way,[47], and to prevent possible unfair or deceptive practices or unfair methods of competition.

case of shipping, however, this traffic is mostly carried without the ship calling at its homeport.

[45] As a matter of fact no government, as a rule, allows a flag-carrier of a third country to operate services having their starting point on its territory or the territory of another State.

[46] Cf. also Part 215.2 "In holding out to the public and in performing air transportation service, an air carrier or foreign air carrier shall use only the name in which its operating authority is issued or a name the use of which has been authorized by the Board."

[47] Cf. Part 399.82(c) Minimum safeguards, to insure the separate identification of the affiliated carriers (Part 399 is only applicable to US carriers, but the CAB in practice appears to apply these limitations to relationships between foreign airlines as well). The limitations imposed on BOAC/BWIA/Air Jamaica are listed in Order E-23280, Docket 15919 et al., adopted Jan. 19, 1966 and approved Feb. 19, and served Feb. 21, 1966; page 2.

The permit of BOAC further stipulates that "BOAC shall not directly or indirectly exercise any private contractual right they may possess or acquire . . . to approve or disapprove any US carrier or supplemental air carrier charter to, from or through Jamaica."

Here again the CAB shows its concern for the possible frustration, in this case by BOAC, of its own regulatory powers, and for any outside (third party) influence on its bilateral relationships with other countries.

Finally in the BOAC and BWIA permits a requirement was imposed for the filing of all existing and future agreements between BOAC/BWIA and Air Jamaica, while in the Air Jamaica permit an additional requirement was inserted concerning the filing for approval of wet lease agreements prior to commencement of the operations.

The Air Jamaica Case has become decisional law and the CAB has applied similar rulings to other wet lease agreements between foreign carriers since then.

In the Air Jamaica (1968) Ltd. Case, however, the Board found that Air Canada did not require a permit, notwithstanding the fact that Air Canada held 40% of Air Jamaica's voting stock and moreover exercised substantial powers over the affairs of Air Jamaica.[48]

In the case of the leased-space agreement between TAP and Alitalia [49], the CAB issued permits to both carriers although the issuance of a separate permit to Alitalia seemed wholly unnecessary.

The question whether lessor or lessee or both require special CAB authorization deserves further attention on the following pages.

IV. SPECIAL WET LEASE OPERATING AUTHORITY

It should be noted that in the case of a wet lease agreement between a US carrier and a foreign air carrier the CAB simply approves or disapproves the agreement, (the transportation concerned to be performed on routes for which the foreign carrier already holds operating authority), while in the case of a wet lease agreement between two foreign carriers the CAB either issues separate permits to the carrier lessee *and* the carrier lessor, or issues an additional permit to the carrier lessor (if the transportation is to be performed on a route or routes for which the carrier lessee already holds operating authority).

Does and should the CAB always require that the carrier lessor, in case

[48] Cf. Order 69-4-3, served April 2, 1969.

[49] Cf. Press Release CAB 66-81, 382-6031. Docket 16692, TAP S.A.R.L., served June 15, 1966, Order E-23820. See further under blocked-space arrangements.

of a wet lease agreement, obtain additional operating authority under the Federal Aviation Act? And does and should the CAB impose passing off restrictions on the carrier lessee?

In our opinion it is necessary to make a distinction between the operational control of the lessor [50] and the possible holding out of air transportation as a common carrier by the lessor on the route or routes of the lessee.

The fact that an aircraft, if leased with crew, remains under the operational control and ultimate safety responsibility of the lessor causes the CAB to consider such lease as a charter or rather a series of charters for which the lessor requires specific permission.[51]

The Federal Aviation Act of 1958, Sec. 101 as amended, provides that "any person who causes or authorizes the operation of aircraft whether with or without the right of legal control is deemed to be engaged in the *operation of aircraft* and subject to the Act."

A corporation engaged in the business of leasing airplanes requires certification as a carrier from the Federal Aviation Agency, if he normally provides his own pilots and facilities. If the lessee furnishes his own pilots, crew and facilities, he may be regarded as the carrier. The purpose of *certification* of course is to provide safe air travel.

Although therefore safety responsibility requires the certification or authorization of the lessor, this in itself should not lead to the conclusion that the lessor is engaging in foreign air transportation on the route or routes of the lessee. In other words, operating an aircraft is not necessarily engaging in air transportation or holding out air transportation as a common carrier. A wet lease agreement in itself would then not require the lessor, as in the case of an off-route charter, to obtain additional operating authority on the route or routes concerned.

If we analyse the "Air Jamaica Case", we see that much more than a wet lease was involved: The lessors held ownership interests in Air Jamaica and these were interests of different nationality than the applicant. They conducted sales, marketing, agency, advertising and other activities, and

[50] This involves such matters as maintenance of the aircraft, scheduling, dispatch, provision of operational and ground services, fuel and lubricants, liability for damage to or loss of the aircraft, control over the cockpit crew in charge of actual flight operations, the safety responsibility for airworthiness, crew member training, etc. of the State of registration of the aircraft.

[51] N.B. To decide this question unilaterally and to avoid confusion as to the true nature of a wet lease agreement between foreign carriers serving the US, the CAB proposed a new Part 218 of its Economic Regulations (EDR-166, June 13, 1969) to which we will revert later and which would apply to on-route interline charters (other than those covered by Part 212 or charters to foreign tour operators or foreign freight forwarders).

so question could arise as to the identity of the person holding out as a common carrier.[52]

"The corporate shell of Air Jamaica, owned substantially by the wet lessors BOAC and BWIA, was made an air carrier through the holding out by BOAC and BWIA through their ticket offices, agency arrangements, advertising, schedule publishing, personnel and so forth. Without the relationships with the wet lessors, in addition to the wet lease, Air Jamaica did not exist a a carrier." [53]

In addition to the Air Jamaica Case, the Leeward Islands Air Transport Services Ltd. (LIAT), Antigua, Case [54] merits attention as establishing decisional law. Here again one of the main issues was the relationship between two foreign carriers, LIAT and BWIA (Trinidad). Moreover LIAT allegedly was substantially owned and effectively controlled by BWIA. The operation of the route applied for by LIAT was provided for in the US-UK bilateral air agreement as amended and LIAT was an officially designated air carrier of the British Government.

In the case the Examiner recommended that LIAT be required "to file annual reports setting forth the steps it has taken to achieve ownership and control by UK nationals." [55]

On this point, however, the Board decided that "a strict requirement for British ownership and control of LIAT could force the carrier into the hands of British investors outside the Caribbean area and impede the formation of a regional airline" (a multinational Caribbean airline owned by nationals of the various Caribbean islands).

While the Examiner further recommended that passing off restrictions be imposed, the Board ruled that no condition requiring that LIAT aircraft wet leased to BWIA carry the livery of BWIA was necessary but that the requirement for identification of the aircraft operator would adequately be met by the posting of a sign inside a wet leased aircraft.[56]

It should be noted that LIAT, as the holder of the permit, is required to post a sign in the interior of aircraft wet leased to BWIA, to show that

[52] Cf. Docket, 18595, Answer of ALM to Motion of Bureau of Operating Rights, September 13, 1967, p. 4.

[53] Cf. Docket 18595, ALM's Answer to Motion of PANAM, September 1, 1967, p. 3.

[54] Cf. Docket 17403, Order E-25175, approved May 22, 1967.

[55] Cf. the standard clause in the US-UK bilateral agreement concerning "substantial ownership and control to be vested in nationals of the Party designating the carrier."

[56] Cf. the Air Jamaica Case where the Board imposed the condition on Air Jamaica as a lessee of aircraft of BOAC and BWIA that the wet leased aircraft carry the livery of Air Jamaica and that a sign be posted in the interior of the aircraft, clearly showing the foreign carrier in operational control of the aircraft, and the crews of said carrier to be operating the aircraft. (The other conditions imposed on LIAT are identical to the conditions imposed on Air Jamaica)

the aircraft is in operational control of LIAT as the lessor. If LIAT wet leases its aircraft to some other carrier, therefore, no such requirement exists. This would seem inconsistent with the intention of CAB to prevent confusion in the mind of the traveling public, but may be explained by the existence of other relationships between LIAT and BWIA. One could conclude that wet lease arrangements are being made subject by the CAB to conditions that prevent passing off only when relationships other than the lease agreement exist between the lessor and the lessee.

One may question, moreover, whether it is necessary to impose passing off restrictions in the permits of both lessor and lessee.

Obviously the CAB has begun to require special authorization for wet lease arrangements, which must be obtained by both the carrier who wishes to wet lease and the carrier who wishes to become lessee.[57]

The Air Jamaica Case and the LIAT Case are examples of the Board's efforts to prevent the public from being misled as to the relationship between carriers of different nationality.

The Board's Policy Statement, laid down in Sec. 399.82, establishes the minimum safeguards in this respect for the relationship between a US carrier and a foreign carrier. These safeguards, by analogy, are also applied to relationships between two or more non-US carriers.

Here again the CAB wishes to keep a foreign carrier from renting out its permit to another carrier who has not been authorized by the CAB to operate the routes concerned in its own right.

A wet lease by itself, in the absence of any holding out by the wet lessor, does not constitute "air transportation" as defined in the Federal Aviation Act.

In the Recommended Decision of Examiner Hyman Goldberg in the matter of ALM's application [58], it is stated that "the crux of the question is whether exclusive direction and control over, and responsibility for, the leased aircraft and crews and the operations performed therewith will reside in ALM. In the determination of this question, the wet lease and sub-wet lease documents are not conclusive but must be considered in the light of all the surrounding circumstances." The examiner found on this point that the wet and sub-wet lease agreements and other relationships and circumstances gave KLM, VIASA and AVENSA "a degree of control over ALM's operations over the routes in issue requiring a conclusion that

[57] Cf. ALM Recommended Decision Docket 18595.

[58] Cf. Docket 18595, Recommended Decision, served July 1968, Findings and Conclusions, p. 38 and ff. ALM, a Dutch designated carrier, applied for a CAB permit to operate routes covered by the US-Netherlands bilateral air agreement, using aircraft leased from KLM and VIASA and AVENSA aircraft sub-leased from KLM.

they will be engaged in foreign air transportation within the meaning of the Act."

ALM's case is noteworthy for a number of reasons: First of all, because of the relationships between ALM and KLM, both being carriers of the same (Dutch) nationality and entitled (designated) under the US-Dutch bilateral air agreement to operate services over identical routes to the US (multiple designation).

Secondly, because of the involvement of the Venezuelan carriers VIASA and AVENSA, leading the Examiner to the finding of the existence of a "joint venture" among ALM/KLM/VIASA/AVENSA.

Thirdly, because of the issue of ALM's "fitness"; and finally, because of the policy of the Kingdom of the Netherlands with regard to the development of an Antillean airline in cooperation with KLM.

As to the first aspect, the Examiner remarkt that "... even as between two carriers of the same nationality, such as KLM and ALM, which have been designated to serve identical routes, there is nothing in the applicable bilateral agreement to suggest that one carrier is authorized to operate in behalf of the other carrier. Certainly, when the Board granted KLM a permit, there was no manifestation of intention to authorize KLM to conduct wet lease operations for another Dutch designated carrier." [59] Surely this reasoning reverses the issue. Under the bilateral it is entirely up to the Government of the Kingdom of the Netherlands to have the routes granted therein operated by carriers designated by it in the manner it sees fit (allowing both carriers to operate identical routes) as long as the carriers do not violate the "substantial ownership and effective control" provisions of the bilateral agreement.

The existence of relationships between KLM and VIASA and between VIASA and AVENSA, although not connected with the ALM/KLM relationships, misled the Examiner to assume a mutuality of interest among ALM/KLM/VIASA/AVENSA underlying the conclusion of the wet and sub-wet lease agreements. Consequently, the Examiner came to the conclusion that permits were required by KLM, VIASA and AVENSA to perform air transportation for ALM, and he recommended the issuance of same.

If, then, other carriers having no relationships whatsoever with KLM or ALM, had concluded the lease agreements, would they not have been required to obtain additional authorization?

As to the third aspect mentioned above, the Examiner concluded that "ALM is not independently fit, willing and able, within the provisions of

[59] Cf. Rec. Dec. Docket 18595, pp. 49 and 58.

the Act, to perform the foreign air transportation it proposes", but "ALM is fit, willing and able by virtue of the wet lease arrangements directly or indirectly with KLM, VIASA and AVENSA." There is no reason whatsoever why ALM should be independently fit, as long as it is fit, etc., because it can rely on KLM, a carrier of the same nationality.

The Examiner proposed a number of conditions to be attached to the permit of ALM and at the same time to the permits issued to KLM, VIASA and AVENSA for the protection of the public interest, to prevent passing off practices and to "assure that ALM moves promptly to achieve a separate, independent identity." A three-year limitation upon ALM's permit was recommended "to provide the Board with an early opportunity to review the progress made by ALM toward independence."

It would seem that the passing off restrictions as recommended would have assured ALM's independent identity so that three-year limitation of the permit would be both unnecessary and in violation of the bilateral air agreement. In effect, and here we come to the last aspect of importance, three-year limitation to assure ALM's progress toward independence, would be imposing US policy upon the Kingdom of the Netherlands, who should be free to determine whether or not, how and when an independent ALM should be created. In this respect it must be mentioned that the Examiner took some pains trying to establish the voluntary character of the KLM/ALM relationship: "In these circumstances, any contention that the relationships between ALM and KLM are exclusively the product of historical political relationships involving only policy matters between the Kingdom Government and the Netherlands Antilles Government is not persuasive."

The circumstances referred to were the fact that "KLM voluntarily entered into various relationships with ALM." In reality KLM voluntarily cooperated in carrying out Government policy, in view of KLM's interest in the Netherlands Antilles and the advantages to KLM of the policy of the Government to promote Antillean air services through cooperation between ALM and KLM.

Let us return to the wet lease as such. In the Recommendation in the ALM Case, the Examiner found that the existing permits of the carriers involved did not authorize them to perform foreign air transportation for one another pursuant to wet lease agreements, and that the KLM/VIASA crew leasing agreement "appears to raise a serious Sec. 402 problem or, at least, a problem of an appropriate notice to the traveling public of the identity of the carrier whose crew is in operational control of the aircraft."

The Examiner expressed the expectation that the carriers concerned would "file application with the Board for appropriate authorization ... or run the risk of enforcement proceedings."

The CAB uses the term "wet lease" to describe an arrangement under which an aircraft is leased to another carrier while the control of and the responsibility for the leased aircraft remains with the lessor (cf. the relationship between the operator and the charterer in case of charter agreements). If, however, the control of and the responsibility for the commercial operation with the leased aircraft and crews and operations with the leased aircraft pass from the lessor to the lessee, a different legal relationship arises. While in the first case the lessor is engaging in air transportation under the lease, he is not in the second case. In the second case operations are governed by the authorizations held by the lessee, and the lessor does not require authority for operations with the leased aircraft.

In other words, a carrier normally – and not only in emergencies – should be free to operate the routes for which it holds authority under bilateral air agreements or unilateral permits, with aircraft and crews leased from other carriers (even of different nationality), as long as the exclusive control of, and responsibility for, the *commercial* operation with the leased aircraft is vested in the lessee.[60] Of course, the operational requirements of the country where the aircraft and crews are to be used must be complied with and the aircraft and crews must conform to the operational, safety, licensing and security standards of that country.

PANAM [61] argued that the "physical operation of KLM, VIASA and AVENSA aircraft by their respective crews into US air space in the service of ALM will constitute 'navigation of aircraft' within the meaning of Sec. 101 (25) and 'operation of aircraft' within the meaning of Sec. 101(26) by these carriers, while the same goes for sub-wet leasing as Sec. 101 (26) speaks also of the person who 'causes' of 'authorizes' the operation of aircraft, 'whether with or without the right of legal control'." PANAM concludes from these arguments that special authorization is required under either Sec. 1108(b) or Sec. 402 of the Act. This interpretation would also "prevent the anomaly of aircraft and airmen of an unfriendly power conducting wet lease operations in US air space without authorization and be physically entrusted with US mail." [62]

[60] Cf. Docket 18595, KLM Brief to Hearing Examiner, March 22, 1968 in the application of ALM Dutch Antillean Airlines, pp. 5 and 6.

[61] Cf. same proceeding PANAM Brief to Examiner, March 25, 1968, pp. 28 and ff.

[62] N.B. The lessee is required to have the FAA agree that its operation specifications cover the use of leased aircraft in its service with crews provided by the lessor and obtain the approval of the application of its operating and maintenance manuals for the aircraft when operated in its service. The FAA proposed a new Rule Making (14 CFR Part 121) on March, 18, 1969, to be able to determine which party is conducting the

This interpretation implies that if the lessor is a carrier who holds an authorization to operate to the US in its own right under a bilateral air agreement or unilateral permit, it will not need special authorization to wet lease aircraft and crews to another carrier which is also authorized to operate into the US. Nor would the lessee! The fact that the lessee may operate with leased aircraft a route which is not covered by the bilateral or permit held by the lessor would be immaterial in the PANAM's view. Moreover the lessee would require special authorization to use wet or even dry leased aircraft to establish in each instance whether the lessee is "fit, willing and able".[63]

Obviously PANAM's interpretation does not allow for a wet lease agreement under which the exclusive control of, and responsibility for, the commercial operation of the routes on which the leased aircraft is used, is vested in the lessee.[64] That operational and technical, safety and security requirements must be met as well, is the equal responsibility of the lessee, under its own operating authorization. It is, in fact, unnecessary to require special authorization for wet lease agreements. Moreover this sets a precedent which impedes the sound development of international air transportation. A wet lease is nothing but the mostly only temporary supplying of a whole aircraft and crew to the lessee for his subsequent control. The lessee does not pass off the services as those of the lessor by virtue of a wet lease. It is the lessee who enters into the contract of carriage with the passengers.

A charter, on the other hand, is the supplying of the *capacity* of the aircraft for use by the charterer.

If there is affiliation between lessee and lessor it would seem, furthermore, that passing off restrictions would be sufficient to prevent any adverse impact of the wet lease agreement upon the competitieve situation on the routes involved and would thus obviate a requirement that a special permit be issued to the lessor.

The CAB normally does not wish to exercise jurisdiction over dry lease arrangements between foreign carriers.

Nevertheless, as in the case of the Transcarga (Venezuela) application [65], the CAB ruled that VIASA required additional permit authority

operation in the case of lease agreements by requiring the provision of copies of wet lease agreements to the Administrator.

[63] Cf. Brief PANAM, pp. 44 and 49.

[64] Cf. also Convention of Guadalajara, September 18, 1961, concerning the responsibility of the carrier: the lessor is not considered to be the carrier with regard to the traffic carried.

[65] Cf. Docket 20541, served Sept. 3, 1969. Cf. also Martin's permit: "Martin's shall

even though Transcarga only dry leased aircraft from VIASA. Here, however, the CAB explained that because of the dominion and control exercised by VIASA over the operations of Transcarga additional permit authority was required. "A wet lease as such is a strong presumption of dominion and control by the lessor",[66] and therefore it is not because of the wet lease or dry lease for that matter that the CAB requires additional permit authority, but because of the dominion and control of the lessor over the operations.

Transcarga owned no aircraft and was a wholly-owned subsidiary of VIASA which VIASA wanted to use to conduct international all-cargo operations. Transcarga was a designated air carrier of the Venezuelan Government and the routes applied for were covered by the air agreement between Venezuela and the US.

The CAB granted Transcarga a foreign air carrier permit but made it subject to prior approval by the CAB of all agreements for lease of aircraft, under which Transcarga is "a lessee or lessor, co-lessee or co-lessor, or sub-lessee or sub-lessor of aircraft." The CAB granted VIASA the right to transportation performed "through" Transcarga.[67]

Summing up, we conclude that a single wet lease (and, a fortiori, a dry lease)[68], if no other relationships exist between lessor and lessee,

- does not affect the substantial ownership and effective control if the lessee, the commercial operation with the aircraft and crew being under its exclusive control;[69]
- does not constitute holding out by the lessor on the routes operated with

not, except in cases of emergency, wet lease or dry lease aircraft to or from KLM . . ." Docket 18016, Sept. 8, 1967, Order E-26146, condition 4(h).

[66] Cf. the ALM Case. See further p. 134.

[67] N.B. Both the Transcarga and the VIASA permit were made subject to "passing off" restrictions, "to protect the shipping public and the US carriers, Transcarga being a non-IATA carrier."

[68] A dry lease of an aircraft of different nationality as a rule requires the authorizations of the civil aviation administrations of the country of registry of the aircraft and the country of the lessee, for the operation of the aircraft by the lessee's crews. Cf. the agreement concluded between the Scandinavian countries, the Netherlands and Switzerland on May 12, 1969, on government supervision of the airworthiness, the operation and maintenance of the aeroplanes involved under technical cooperation agreements between SAS, KLM and Swissair. In Annex 2 concerning Flight Operations, it is stated that the flight operation of an aircraft involved shall be supervised by the civil aeronautics administration of the operator employing the flight crew responsible for the flight operation.

N.B. A dry lease if used as a means to share in another carrier's route would be objectionable to the CAB. Sharing aircraft as such, however, is fully acceptable to the CAB.

[69] Of course, if the lessee has no aircraft of its own and is entirely dependent for its operations on aircraft leased from another, the lessee may in fact be only an "empty shell".

leased aircraft under the exclusive control of the lessee, as the operations are conducted in the lessee's name under his full responsibility and complete and exclusive public liability is assumed by lessee;[70]

- does not affect, therefore, the fitness, willingness and ability of the lessee;
- does not, therefore, constitute passing off the identity of the lessee as that of the lessor;
- is not an affiliation between the lessor and the lessee as the lessor retains no interest in, responsibility for or control over the lessee's operations with the aircraft and crew under the lease agreement;
- does not, therefore, give the lessor undesirable control over the lessee – gives in fact, no control at all;
- does not constitute hiring out the lessee's permit to the lessor.[71]

CAB doctrine in the Air Jamaica Case ("established decisional law") cannot therefore apply to simple wet lease agreements, insofar as the requirement of additional permit authority for the lessor is concerned, but may be applied only to the passing off restrictions imposed upon the lessee.

Nevertheless the CAB wishes to require the carrier who leases its aircraft and crew to another carrier to hold a foreign air carrier permit authorizing the operation under the lease agreement (a wet lease permit) and to submit the lease agreement to the CAB for approval, probably on the assumption of the possible existence of mutuality of interest beyond the lease agreement itself.

This would apply:

a) If the leased aircraft is used on a route which the lessor has *no* authority to operate, or has no authority to operate in the way the lessee uses the aircraft (turning the aircraft around at a point which the lessor is allowed to use only as an intermediate stop on the route); such a situation would require the granting of additional permit authority by the CAB to the lessor to conduct operations *under the lease agreement* on that route or to operate turn-around services pursuant to the lease agreement to and from the intermediate point where the lessee turns the aircraft around.[72] This requirement would be designed to ensure

[70] In such a case, the lessee has included these operations in its public liability coverage.

[71] See however note 69 above.

[72] Cf. Order E-25867, Docket 18595, October 23, 1967, ALM, Dutch Antillean Airlines: "Moreover the operation of turn-around services by VIASA between the Netherlands Antilles and New York is prohibited by a long-haul restriction in VIASA's permit which requires that all New York flights originate at a point in Venezuela, other than Maracaibo." Even without such a long-haul restriction the doctrine would be applicable.

that the lessee is not hiring out its permit to the lessor and the lessor is not sharing in lessee's route.

b) If the operations with the leased aircraft are conducted over a route for which the lessor already holds operating authority. Here the issuance of additional permit authority to the lessor may be explained as the CAB's wish to ensure that no undesirable form of cooperation exists between the lessor and the lessee in the operation of the route concerned.

But should such additional operating authority be required if no relationship exists between the lessor and the lessee which might create doubts as to who is holding out as a common carrier on the routes operated under the lease agreement, and if no undesirable forms of cooperation exist between the lessor and the lessee with regard to the operation of the routes under the lease agreement?

The requirements of additional permit authority and approval of the lease agreement seem unnecessary. They place undue burdens on carriers operating to and from the US, limiting their flexibility of operation and their efforts to obtain optimum utilization of their aircraft and additional revenue by interchanging aircraft (leasing aircraft to each other). As a matter of fact an interchange presupposes that the operator(in a technical sense) has no traffic rights to operate the routes concerned. The CAB should not require carriers (lessors and lessees) to prove that their relationships do not involve irregularities, such as a mutuality of interest, unless it has proof of such irregularities.[73]

Making requirements in advance means asking carriers to prove their fitness every time they enter into a wet lease agreement with another carrier. Such a system hardly seems adequate or justified.

Moreover, apart from emergency considerations, the CAB adopts, as the main criterion for granting wet lease authority to foreign carriers, the public interest of the US (Sec. 102 of the Act), which leaves foreign carriers

[73] Cf. e.g. Docket 18791, Enforcement Proceeding, VIASA July 13, 1967: "By virtue of the extent of VIASA's participation in CDA's operations in foreign air transportation, utilizing CDA's foreign air carrier permit, VIASA has engaged and will continue to engage in foreign air transportation between Santo Domingo and San Juan and between Santo Domingo and Miami for which VIASA has not been granted authority by the Board" (Cf. p. 8 of the Complaint), and, "... VIASA has violated and will continue to violate the provisions of Sec. 402(a) of the Act" (49 USC 1372(a), and again, "VIASA ... has passed off its services as the services of CDA; has passed off CDA's services as the services of VIASA; and has passed off the services of either or both of them as part of a unified system of which each is a part."

Finally, "... VIASA has engaged in unfair or deceptive practices or unfair methods of competition in air transportation as meant by Sec. 411 of the Act (49 USC 1381)." Cf. p. 10 of the Complaint. On June 26, 1968, the Board ordered VIASA to cease and desist from violating the Act (Cf. Order E-26975).

completely in the dark in each particular case as to whether or not a wet lease agreement will be authorized or not. Granting a wet lease permit may, in practice, be dependent upon the absence of other relationships between the lessor and the lessee and in general on the circumstances prevailing in each case.

The CAB derives the right to require additional operating authority, that is to require a wet lease permit to operate in the name of or on behalf of another carrier, and to impose limitations and conditions, partly from its arbitrary interpretation that bilateral agreements do not expressly grant the right to the designated carriers to engage in foreign air transportation with the use of the crews and equipment provided by another carrier, or at least a carrier of another nation, nor to conduct foreign air transportation for a foreign air carrier of another nation.[74]

This argument seems fallacious. Nothing in standard bilateral agreements prevents a designated carrier from leasing aircraft and crew from another carrier as long as the standard provision in bilateral agreements concerning the substantial ownership and effective control of the designated carrier is not violated and the carrier complies with the applicable national laws (in the case of the US the provisions of the Federal Aviation Act); also it is at least questionable whether the lessor can be said to conduct foreign air transportation for the lessee.

In its Decision in the ALM Case [75], the Board ruled that KLM required a wet lease permit to lease its aircraft with crew to ALM because KLM's control (control of aircraft, maintenance, schedules, liability for loss or damage to aircraft and the provision of services, supplies, personnel and insurance) over ALM's Antilles-New York operation "will be sufficient to cause it to be engaged in foreign air transportation on behalf of ALM" and "KLM's existing permit does not authorize the carrier to engage in air transportation on behalf of ALM."

This finding was made "in the light of the lease and other cooperative arrangements between the carriers." The Board further stated that its "experience justifies a strong presumption that the carrier furnishing both aircraft and crews will actually exercise dominion and control over the operation, even if the lessee can direct some aspects of the service. Carriers who contend that a wet lease is not a charter carry a heavy burden of

[74] Cf. Rec. Decision p. 15 Docket 16692, and Rec. Decision p. 57 ff. Docket 18595. Cf. also the "ONA doctrine", CAB 1962, affirmed by the US Court of Appeals, District of Columbia, to the effect that the lessor requires operating authority.

[75] Cf. Docket 18595, Decided Dec. 12, 1968, served Febr. 4, 1969.

showing that the owner of the aircraft will in fact surrender control to the lessee." [76]

Apparently, the beneficiary ownership (of the lessee) is of secondary importance to the CAB, and the possibility that a wet lease contract can provide for possession and control to be vested in the lessee is ignored.

Illustrative of CAB thinking on these aspects is the VIASA/CDA Enforcement Case: "The commander of the aircraft is the person who governs the destination of each flight." [77] The Examiner recommended that VIASA be ordered to cease and desist from violating the Act by operating under a wet lease charter agreement with CDA on a route for which VIASA holds no foreign air carrier permit; by conducting such operations as a joint venture; and by passing off the services of CDA as its own. (The first two points allegedly in violation of Sec. 402 (a) and the third point in violation of Sec. 411 of the Act.) [78]

This recommendation was strongly influenced by the evident partnership between VIASA and CDA and by the fact that the operations in which VIASA was involved constituted the bulk of CDA operations. A substantial number of different factors, or the sum of circumstances, rather than one single aspect of the relationship between VIASA and CDA, determined the decision of the Examiner. The Examiner concluded that CDA was completely dependent upon VIASA and argued that the lessor was engaged in foreign air transportation as defined in the Act in Sec. 101 (21): "foreign air transportation means 'the carriage by aircraft' of persons or property as a common carrier for compensation or hire, or the carriage of mail by aircraft, in commerce between [–(c)] a place in the US and any place outside thereof."

Opposing passing off, the Examiner referred to the minimum safeguards listed in Sec. 399.82 of the Board's policy statements, which refer

[76] Cf. ditto pp. 4 and 5.

[77] Cf. Initial Decision of the Examiner, VIASA Enforcement Case Docket 18791, served May, 1968, p. 27. The newly proposed Part 218 provides in 218.3.b.4 that even if the pilot in command of the aircraft "has been employed by the lessor prior to the lease and his employment by the lessee is co-existensive with the period or periods for which the aircraft is available to the lessee under the lease agreement", the proposed regulation will apply, meaning that a special wet lease permit will be required by the lessor, unless both the lessor and the lessee can demonstrate that "true operational control and safety responsibility for the air transportation services to be provided are in the hands of the lessee rather than the lessor."

[78] N.B. In case of a lease agreement between a US air carrier and a foreign air carrier the requirement of approval of such agreement by the CAB as far as the US carrier is concerned is based upon Sec. 412 of the Federal Aviation Act of 1958 as amended, and for exemption authority in order to perform the service on Sec. 416(b) and Sec. 401 and 403 of the Act.

only to affiliation between a US and a foreign air carrier but are applied to affiliations between two foreign carriers, as well.

The VIASA/CDA cooperation agreements were entered into for a period of five years and constitued a package deal.

In effect the Examiner considered CDA to be an empty shell without the ability or proper means to control the operations conducted by VIASA under a wet lease agreement with CDA. As the CAB wanted to prevent a carrier from starting operations on the assumption that the CAB has no jurisdiction over the operation and then have to resort to enforcement action, it proposed a new Regulation requiring prior approval of wet lease agreements.[79]

The CAB, in effect, would require the lessor to obtain under Part 218, whether it concerns an on-route operation or an off-route operation, and regardless of the absence of other relationships between lessor and lessee, a special permit to operate in the name of or on behalf of another carrier, unless the parties to the lease agreement indeed would be able to carry the burden of proof that the lease agreement is not a charter. In that case the lessor obtains a disclaimer of jurisdiction. However, by establishing a presumption that true operational control and safety responsibility are exercised by the lessor where the lessor furnishes both the aircraft and the crews and that in such case the lessor is engaged in foreign air transportation (Part 218.6), the CAB makes it practically impossible to prove that no permit is required under Part 218, if adopted. The new regulation would apply to interline wet lease (or charter) agreements for on-route operations of the lessee.

The CAB considers the lessor to be engaged in air transportation. As a consequence US supplemental air carriers would require designation by the US government to be allowed to operate on behalf of a foreign route carrier. They would also have to qualify under the laws of the foreign country concerned.

In our opinion lessee's permit is decisive. Most countries hold that view. In the case of the US, this means that on the basis of lessee's permit, under wet lease agreements the lessor may perform scheduled air services, on-route charter operations and off-route charter operations on behalf of lessee. It is clear that special authorization is required for operations that are off-route for both lessor and lessee.

Bilateral air agreements do not prohibit a designated air carrier to use foreign aircraft with crew as a lessee for (lessee's) on-route operations, nor

[79] Cf. Proposed Rulemaking New Part 218, EDR-166, June 12, 1969, Docket 21080, p. 4.

do they prohibit on-route operations, as a lessor, on behalf of another carrier.[80]

Therefore, wet lease operations should be permitted if they are on-route either for lessee or lessor. Of course this applies to bona fide cases only: a carrier should not engage in such operations exclusively and wet lease agreements should be concluded for limited periods only.[81]

V. WET LEASE AGREEMENTS WITH CHARTER CARRIERS

Further illustrations of the CAB's concern with affiliations and wet lease arrangements are the charter permit cases of Condor and Martin [82], a West German and a Dutch irregular (non-scheduled or charter) carrier, respectively affiliated to Lufthansa and KLM. These are cases of affiliation between a regular and an irregular carrier of the same nationality, and wet lease agreements are involved. The Bureau of Operating Rights of the CAB in its Brief to the Examiner [83] stated that if the operations of Martin and KLM were to remain separate, wet and dry leasing of equipment must be prohibited [84] and that divestment by KLM of its stock interest in Martin would be the only sure way to eliminate the danger of Martin referring business to KLM and vice versa which would ensure that Martin's proposed charter operations to and from the USA were conducted wholly independent of and separate from the operations of KLM.[85]

However, in its decision in the Martin Case, the Board ruled that "no limitation would be imposed on KLM's stock interest in Martin's"; that "a rate condition should be imposed to avoid the possibility that Martin's by reason of its affiliation with KLM might file unreasonably low tariffs in a manner which would constitute an unfair competitive advantage over US supplemental carriers"; and that, as requested by Martin's, "wet or dry leasing aircraft to or from KLM would be permitted in cases of emergency".[86]

Rather severe conditions were imposed to preserve the separate identity

[80] N.B. Normally a carrier will not operate his own routes on behalf of another carrier to whom the operation is off-route.

[81] Cf. also Part 399.19.

[82] Cf. Order E-26147 Docket 17233 approved Dec. 18, 1967, and Order E-26146, Docket 18016, approved December 18, 1967.

[83] May 8, 1967, Docket 18016.

[84] The Examiner recommended this condition to the Board.

[85] The Examiner recommended that KLM be required to dispose of its stock interest in Martin's, prior to the next renewal of Martin's permit.

[86] Cf. Docket 18016, Order E-26146, and Permit, approved Dec. 18, 1967. Point 7 of the permit (suspension without hearing of charter tariffs filed by Martin's and paragraph (h) of the Order (leasing aircraft to or from KLM).

of the affiliated carriers in their operations to and from the USA and to their relationships within the USA [87]:

a) No joint public relations activities, advertising or promotion with KLM;
b) separate offices, telephone listings, personnel;
c) Martin's personnel shall preserve the individual identity of the carrier in all public dealings;
d) Martin's shall not serve as agent, general agent or general sales agent for KLM, nor permit KLM to serve in a similar capacity;
e) Martin's shall not, with respect to KLM, accept or exchange tickets, baggage checks, exchange orders, etc.;
f) Martin's shall not directly or indirectly hold out or offer to charter groups it carries onward transportation in Europe on KLM's scheduled services;
g) Martin's shall not use any KLM facility, including terminal and aircraft handling facilities; and shall not perform any service, including baggage handling and ticket collection and processing, for KLM;
h) Martin's shall not, except in cases of emergency, wet lease or dry lease aircraft to or from KLM for use in the performance of air transportation to and from the US.

Considering Condor's application, the Bureau of Operating Rights of the CAB [88] took an extreme attitude: "Condor's primary purpose is to allow Lufthansa to avoid the regulatory systems prevailing in Europe, including the IATA resolutions, and by doing so to participate in the large and growing European IT market" and, "DLH will possess through Condor the sum authority under which US scheduled and US supplementals operate ... and this sum is greater than the arithmetic sum of the authority the two types of US carriers possess individually."

It was noted that route carriers are given charter rights outside the bilateral and these rights were therefore reducible or revocable by the US. Any independent irregular carrier can have entry into the charter market on the basis of reciprocity.

The Bureau of Operating Rights stated that the possession of scheduled and supplemental authority by a single carrier constitutes "a critical mass which could seriously disrupt the regulatory system now prevailing in the

[87] Cf. Order No. E-26146 appr. Dec. 18, 1967, p. 2 and Order 68-12-121, Dockets 19570 & 19745, appr. Dec. 20, 1968, Martin's amended Foreign air carrier permit. p. 2. Cf. also Order appr. Febr. 19, 1966, No. E-23280, Air Jamaica, p. 2, and note the differences.

[88] Cf. Docket 17233 of January 6, 1967. Brief of Roy Pulsifer.

transatlantic market." The answer to this by Condor was that "the Board has always focused on the exchange of transportation rights themselves rather than on the make-up of the foreign instrumentality concerned." [89]

The Condor case, Condor being a non-IATA carrier, gave rise to sharp criticism of IATA.[90] "Condor may be used (by Lufthansa) to evade IATA resolutions and as a "fighting ship" to combat privately-owned non-scheduled carriers serving the IT charter market." [91]

In its answer to the Bureau, Condor and Lufthansa pointed out that with Condor agreeing to include a minimum pricing condition in its permit, the fighting-ship issue is eliminated. Condor had suggested three fair-trading conditions to be included in its permit:

1. A rate floor for its charters geared to the lowest charter rate of a US supplemental carrier for parallel types of equipment, accommodation and service.
2. No use of Lufthansa employees and sales personnel and no public holding out of any relationship between the two companies.
3. In its dealing with IATA agents also appointed by Lufthansa, Condor would abide by the same restraints as those observed by the IATA carriers.

In its final decision, the Board considered that it was not obliged to impose conditions in foreign air carrier permits to prevent evasion or subversion of IATA resolutions unless such a condition were necessary to prevent detriment to US carriers. A condition was imposed which assured that Condor's tariff rates would not unfairly undercut those of *US* supplemental carriers. Possible violations of IATA resolutions by Lufthansa through its relationship with Condor posed no real threat. As a matter of fact, the CAB does not require US or foreign carriers to be members of IATA.[92]

The recommendation of the Examiner that Lufthansa divest itself of all ownership and control of Condor, a requirement declared unacceptable both by Condor and Lufthansa, was not taken on by the Board, as the Board, in the absence of any adverse impact on US carriers, did not wish

[89] Reply Brief of Condor to Examiner, February 1, 1967, Docket 17233, p. 6.

[90] Roy Pulsifer: "Instead of making the scheduled system competitive in terms of price and service . . . high fixed fares and rigid commercial practices determined within IATA continue to obtain. Therefore now wholly-owned subsidiaries are used to operate outside the traditional regulatory framework."

[91] Pulsifer, p. 3.

[92] Cf. Order E-26147, served Dec. 21, 1967, Opinion p. 8. N.B. Cf. also, Order 70-2-125, adopted Febr. 27, 1970: ". . . the Board views with concern any governmental actions which would in effect require the non-IATA supplemental carriers to adhere to rates agreed upon by IATA carriers." See also Appendix I.

to attempt to impose US policy for regulation of US carriers on the German Government.[93]

The Board considered it to be sufficient to impose conditions designed to require that:

a) operations on the part of Condor would be conducted independently of DLH;
b) holding out any identity or relationship between the two carriers would be eliminated.[94]

The Board did grant Condor authority to wet lease or charter to Lufthansa for the performance of Lufthansa's on- and off-route charter and individually-ticketed and way-billed services, subject to prior Board approval. "The interior of the aircraft shall contain a sign prominently displayed and clearly showing that Condor is in operational control of the aircraft and the fact that its crews are operating the aircraft."

The, for the CAB liberal, attitude in both cases was explained by the Board itself as being based upon considerations of international comity, the support given to the applications by the governments concerned and the liberal attitude of the Dutch and German Governments vis-à-vis US carrier operations to their countries (reciprocity).

The relationship between Lufthansa and Condor was not viewed as a monopolization of the market in view of the fact that the US-German charter market is served by two US-flag scheduled carriers and six supplemental carriers as well as the German (at that time still independent) charter carrier Sudflug.

There are some differences in the Martin's and Condor permits:
Martin's cannot have KLM provide ground handling, a restriction which was not imposed on the Condor/Lufthansa relationship. Condor and Martin's are both prohibited from wet or dry leasing aircraft to or from Lufthansa and KLM, except in cases of emergency (Martin's), but Condor is authorized to wet lease or charter its aircraft *to* Lufthansa for the on-route (including off-route charter authority subject to the provisions of Part 212) operations of Lufthansa service for the carriage of Lufthansa

[93] "We assume for present purposes that the Board would not authorize a US route carrier to acquire control of a supplemental carrier. The German Government, however, makes no distinction between a supplemental carrier under exclusive private ownership and a supplemental carrier that is a subsidiary of a scheduled carrier and this policy is applied both in respect to German carriers and carriers of other nationalities without discrimination."

[94] Idem p. 15.

traffic under tariffs subject to CAB special permission in each case, and the posting of an appropriate sign in the interior of the aircraft.[95]

It should be noted that the attitude of the CAB with regard to affiliation [96] and wet lease agreements [97] depends on the character of the relationship between lessor and lessee, and who is the lessor and who the lessee:

a) a US route carrier (lessor) and a foreign scheduled or charter carrier (lessee);
b) two foreign scheduled carriers;
c) a foreign charter carrier (lessor) and a foreign route carrier (lessee) or vice versa;
d) a US supplemental carrier (lessor) and a foreign scheduled carrier (lessee);
e) a US supplemental carrier (lessor) and a foreign charter carrier (lessee).[98]

The CAB does not permit cooperation among US carriers.[99]

It would seem that in practice no great difficulties need be expected in obtaining a wet lease permit in the case of wet lease (or charter) arrangements between foreign carriers for operations which are on-route for the lessor and the lessee. Wet lease arrangements between a foreign route carrier (lessee) and a foreign charter carrier (lessor) are not welcomed by the CAB.[100] Wet lease or charter arrangements between a foreign carrier as a lessor and a US (route) carrier as lessee in general are not possible.

[95] Cf. also the KAR-AIR permit and the FINNAIR permit. Docket 19632, served October 21, 1968 and Order 8-10-107: Permit authorizing FINNAIR to engage in wet lease charter operations for KAR-AIR with respect to persons and property chartered by KAR-AIR pursuant to KAR-AIR's authority. Permit authorizing KAR-AIR to engage in wet lease operations for FINNAIR with respect to persons, property and mail individually-ticketed or waybilled or chartered by FINNAIR pursuant to FINNAIR's authority, including off-route charters (the permit states "by and only by charter agreement with FINNAIR resp. KAR-AIR"). All flights still require specific Board approval: Unless specifically authorized in advance by the Board, Finnair and KAR-AIR shall not wet or dry lease aircraft to or from each other, for use in the performance of air transportation to and from the USA.

Finnair (who owns KAR-AIR) and KAR-AIR shall not, directly or indirectly, hold out or offer to charter groups carried by KAR-AIR onward transportation in Europe on Finnair's scheduled services. (N.B. The language used by the CAB shows again that no distinction is made between wet leasing and charter operations).

[96] Cf. Sec. 408.

[97] Cf. Sec. 412.

[98] Cf. respectively e.g. (a) PANAM/Air Afrique, (b) TAP/Alitalia, BOAC/Air Jamaica, (c) Martin's/SAS, DLH/Condor, (d) Flying Tiger/KLM, Airlift International/Alitalia, (e) ONA/Martin's, etc.

[99] Except interchange agreements to provide one-plane through services (end-on interchange).

[100] Cf. CAB Order 69-2-22, denying Caledonian to operate charter flights for BOAC.

In case the lessor does not otherwise serve the USA or has no other airline operations, the CAB may more easily accept the lessee's control of the wet lease operation and consequently approve the arrangement.

To date it seems to have made no difference to the CAB, where two foreign carriers are involved, whether the lessor and the lessee are carriers of the same nationality or not, except for the fact that the CAB apparently does not wish to impose limitations on the stock interests of one carrier in the other or at least of a regular carrier in a charter carrier of the same nationality. Of course, bilateral air agreements do impose limitations upon the stock interests of nationals of another State in the carriers designated by the parties to the bilateral.

While the affiliation of, or joint venture between, foreign carriers leads the CAB to require permit authorization under Section 402 for the operations of the participants and impose passing off restrictions, a single wet lease agreement makes the CAB suspicious that an affiliation, a joint venture or at least a mutuality of interest exists, which is why the CAB in such cases wishes further to require an application by the lessor for additional Section 402 permit authority to conduct the operations under the wet lease agreement.[101]

We have explained that we are not in favor of these requirements. Moreover a standard provision in CAB Section 402 (foreign air carrier) permits reads: "This permit shall be subject to the condition that in the event a practice develops which the Board regards as inimical to sound economic conditions, the holder and the Board will consult with respect thereto and will use their best efforts to agree upon modifications thereof satisfactory to the Board and the holder." Such consultation procedures seem more adequate than strict prior approval of wet lease operations by foreign air carriers, whether or not an affiliation or a joint venture exists beyond the wet lease agreement.

VI. BLOCKED-SPACE ARRANGEMENTS

While a carrier may lease an entire aircraft and crews, whereby the control over and the responsibility for the operation with the aircraft and crews passes from the lessor to the lessee, and while a carrier may also enter into a lease without the control and responsibility passing to the lessee (the

[101] Interline charters to conduct off-route operations are prohibited except in cases of emergency (Part 212). Interline charters or wet lease agreements will be subject to special Board approval if proposed Part 218 is adopted.

CAB calls this a charter), the carrier leasing the capacity of the aircraft as it would in a charter agreement, a carrier may also lease only a number of seats or an amount of cargo space. Such an arrangement is called a blocked-space agreement and a Sec. 402 permit is required for it.

The multi-national air carrier Air Afrique started operations to the USA (New York) on the basis of an "Air Transport Development Agreement", leasing a number of seats and proportionate cargo space from PANAM. For this operation Air Afrique required a foreign air carrier permit from the CAB and PANAM required both approval of the agreement by the CAB and exemption authority for the joint operations.[102] The Board in this case applied the following criteria: "First, arrangements such as these are considered as a valid transitional instrument for the development of air transport relations with less developed countries where the operation and arrangement are desired in its own interest by a US-flag carrier. Second, the provision of service under the arrangement is warranted on economic grounds. Third, the market is presently inadequate to support normal service by both the US flag and the foreign flag carrier. Fourth, it can be reasonably anticipated that a normal exchange of traffic rights would be economically feasible at some future date. Fifth, the foreign flag carrier is organized on a rational economic basis, and the proposed arrangement is likely to contribute toward its economic viability. Sixth, the arrangement supports such US objectives as encouraging regional carriers for long-haul operations of several nations.[103]

In this respect the LANICA/TAN joint Operating Agreement deserves attention.[104] This agreement, of September 28, 1967, contains both blocked-space and wet lease arrangements.

The agreement is essentially an arrangement for sharing capacity, each carrier being allocated an equal number of passenger seats and half of the cargo space of LANICA's jet aircraft on all flights between San Salvador and Miami via intermediate points, the carriers exercising only such traffic rights as they possess in their own name. The agreement does not provide for any pooling of revenues for any traffic carried. Although the names of both carriers appear on the fuselage of the aircraft, the aircraft remains under the full control of LANICA while jointly used. No other

[102] Cf. Order E-21129, Air Afrique permit, adopted July 23, 1964. Order E-20781, adopted May 1, 1964, granting exemption authority. CAB 17500, agreement PANAM/Air Afrique. Orders E-22160 and E-22843 of May 13 and Nov. 4, 1965. Air Afrique's permit was extended by Order E-24597, adopted Dec. 1, 1966, PANAM's by Order E-24596. The inter-carrier (amended) agreement (CAB 17500) was adopted by the same Order E-24596, December 1, 1966. See also note 41 above.

[103] Cf. Order E-24596, December 1, 1966, p. 3, Note 6.

[104] Cf. Docket 19601, served September 12, 1968.

relationships exist between the carriers. The agreement is a device allowing both carriers to operate jet service to the US at minimal capital and operating cost.

The Examiner considered that LANICA required additional authorization for the carriage of traffic for TAN between San Pedro Sula and Miami and between San Salvador and Miami, which TAN ticketed, as LANICA's permit authorized traffic operations in foreign air transportation only in LANICA's own name and right over a Managua-San Salvador-Miami route.[105]

For TAN the case was a different one and the fact that TAN's traffic would be carried in space aboard LANICA's aircraft with a LANICA crew in operational control did not necessitate an additional authorization for TAN; where TAN cockpit crew would be operating the aircraft carrying LANICA traffic, TAN would still not be engaging in foreign air transportation on behalf of LANICA as LANICA, under the terms of the agreement, would be exercising direct supervision and control over the crew members, and consequently would not need new authorization.[106]

The use by TAN of LANICA's jet aircraft was considered to be in the public interest, for it enabled TAN to upgrade its own operations from propeller to jet services under an agreement which was a first experimental step towards the ultimate formation and operation of a single multinational airline serving the interests of the area and owned by nationals of the small countries involved and it would not be in the long-term interests of the US to force the national carriers of Central American nations to continue uneconomic forms of operation.[107]

In terms of blocked-space arrangements, the allocation of seats to each of the carriers under the LANICA/TAN agreement, left room for the use of a part of the other carrier's allocated seats if need be. The tickets for the space allocated or released to each of the carriers should be issued and honored by the carrier concerned.[108]

A blocked-space agreement for the lease of seats (a wet lease of part of an aircraft) is exceptional,[109] as normally such agreements concern the lease of cargo space.

[105] Cf. idem page 27.

[106] Cf. *idem* p. 31. The Board in its Decision of December 4, 1968, Docket 19601, Order 69-2-7, agreed with the Examiner but modified certain proposed passing off conditions: instead of the Condor type (affiliate relationship) conditions, conditions were imposed as for AUA/Sabena and TAP/Alitalia. The Board did not adopt the Examiner's observations on the possible formation of a Central American airline consortium (see note 107).

[107] Cf. position of PANAM and the Examiner, p. 28/29.

[108] Cf. *idem* p. 9.

[109] Cf. e.g. also TAP/ALITALIA blocked-space agreement, Docket 16692, Order

Many of such blocked-space cargo arrangements have been made between carriers, one carrier making available to the other an agreed amount of capacity (normally defined in terms of pallets) at a point on its flights against payment of a charge per unit (pallet), regardless of the amount of cargo loaded on each pallet.[110]

The carrier leasing space from another carrier usually publishes the availability of the leased space by giving the flight or service concerned a line number of its own with the annotation that the service is operated by the lessor.[111]

Dual aircraft identification has become common as carriers endeavour to obtain greater utilization of their aircraft by leasing arrangements. In the US this practice has existed for a long time under equipment interchange agreements.

In the case of lease agreements it happens that an aircraft carries the livery of both carriers, one on each side.[112] A more simple lessee identification on a leased aircraft is a sign, for instance: "Rented by . . . (name of lessee)." In such cases the lessee is the operator even while the aircraft is owned and flown by crews of the lessor.[113] In cases where the control of, and the responsibility for, the operation remains with the lessor or charterer, any doubt of who the operator is may be dispelled by the indication: "Operated by . . . (name of the carrier supplying the aircraft and crew)."

In the case of blocked-space arrangements it should be noted that the lessor remains the commercial operator of the route concerned next to the

E-23820, concerning the route Lisbon-New York, served June 15, 1966, and the AUA/ Sabena blocked-space agreement concerning the Vienna-Brussels-New York route, AUA leasing half of the entire capacity of Sabena aircraft; Docket 19893, served November 22, 1968. "Should it arise that one carrier needs more seats than the other, an exchange of interline passengers will be effected in accordance with standard interline procedures."

110 Cf. e.g. Seaboard World/TMA blocked-space cargo agreement, Order E-24943, April 4, 1967, on the sector London-Frankfort of Seaboard's New York-Frankfort flights; TWA/ELAL agreement relative to the purchase by ELAL of cargo space (pallets) on aircraft operated by TWA between New York and Tel Aviv. There is no provision in the agreement providing for public identification of ELAL's service or for any substantial measure of ELAL control over TWA's schedules. Approved by the CAB as being in the public interest and not in violation of the Act, the agreement not having any adverse effect on other US carriers; Order No. E-26685, adopted April 18, 1968. Disapproval of cargo blocked-space agreements because of an adverse effect on other US carriers: See Orders E-20553, March 6, 1964 and E-20770, April 29, 1964, involving TWA and Air France.

111 Cf. Swissair-Seaboard blocked-space cargo arrangement, Order E-21042, July 9, 1964, which was published as a Swissair service.

112 Cf. KLM/VIASA interchange.

113 Cf. also Trans International Airlines, Order E-23861, June 27, 1966, lease with crew to CPAIR (operation under CPAIR's permit).

lessee. The leased-space agreement between TAP and Alitalia for the inauguration of TAP's services to New York involved transportation by Alitalia between Lisbon and New York for which Alitalia held permission under its own CAB permit on a route between Italy and New York. The CAB, however, issued permits to both carriers, ruling that since TAP's flight operations would be conducted by Alitalia under a leased-space arrangement, the transportation should be limited to transportation performed pursuant to the leased-space agreement between the Italian carrier and TAP and that all flights operated by Alitalia should originate and terminate at a point in Italy. Alitalia would not enjoy, in effect, the benefits of a permit to engage in air transportation between Portugal and the USA.[114]

It is not wholly clear why it was necessary to issue a separate permit to Alitalia, as this permit limited possibilities which the carrier would not have had in the first place under the permit issued to TAP. The reason for issuing a separate permit to Alitalia was not to limit Alitalia's possibilities in the Lisbon-New York market, but to expressly authorize Alitalia to perform transportation pursuant to the leased-space agreement with TAP between Lisbon and New York, which, according to CAB doctrine (the Air Jamaica Case), could not be allowed without special CAB authorization. Further conditions were imposed which were designed to make clear to the public the respective roles of TAP and Alitalia in providing the authorized transportation.

In the case of blocked-space arrangements and wet lease agreements it could be argued that under bilateral air agreements the designated carriers are free to use their aircraft and capacity in the way they deem fit, including operation on behalf of another carrier under a lease agreement, so long as it concerns on-route operations and the substantial ownership and effective control of the designated carrier with regard to the operation of the agreed routes cannot be questioned.

On the other hand, designated carriers should be free to exercise the rights under bilateral air agreements in the way they see fit, including the use of aircraft and capacity leased from another carrier for on-route operations, so long as the substantial ownership and effective control of the operations on the agreed routes remain with them.

The CAB Bureau of Operating Rights has consistently held that bilateral air agreements do not cover operations performed by carriers other than the carriers of the parties to the agreement.[115] Therefore the CAB requires,

[114] Cf. Docket 16692, Order E-23820, served June 15, 1966.

[115] Cf. for instance, Recommended Decision TAP, Docket 16692, March 28, 1966, page 4.

as a rule, new and special permits for each party to a lease, including blocked-space, agreement authorizing the transportation to be performed pursuant to such agreement. Whether or not the CAB grants the required permits depends upon the merits of each particular case.

VII. SUMMARY

The CAB applies "fit, willing and able" criteria to foreign air carriers applying for a foreign air carrier permit and examines capital, management, liability, organization (sales offices), operations and ground handling of the applicant. In addition and of overriding importance is the criterion of public interest.

If a carrier is already operating to the US, it is deemed to be fit, willing and able to perform the proposed transportation so long as the transportation already being performed is substantially similar in character to, and as extensive as, the transportation proposed.[116]

In the case of Quisqueyana, it was found that its management was without persons with airline experience and that the carrier was not financially sound and not able to finance the proposed transportation.[117] Nevertheless the carrier was found fit, willing and able, because it was already operating and, as may be noted, the proposed operation was felt to be in the public interest, Quisqueyana being designated in conformity with the bilateral agreement between the US and the Dominican Republic.

In the Air Jamaica Case [118] it was found that Air Jamaica was neither fit nor able to perform the proposed transportation on behalf of itself. BOAC and BWIA were found to be fit, willing and able, however, and the CAB concluded that the fitness, etc. of the wet lessors (BOAC and BWIA) could be imputed to the lessee (Air Jamaica). This conclusion was reached because the proposed transportation was felt to be in the public interest in view of the reciprocity extended by Jamaica to US carriers and because Jamaica was a friendly and neighboring country.

Noteworthy also is that in the Decision in the ALM Case [119], the Board argued that ALM would not be required to move towards independent operations, because the Netherlands carriers should not be forced to abandon cooperative arrangements in accordance with their Government's policy in favor of totally independent operations.

[116] Cf. Part 399 of the Procedural Regulations of the CAB.
[117] Cf. Order E-24233, served September 28, 1966.
[118] Cf. Order E-23280, p. 7.
[119] Cf. Decision of December 12, 1968, Docket 18595, p. 3.

This might have been different for carriers of different nationalities unless the Governments of the carriers concerned had agreed beforehand on joint operations and common aviation policy. During discussions on the formation of an "AIR UNION" in Europe, governmental agreement, influence and management within AIR UNION were found necessary for acceptance by non-participating governments (the USA) of these joint operations.

On another occasion,[120] however, the CAB ruled that it is not in the public interest for the holder of a foreign air carrier permit which may be in competition with US certificated flag carriers to render itself fit, willing and able properly to perform the air transportation required by its permit through leasing, on an indefinite basis, the equipment, operating staff and other resources of a *US* carrier.

In would seem, therefore, that if a carrier is designated in conformity with a bilateral air agreement with the US, the CAB has difficulty finding such a carrier not fit, willing and able on the grounds of having concluded a cooperative arrangement with another foreign carrier. Examples are the TAP/Alitalia lease arrangement and the Austrian Airlines/Sabena lease arrangement, both of which were approved by the CAB.[121]

But if the CAB finds that the operation as proposed is adverse to the public interest, which in practice means that the operation may have an adverse impact on US carrier operations, no permit will be recommended. Refusal may depend on the extent of the cooperative arrangements between the applicant and other carriers, or on the reliance upon the resources of a US carrier, or upon the fact that the applicant is not designated in conformity with a bilateral agreement, or is not yet operating into the US. All are reasons for the CAB to find the applicant not fit, willing and able on the grounds of its having concluded some cooperative agreement with another carrier.

In this respect it should be noted that the CAB interprets "in the public interest" as meaning that a positive advantage (reciprocity) must ensue from the grant of a permit to US carriers and that it is not sufficient that

[120] Cf. Order 1708, 1953, Seaboard aircraft lease to Irish Airlines.

[121] Cf. AUA, Docket 19893, served Nov. 22, 1968, Order 68-11-79. Foreign air carrier permit issued to AUA and a wet lease permit issued to Sabena: "Because of limited financial resources and the requirement of substantial capital investments, AUA has taken the means of a 'blocked-space agreement' with Sabena to engage in foreign air transportation between its country and the US." Sabena entered into the blocked-space agreement to improve its earnings. The wet lease permit was granted to Sabena for a period of three years.

US carriers will not be affected one way or another by the grant of a permit to a foreign carrier.[122]

In the ALM Decision, the Board clearly wanted to retain its "existing" licensing authority over wet lease arrangements, "in view of the competitive impact on US carriers." Apart from reasons of policy, the Board advanced the argument that "apart from the customary permit language, the Board was not presented with any issue of KLM operations for other carriers when granting KLM's existing permit. Its award was not intended to confer any rights exceeding those applied for."

In other words, the US wanted to make the granting of such rights subject to reciprocal advantages for US carriers. Whether or not the other party (the Kingdom of the Netherlands) allows US carriers to operate for other carriers without the need for special authority, was not considered.

The requirement of a special wet lease permit is objectionable inasmuch as such a permit may be refused solely on the grounds of the competitive impact of the lease on US-carrier operations.

It may be noted here that it is not primarily the use by a carrier of aircraft leased from another carrier, but rather the operation of aircraft by a carrier in the name of and on behalf of another carrier, which preoccupies the CAB. A wet lease permit will be refused by the CAB if the competition with US carriers will increase as a result of the wet lease operations and the share of the foreign carrier of the market concerned will improve. In such cases the lessor will not receive a wet lease permit, since it would improve the positions of both lessor and lessee. Foreign carriers should operate their routes to the US with their own aircraft and rely mainly on their own resources.[123]

Is it necessary for both the lessor and the lessee to enjoy traffic rights in their own name on the routes over which the transportation is to take place in order to be granted new and separate permits authorizing the lease operations? This appears not to be the case.

One could hold, of course, that a lease agreement gives an undue advantage to the lessor in competing for traffic to which it is not entitled (off-route operations), or to which it has only a secondary claim, if it concerns transportation between points one of which the lessor is authorized to serve only as a secondary objective as in the case of the Alitalia/TAP leased-space agreement.

[122] Cf. AUA Docket: "A substantial community of interest exists between Austria and the USA."

[123] It may be noted that a lessee normally relies on its own resources for the payments to be made for the lease of aircraft.

Here again it should be stressed, however, that the lessor is not the carrier which commercially operates the routes for which the lessee has leased its aircraft. The lessor therefore need not hold in its own name traffic rights which the lessee intends to exercise with the leased capacity in order to be granted permission by the CAB to perform transportation pursuant to the lease agreement.

However, as a rule, the CAB does impose conditions designed to ensure the separate identity of lessor and lessee to protect the public by requiring appropriate identification showing that the aircraft is leased to another carrier and that the lessor is in operational control of the aircraft.

Apart from this more or less established policy, opportunism plays an important role:

A case in point is the TAP Decision cited above, in which the Examiner considered that US carriers would operate substantially more flights than the one Portuguese carrier. Thus "reciprocity and comity alone would require that a Portuguese carrier be permitted to operate over the Lisbon-New York route. A substantial community of interest exists between Portugal and the United States and, of course, Portugal is a NATO ally. Trade between the US and Portugal is on the increase and the balance of trade is in the US' favor." After mentioning that the statistics on immigration illustrate a like community of interest, the Examiner concluded that these considerations were "compelling factors in favor of the grant of the application."

In its Decision the Board showed serious concern over the recent disapproval by Portugal of the increase of frequencies proposed by US carriers, but argued that it would not be in the public interest to withhold issuance of TAP's permit pending resolution of the frequency problem.[124]

The above shows that, contrary to official policy, civil aviation relations are (sometimes) considered part of overall bilateral relationships between the US and other countries. Moreover, the nature of each particular case governs the CAB's choice of which aspect to emphasise in argumentation justifying their recommendation to the President of approval or disapproval of an application.

Finally, apart from legal considerations, the practice of operating with leased aircraft as an economic necessity will have to be accepted if a State has no choice but to operate with leased aircraft to be able to compete effectively and maintain or obtain a share of the international traffic market under the bilateral agreements it has concluded. This makes the

[124] Cf. Docket 16692, Order E-23820, served June 15, 1966, page 4.

acceptance of this practice by other States dependent on the continued exercise of reciprocal rights.

Thus national sovereignty over air space may force States, having entered into bilateral agreements with each other, to accept each other's carriers regardless of the way in which these carriers choose to operate their services, subject only to safety requirements.

The CAB requirement that a national carrier be fit, willing and able, (that it have an own organization, aircraft fleet, competent personnel, adequate financial basis, etc.) and that it operate independently, may become obsolete in these cases, since it is in the public interest of the US to accept without question the fitness, willingness and ability of the designated carriers of other States. Maybe it is, therefore, that the CAB proposed a new economic regulation (Part 218), requiring that only the lessor obtain a special wet lease permit, thereby indirectly limiting the possibilities of foreign air carriers to operate their routes with wet leased aircraft.[125]

In this respect it may finally be remarked that US policy disregards the advantages of cooperation between US and foreign air carriers, especially aircraft pooling and interchange agreements.

For instance, end-on interchange arrangements under which one-plane through services are provided by combining routes of different air carriers and using the same aircraft, can substantially contribute to the further development of the international air transportation system. Under such arrangements each carrier retains control over the operation of its own route (dry lease).

The US attitude on airline cooperation is anachronistic. The US wishes to reserve control over US carriers to US citizens as these companies are considered of vital security interest to the country. This attitude does not leave room for foreign air carrier participation in US air transportation. It makes integration of airline operations with US carriers as partners, in the interest of the traveling and shipping public, a far-off dream.

[125] For a summary of the attitude of the CAB towards cooperative agreements, see also Burton A. Landy: "Cooperative agreements involving foreign airlines: a review of the policy of the United States Civil Aeronautics Board." JALC, Autumn 1969, p. 575 ff.

CHAPTER FIVE

CONCLUSION

In 1861 John Stuart Mill stated that a State is a uniform ethnic entity. Sir Ernest Barker, however, predicted that each nation (ethnic entity) would form a State and each State would then be a nation.

To draw a parallel we could technically define a uniform air traffic market as a State. We can, however, predict that from an economic point of view each city, each area, each region within the State will become an independent air traffic market and that the technique of civil aviation regulation will have to recognize each such separate traffic market for the establishment of air relations with other similar areas.

Although the State undoubtedly will remain the authority which negotiates and decides upon the establishment of international air services, the central government will be forced by the developments within its air traffic markets which show a continuing tendency towards regionalization within the States to subdivide the national traffic market and treat the various regions as independent markets within the State.

If this is true, and the future will bear us out, it will become necessary to abandon the present-day system of horse trading between States. This system translates national markets into property which can be bought or exchanged for something of equal value. A denationalized approach to the international air traffic market will become necessary and the participation of each national carrier will become dependent on the services it can provide based on its specific relation to each of the different and separate markets.

This relationship must be viewed, at the same time, in the light of the interrelationship among these separate markets and the place within the overall international air traffic market as reflected by the worldwide pattern of air services. In other words the relation between a carrier and the separate markets, the interrelationships among these markets and their place in the network of that carrier, and the position of that network within the overall pattern of international air services will determine the rights which that carrier should be able to exercise.

In our view, there are no national markets, but only nationally-controlled markets. There is one big international air traffic market, divided into numerous sub-markets, each with its specific requirements as part of the greater pattern of the total international air traffic market.

The technique of international civil aviation regulation should be based on the reality of these factors. Since national governments are the ones to implement such regulation on a bilateral basis, they should see bilateral markets in accordance with this reality.

Technically the international air traffic market should be taken as a whole and not broken down into as many separate independent markets as there are States, nor into separate bilateral markets where each route is a separate market defined by traffic with "origin" and "destination" at the terminals of the route or route sectors. Each route should be viewed as an integral part of the worldwide pattern of air connections. Each separate market and each bilateral market should be viewed as a part of the overall international air traffic market. Each carrier should be treated in terms of the market which it is able to reach and develop with a network whose hub is the carrier's home territory.

Each route, technically, provides a separate opportunity to participate in the international carriage of the world's air traffic and constitutes a separate means to obtain a share of the international air traffic market.

Although each route represents a separate opportunity, its value to the air carrier will depend not only on the traffic moving over it but also on its possibilities for integrating this route into the airline's entire network and the network into the worldwide pattern of air services. A route, therefore, should not be sealed off from the rest of the international routes by confining its use primarily or exclusively to traffic defined by origin and destination, nor should its granting be dependent on traffic demands as so defined.

The advent of the wide-bodied jet aircraft will stimulate wholesale marketing of the expanded capacity both for passenger (group and IT) traffic and cargo traffic (incremental pricing). This development intensifies competition between route and charter carriers.

On the other hand, the need for cooperation among air carriers (through aircraft pooling, blocked-space and revenue pooling arrangements) will increase.

It will be harmful to the economic operation of wide-bodied jet air services if governments subject the use of the capacity and the cooperative arrangements concerning the operation of these aircraft to bargaining for additional advantages under their bilateral air agreements. Flexibility of airline operation should not be traded for additional traffic rights.

International air traffic continues to grow at a fast rate. The air carriers on the other hand are engaged in a continuous struggle to obtain and maintain economic conditions for the operation of their international air services. There is no way for them to be sure that also in the future a profitable operation of their air services will be possible. It remains necessary for them to invest heavily in new equipment, to expand their services continuously (new routes, more capacity, – bigger and faster aircraft and more frequencies – better schedules, greater variety of fares and rates) in order to meet competition. To the extent that they are forced to bring fares and rates down they must obtain bigger volumes of traffic in compensation. As costs rise, efficiency must be improved.

As protectionism increases and the markets available to the air carriers are limited, the fight for traffic becomes fiercer.

It is no wonder that States, in order to provide a basis for their air carriers to survive, turn to the doctrine of a State's own traffic, that is, the right to traffic to, from, via and passing over its territory. Thus civil aviation policy is turning into the most elementary form of power politics. The materialistic approach to international civil aviation, the efforts to arrive at a balance, no longer primarily between capacity offered and traffic demand, but between the benefits derived by carriers from the carriage of traffic between their territories (third and fourth freedom traffic mainly), the complete disappearance of more idealistic considerations to try and build up traffic together to the benefit of all, leads to the disintegration of the international air traffic market at the expense of all.

States try to obtain for their air carriers a proper share of the international air traffic market. This proper share is defined in terms of power. No or little account is taken of economic considerations: the right to transport traffic overshadows the requirements needed to transport traffic in the most economic and efficient way, and the resources and efforts needed to do so.

The product changes, expands, diversifies. The qualitative and quantitative demands increase with it. The need for a broader basis of regulatory measures grows. Bilateralism as a regulatory mechanism can be adequate only insofar as multilateral standards are applied.

Capacity regulation, frequency regulation, multiple designation, precise definitions of the various products, subdivision of the air traffic market geographically and otherwise, flexibility in aircraft use- in short, denationalization of civil aviation regulation in order to regulate competition, not on the basis of a nation's rightful share but on the basis of the situation as it presents itself, the situation of the carriers offering a product and the subsequent demand, all require a technical approach.

Priority rights of carriers can no longer be based on their right to carry their own traffic, but should be based on the possible contribution they can make to the further sound development of the international air traffic market.

APPENDIX I

STATEMENT ON US INTERNATIONAL AVIATION POLICY

On January 15, 1970, the task force on the new Nixon policy on international aviation, headed by Professor Paul W. Cherington, released a draft of a proposed US international aviation policy. The draft Statement encourages charter services as a way of creating new and cheaper travel opportunities. It takes a hard line on a larger share of world air traffic for US carriers.[1] It also reaffirms the need to encourage open competition; the Bermuda provisions as the basis for the exchange of air transport rights and the need to ensure "fair and equal opportunity" for US carriers; the desirability of studying an exchange of routes and traffic rights (including charter rights) on a multilateral basis.

The doctrine of an "equal exchange of economic benefits" is not mentioned, although the rights exchanged should assure US carriers the opportunity to achieve benefits no less than those available to the foreign air carriers.

The draft policy seeks to improve the quantity or variety of service in many major and secondary markets by certification of new US carriers to operate international routes (point-to-point competition among US carriers, direct services to secondary markets, charter services). This could mean a more extensive use of the multiple designation possibilities present in existing bilateral air agreements.[2]

[1] The US carrier position in international air transportation was felt to be insufficient. Also the economic condition of the US carriers was a topic of the greatest concern: "The rate of return on investment, which has been used by the CAB as a measure of the economic viability of the airlines, fell to 3.7% from the level of six percent of the year before." Secor D. Browne, Chairman of the CAB, in an address in Oakland, California, January 22, 1970.

[2] Cf. e.g. the collateral Exchange of Notes following the 1965 US-Japan consultations: "(2) A designation at any time of one or more airlines to operate air services on any of the air routes specified in the Schedule attached to the Agreement does not prejudice the right of a contracting party to designate at a later date one or more additional air-

In his book,[3] however, Wheatcroft states that "there is no evidence that parallel licensing will lead to a larger share of the total traffic but that there is a serious possibility that this development would come into conflict with the aims of national policy in air services agreements." Mr. Roy Jenkins, then Minister of Aviation in the UK, stated on February 17, 1965: "So far as scheduled services on international routes are concerned, I am not convinced that the national interest is, in general, served by more than one British carrier operating on the same route." [4] Moreover, the balance of international relations might be upset by the use of multiple designation possibilities by one of the parties to a bilateral air agreement.

The main question is whether the market can support a greater number of carriers competing for the same traffic: Many of the existing carriers will be operating the wide-bodied jet aircraft and additional licensing may create overcapacity. The statement of Cherington that "there is room for both scheduled and charter service", therefore, should not lead to licensing charter carriers to compete in markets catered to by scheduled carriers. However, the draft policy states: "both scheduled and supplemental carriers should be permitted a fair opportunity to compete in the bulk transportation market. We consider passengers traveling at group rates on scheduled services to be part of that market."

As the draft policy statement, furthermore, advocates the conclusion of intergovernmental agreements covering charter services and states that there should be no trade-off as between scheduled service rights and charter service rights, the question arises whether the apparent equation of charter service and group and bulk travel will lead to separate intergovernmental agreements, governing all services exploiting the bulk travel market (thereby restricting IATA to the setting of individual fares?).

A problem is that most countries have only one national air carrier (often regarded as chosen instrument) operating both international scheduled and charter services, which will prevent international acceptance of a system of intergovernmental agreements covering charter services as distinct from agreements covering scheduled services, at least if this would result in multiple designation of both scheduled and charter carriers to compete for the same traffic.[5]

lines to operate air services on the same specified route." This provision shows the US concern to ensure the possibility of multiple designation, normally opened by the use of the plural sense of designated carrier in bilateral air agreements.

[3] Air Transport Policy, 1964, p. 171.

[4] Cf. Edwards Report, p. 293.

[5] Cf. also the comments of the Air Transport Association on the proposed policy: "There can be no doubt that when, in 1962, Congress created the supplemental air carriers to supplement the scheduled services . . . it did not authorize them to compete

Another statement made in the draft which merits attention is the one referring to sixth freedom traffic: "There is some evidence that the incidence of air services by foreign air carriers from points behind their home countries may continue to increase."

Cooperation among carriers is inadequately treated in the draft Policy. Nothing is said about the need to cooperate in the utilization of the wide-bodied jet and supersonic aircraft. Mention is made only of the need of developing countries to cooperate in the formation of multi-nation airlines.

The draft policy states that revenue and traffic pools between US and foreign air carriers are anti-competitive and as a rule should be discouraged. Blocked-space agreements, however, are acceptable.

The most noteworthy implication of the draft policy is the attack on the traditional privileged position of the scheduled air carriers under intergovernmental agreements and the fare-setting monopoly of IATA. The emphasis is placed on the interests of the consumer and the role of US carriers, both scheduled and charter carriers, in the bulk air transportation market.

It is questionable, however, whether this change of emphasis will serve the interests of the traveling and shipping public in a period when the route carriers are facing jumbo-sized problems in filling their aircraft. After all, the route carriers are the mainstay of international air transportation.

The bulk travel market is the very market the scheduled carriers need to fill their wide-bodied jet aircraft and to continue the growth commensurate with the possibility for maintaining a profitable operation.

No answer is given in the draft policy on how to separate charter service from individually-ticketed service, while the equation of charter service and group and bulk travel is not accompanied by suggestions on how to solve the problem of regulating competition between air carriers, something which will be of major concern to the rest of the world.

By calling for greater emphasis on the role of charter carriers, the draft policy may complicate the regulation of competition between the carriers of the world, although "geographical limitations, charter definitions and volume restrictions" are mentioned as licensing tools.

Strong opposition of the US scheduled air carriers led to some language changes in the wording approved by the President on June 22, 1970.

with the scheduled services. To supplement and to compete are mutually exclusive concepts." Aviation Daily, February 11, 1970. A country like Australia, for instance, limits the role of supplemental/charter carriers to the performance of own use and affinity charter flights. Affinity charter flights may be performed only when the charter passengers originate in and return to the home country of the carrier.

APPENDIX II

DEFINITIONS

1. *Charter trip* means air transportation where the entire capacity of one or more aircraft has been engaged for the movement of persons and their baggage or the movement of property, on a time, mileage or trip basis:

(i) by a person for his own use; or

(ii) by a representative (or representatives acting jointly) of a group for the use of such groups (provided such representative(s) is not professionally engaged in the formation of groups for transportation or in the solicitation or sale of transportation services). (cf. Part 212, Ec. Reg. USCAB)

2. *Single entity* (or *own use*) *charter* means one for which the cost thereof is borne by the charterer and not by the individual passengers.

3. *Pro rata* (*or affinity group*) *charter* means one for which the cost thereof is divided among the passengers transported, the passengers forming a group with sufficient affinity.

4. *Affinity group* means a group which has principal purposes, aims and objectives other than travel and sufficient affinity prior to the application for charter transportation to distinguish it and set it apart from the general public, subject to such conditions as:

a) no charter may be operated for a group, the membership of which exceeds 20,000 (or 50,000 for the North Atlantic), the membership having existed at least six months prior to the date on which the charter operations are to be commenced;

b) the group's principal purposes, aims and objectives are pursued in practice and are not merely theoretical or fanciful;

c) the group is not formed as a result of "public solicitation", (cf. IATA Resolution 045)

5. *Inclusive tour charter* means one for the conduct of a circle or round-

trip tour which combines air transportation and land services and which (i) extends over a period of at least seven days between departure and return; (ii) provides overnight hotel accommodations at a minimum of three places at least 50 miles apart other than the point of origin; (iii) includes, in the tour price, all hotel accommodations and necessary air and/or surface transportation; and (iv) costs no less than 110 percent of any available fare or fares charged by certificated route carriers for individually ticketed services between the points involved in the tour (or 130 percent of CBIT fares). (cf. Part 378, as amended, of the CAB's Special Regulations)[1]

6. *Open jaw* means a round trip, pro rata charter which operates from a point in the country of origin to a point in another country and returns from a different point to the point of departure in the country of origin.

7. *Split charter* (as distinct from planeload charter) means a pro rata charter on which more than one affinity group is transported.

8. *Resale charter* means one where a person or corporate body charters an aircraft for the purpose of reselling individual passages to members of the public. (cf. inclusive tour charters)

9. *Student charter* means one which is performed on behalf of a single college or university, providing air transportation of a group of students, enrolled in one or more universities on a full time basis, for the purpose of pursuing further studies abroad of not less than six weeks duration. (cf. IATA Resolution 045)

10. *Origin and Destination* (Directional Origin and Destination) of an airline passenger are the first and last points on a one-way ticket and the first and last points on each of the two directional parts of a "round trip", "circle trip", "open jaw" or "round-the-world trip" ticket. The final destination according to the ticket is determined by the farthest point from the origin, measured in terms of great circle distances of the actual stages flown. (cf. ICAO Panel on O and D Statistics, 1959-1963)[2]

11. *Part charter* is one which engages part of the capacity of an aircraft operating a scheduled air service, the remaining capacity being available for sale to other persons or groups or to individual members of the general public.[3]

12. *Blocked off flight* is an on-route charter flight performed over the

[1] Note that a travel agent may not charter an aircraft, except in the case of inclusive tours (tour operator).

[2] N.B. Using the ticket information to define the passenger trip inevitably introduces arbitrary simplifications.

[3] Note that part charters, unlike group and BIT travel on line services and inclusive tour charters, are not subject to fare limitations. Part charters are not allowed by IATA.

route and with an aircraft which would otherwise have been engaged in the operation of a scheduled flight.[4]

13. *Blocked space agreement* means an inter-carrier arrangement whereby one carrier leases a determined portion of the capacity of aircraft of another carrier at an agreed price payable regardless of the utilization made by the lessee of the leased space.

14. *Supplemental air transportation* means charter trips, including inclusive tour charter trips, in air transportation, other than the transportation of mail by aircraft, rendered pursuant to a certificate of public convenience and necessity issued pursuant to section 401(d)(3) of this Act to supplement the scheduled service authorized by certificates of public convenience and necessity issued pursuant to sections 401(d)(1) and (2) of this Act. Nothing in this paragraph shall permit a supplemental air carrier to sell or offer for sale an inclusive tour in air transportation by selling or offering for sale individual tickets directly to members of the general public, or to do so indirectly by controlling, being controlled by, or under common control with, a person authorized by the Board to make such sales. (Sec. 101 (33), Fed. Av. Act of 1958, as amended)

[4] Note that such flights will be less frequent after the introduction of wide-bodied jet aircraft on line services, with the possible exception of part charters and split charters, if allowed by IATA.

INDEX

(references are to pages and the footnotes thereto)

AAFRA 112.
access to market 18, 31, 39.
accident of geography 18 n.3, 47.
advertising 67 n.28.
Aeronaves 107 n.8.
Aerotransportes entre Rios S.R.L. 54 n.4.
affiliate carrier 96ff., 99, 101, 120ff., 137, 141.
affinity charter 66, 70, 72ff.
Air Afrique 107, 121 n.41, 143 n.102.
aircraft commander 135.
Air France 29, 45, 145 n.110.
air freight forwarder 81 n.68.
Air Jamaica 121ff., 124, 132, 147.
Airlift International 120 n.35.
air navigation 43, 116, 129.
Air Union 46, 148.
Alitalia 45 n.47, 70 n.41, 88 n.83, 120 n.35, 123, 144 n.109, 145, 148.
all-cargo service 59ff., 99.
ALM 101 n.114, 125, 126ff., 132 n.73, 134ff., 147, 149.
Annex 6, Chicago Convention 116 n.21.
anti-trust 100, 111.
AVENSA 126ff.
AUA 107, 148, 149 n.122.

Balance of payments 8, 69.
basic entitlement 76, 86.
BEA 108.
Bermuda principles 6, 18, 22ff., 45 n.49, 61, 62 n.20, 104, 105 n.3.
beyond-homeland restriction 34, 35, 43 n.42.
Bin Cheng 115.
blind sector traffic 42ff., 44.
blocked-space 63, 142ff., 148 n.121, 158.
BOAC 42 n.39, 53 n.3, 108, 121ff., 125, 147.
Boitreaud J. 16 n.19, 46 n.51.
Bradley M. A. 47 n.54, 80 n.63.
Brenner Mel 20 n.4, 92 n.91.
Browne Secor D. 156.
BUA 53 n.3.
bulk fare 70, 81.
bulk transportation 77, 157.
Burnstein Robert S. 77.
BWIA 121ff., 125ff., 147.
Caledonian 34, 35, 53 n.3, 87 n.79.
Calkins Nathan G. 44 n.45.
capacity control 13, 23, 45 n.49, 90 n.88.
CBIT 70, 77.
CDA 133 n.73, 135ff.
charter carrier 51ff., 93, 96ff., 137ff.
charter service 55ff., 82ff.
Cherington Paul W. 37 n.30, 50 n.60, 53 n.3, 156, 157.
Chicago Convention 52, 59, 79, 80, 107, 112, 115, 116 n.21.
chosen instrument 157.
CMA 97 n.104.
combi service 60.
comity 150.
commercial agreement 9.
commingling 42ff., 62.
common carrier 79.
common policy 66 n.27, 90ff., 93 n.93, 98, 148.
competition 7, 99.
Condor 96, 138ff.
CPAIR 145 n.113.
Crooker John H. 36.

De-nationalization 50, 152.
directional balance 85ff.
directional imbalance 62.
designation 53ff., 57, 99, 116, 136, 151.
diversion 52, 66ff., 90 n.87.

divestiture 96, 139.
double designation (see multiple designation).
double tracking 39.
dry lease 113, 130, 131 n.68, 137, 151.
duplicative authority 96.

EARB 112.
ECAC 62, 84ff., 94, 105 n.3, 116 n.21.
Edwards Report 14 n.15, 36ff., 53 n.3, 57, 58 n.14, 61 n.19, 92, 110 n.11, 157 n.4.
Eisenhower D. 26.
ElAl 119, 145 n.110.
emergency 133, 137ff., 140.
empty leg 87.
end-on interchange 108 n.10, 141 n.99, 151.
enlightened protectionism 11.
entity charter 76, 82 n.71.
equal exchange of economic benefits 8, 21, 100, 156.
equal opportunity 31, 46ff., 88.
equitable exchange of economic benefits 12, 26ff., 31, 156.
exchange of routes 20ff., 37ff., 46ff.
exemption authority 28, 53 n.2, 101 n.113, 135 n.78, 143.
ex post facto review 23, 45 n.49.
extra-national approach 5, 12.
Europair 46.

Fair and equal opportunity (see equal opportunity).
fare limitation 55, 88ff., 139.
fares (see IATA).
Ferreira E. A. 29.
Finnair 141 n.95.
fit, willing and able 5, 117ff., 130, 147, 151.
Flying Tiger 120 n.36.
foreign aircraft permit 79.
foreign air transportation 135.
freedom of the air 6, 11.
freedoms of the air 7 n.7, 22ff., 38.
freight forwarder 81 n.68.
frequency restriction (see volume restriction).

Garuda 112.
gateway 46.
Gazdik J. 80ff.
Gillilland W. 44 n.44.
GIT 68 n.35, 69, 70.
Goedhuis D. 5 n.3.
Goldberg H. 126.
GTD 68 n.35.

Holding out 40, 52, 80ff., 83, 122 n.46, 124, 139ff.
Hourani C. 2 n.1.

IATA 4, 14 n.15, 55, 56 n.10, 63, 68 n.35, 70, 81 n.68, 82 n.71, 83ff., 88 n.83, 139, 157.
Iberia 41 n.37, 107.
ICAO 4, 15, 17 n.1, 54, 55, 90, 91, 106, 113.
ICC 67 n.28, 91.
identity 97, 100, 121, 138, 140, 145, 150.
imbalance (see directional imbalance).
indirect air carrier 81.
indirect routing 62.
INS 113.
interchangeability of aircraft 99, 133.
interchange agreement (see end-on interchange).
interline charter 142 n.101.
International Air Services Transit Agreement 41ff., 79.
internationality of aircraft 115.
internationalization 12.
Irish Airlines 148 n.120.
irregular carrier (see charter carrier).
irrespective of payload 91.
ITA 27 n.14, 60 n.16, 91, 112 n.13.
IT basing fare 56.
IT charter 51, 55ff., 79ff.
IT traffic 63ff.
ITX 70, 89.

JAL 95 n.97.
Jenkins Roy 157.
joint registration 115.
joint venture 108ff., 135.

KAR-AIR 141 n.95.
Kennedy J. F. 26.
Keyzer M. J. 9 n.10.
KLM 20, 29, 44 n.43, 56 n.10, 96, 97, 100, 107, 126ff., 131 n.68, 134ff., 137ff., 149.

Landy Burton A. 151 n.125.
LANICA 143ff.
Landry J. E. 47 n.55, 48 n.58.
lease agreement 113ff., 129, 137ff., 149ff.
LIAT 125ff.
liberalization 50, 101, 105 n.3.
long-haul restriction 132 n.72.

Loy Frank E. 18 n.3, 26, 37 n.30, 39, 47, 48, 85, 107 n.7.
Lufthansa (DLH) 37 n.33, 41 n.37, 45, 74 n.52, 96, 100, 137ff.

Magnuson Warren G. 27.
Mankiewicz R. 106 n.5.
Martinair 73 n.50, 87 n.79, 96, 130 n.65, 137ff.
McCarroll John C. 105 n.3.
mercantilism 28 n.16.
minimum selling fare 68 n.25, 89.
mirror reciprocity 31, 39, 48 n.58.
multi-destination traffic 90 n.88, 91.
multilateral agreement 9, 98, 156.
Multilateral Agreement on Commercial Rights in Non-Scheduled Service within Europe 55, 98.
multi-nation cooperation 107, 143, 144, 158.
multiple designation 37, 53 n.3, 99, 157.
multiplier effect 64.
Murphy Charles S. 6 n.6, 10 n.11, 27 n.14, 69 n.38, 85.
mutuality of interest 127, 133.

NACA 70 n.41, 73 n.49, 83.
Naveau Jacques 115 n.18.
Nigeria Airways 107, 112.
Nilsson Carl 37 n.32, 50 n.60.
Nixon R. 28.
non-scheduled carrier (see charter carrier).
non-scheduled service (see charter service).
NorthWest 75 n.53, 108 n.10.

OARB 112.
off-route 24, 53, 65, 73ff., 95 n.98, 132ff.
Olympic Airways 95 n.97.
on-route (see off-route).
open-jaw 73.
open-rate situation 70 n.41.
operating permit 116ff.
origin and destination 8, 20, 22, 24ff., 32 n.22, 47, 62 n.20, 153.
overcapacity 94.
own market 29ff., 35, 50.
own traffic 29, 51.
own-use charter 76, 82 n.71.

PAL 107 n.8, 112.
pallet 145.
PANAM 34 n.23, 36, 44 n.43, 68, 75 n.53, 97 n.104, 101 n.114, 107, 108 n.10, 119 n.29, 120 n.33, 121 n.41, 129, 143.
Pan-Arab Airline 113.
parallel licensing 157.
part charter 71.
passing off 100 n.111, 120ff.
penetration of the market 90.
Perez y Bouras J. 107 n.8.
planeload charter 72.
point-to point competition 156.
pool agreement 9, 107ff.
positioning flight 42 n.39.
primary entitlement 18, 33, 37, 76, 86.
primary traffic 22, 76, 86.
prior permission 55, 79.
promotional fares 68.
pro rata charter 76, 82 n.71.
protectionism 11, 16, 30, 50, 101, 154.
public interest 100, 117, 119, 133, 147, 148.
public solicitation (see solicitation).
public transport 80ff.
public utility 10.
Pulsifer R. 138 n.88, 139 n.90.

Quid-pro-quo 7, 11.
Quisqueyana 147.

Reciprocity 37ff., 86, 88, 95, 97, 140, 148.
registration 114ff.
retaliation 28, 103.
Riche Jean-Marie 16 n.19.
route carrier 93.
route exchange 13, 37, 46ff., 51.
route specification 40ff.
royalty 31.
Rubio Garcia-Mina J. 29 n.17, 114 n.15.

Sabena 107, 148.
SACAA 113 n.14.
SAS 37 n.32, 45, 46, 50 n.60, 131 n.68.
Sauveplanne J. G. 13 n.14.
Sayre Eugene G. 67 n.29.
scheduled service 54ff., 80ff.
scheduled traffic 54.
Seaboard World 145 n.110, 148 n.120.
Seaver Robert E. 73 n.50.
secondary entitlement 33, 37.
secondary traffic 23.
security 129, 151.
single entity charter (see own-use charter).
SIT 70.
Six Pool 112.

sixth freedom 7 n.7, 18ff., 27, 30, 32ff., 48, 73, 158.
Smathers Report 18, 20, 22.
Sohn L. B. 11 n.12.
solicitation 67 n.31, 70, 82 n.71.
sovereignty 6, 9, 13, 43, 151.
Spencer John H. 47 n.56, 86.
split charter 69 n.37, 72, 73, 76ff., 82ff., 94.
Statement of Authorization 74ff., 89 n.85.
statistics 25, 112ff.
Stoffel Albert W. 22 n.5, 23.
stopover 42 n.39.
subsidy 31ff.
substantial ownership 56, 96, 114, 119 n.28, 122, 131, 134.
supplemental carrier 52ff., 67ff., 83.
Swissair 131 n.68, 145 n.111.

TAN 143ff.
TAP 120 n.35, 123, 144 n.109, 145, 148, 150.
tariffs (see IATA).
Taylor Thomas K. 38 n.34, 110 n.11.
technical stop 41.
terminal market 20, 48 n.58.
TIA 145 n.113.
Tipton S. 16 n.18, 105 n.1.
TMA 145 n.110.
Toda B. 107 n.8.
tourism 8, 64.
tour operator 63, 81.
traffic attraction 86ff.
traffic forecast 4, 61 n.19, 72.
traffic generation 86ff.
Transavia 87 n.79.
Transcarga 131.
transit market 20.
transit traffic 42 n.39, 44.
turn-around service 132.
TWA 36, 68, 75 n.53, 110 n.11, 120 n.33, 145 n.110.

Unfair competition 101, 133 n.73.
uplift ratio 74.
UTA 29.

Value of the market 7, 18ff., 48.
VARIG 30, 107.
Veres V. 69 n.38.
VIASA 107, 126ff., 132 n.72, 133 n.73, 135ff.
volume restriction 88ff., 158.

Wassenbergh H. A. 6 n.5, 13 n.14, 106 n.6.
Wheatcroft Stephen 16 n.17, 20 n.4, 106 n.4, 157.
World Airways 119.

Zambian Airways 31 n.20, 112.

GPSR Compliance

The European Union's (EU) General Product Safety Regulation (GPSR) is a set of rules that requires consumer products to be safe and our obligations to ensure this.

If you have any concerns about our products, you can contact us on ProductSafety@springernature.com

In case Publisher is established outside the EU, the EU authorized representative is:

Springer Nature Customer Service Center GmbH
Europaplatz 3
69115 Heidelberg, Germany

Batch number: 10830943

Printed by Printforce, the Netherlands